Lecture Notes in Artificial Intelligence 4438

Edited by J. G. Carbonell and J. Siekmann

Subseries of Lecture Notes in Computer Science

Lutz Maicher   Alexander Sigel
Lars Marius Garshol (Eds.)

Leveraging the Semantics of Topic Maps

Second International Conference
on Topic Maps Research and Applications, TMRA 2006
Leipzig, Germany, October 11-12, 2006
Revised Selected Papers

 Springer

Series Editors

Jaime G. Carbonell, Carnegie Mellon University, Pittsburgh, PA, USA
Jörg Siekmann, University of Saarland, Saarbrücken, Germany

Volume Editors

Lutz Maicher
University of Leipzig
Department of Computer Science
04109 Leipzig, Germany
E-mail: maicher@informatik.uni-leipzig.de

Alexander Sigel
University of Cologne
Department of Information Systems and Information Management
Pohligstraße 1
50969 Köln, Germany
E-mail: sigel@wim.uni-koeln.de

Lars Marius Garshol
Ontopia AS
N- 0656 Oslo, Norway
E-mail: larsga@ontopia.net

Library of Congress Control Number: 2007924602

CR Subject Classification (1998): I.2, H.4, H.3, J.1, K.3-4

LNCS Sublibrary: SL 7 – Artificial Intelligence

ISSN   0302-9743
ISBN-10   3-540-71944-X Springer Berlin Heidelberg New York
ISBN-13   978-3-540-71944-1 Springer Berlin Heidelberg New York

Springer is a part of Springer Science+Business Media

springer.com

© Springer-Verlag Berlin Heidelberg 2007
Printed in Germany

Typesetting: Camera-ready by author, data conversion by Scientific Publishing Services, Chennai, India
Printed on acid-free paper   SPIN: 12048717   06/3180   5 4 3 2 1 0

Preface

The papers in this volume were presented at TMRA 2006, the International Conference on Topic Maps Research and Applications, held October 11–12, 2006, in Leipzig, Germany. TMRA 2006 was the second conference of an annual series of international conferences dedicated to Topic Maps in research and industry.

Topic maps are continuously gaining more and more attention in science and industry; they are "crossing the chasm." The TMRA series provides a platform for researchers in the topic maps community to meet for exciting exchanges in a stimulating setting. The uniqueness of TMRA is its focus on both sides of the same coin: scientific research on topic maps and upcoming applications in industry.

In the autumn of 2005 the first TMRA conference took place in Leipzig. The proceedings have been published in this LNAI series as volume 3873. It was amazing to see how ideas and solutions from TMRA 2005 matured within the last year to full products or projects. The overall success of TMRA 2005 encouraged us to improve this conference series for the topic maps community: More people were attracted, and the scientific quality was enhanced.

The TMRA 2006 program attracted a very international crowd of about 80 attendees, hosted in the completely new media campus of the Leipzig Media Foundation. The scientific quality of the conference was ensured by significantly enlarging and diversifying the international Program Committee to 34 members. From 52 submissions, 34 were accepted for presentation at the conference. Every submission was carefully reviewed by three members of the Program Committee. In this proceedings volume, 15 full papers, 6 short papers, the invited keynote, and one invited report from both the poster and open space sessions are published.

Parallel sessions focussing on different areas were introduced to better address the different needs of science and industry. The papers were grouped into nine paper sessions.

Smoothly moderated by Steven R. Newcomb, a poster session with six posters took place for the first time. In parallel, there were three system demonstrations. Even the success story from last year was kept in the conference program: The open space sessions, once more moderated by Lars Marius Garshol, have proven to be an exciting playground for visionaries and early ideas. These kinds of sessions will also be part of the TMRA 2007 conference.

For the first time, the TMRA conference was preceded by a full day of in-depth tutorials, called tutorials@TMRA, which were held in parallel. Due to the vital interest, the tutorials will remain an important part of upcoming conferences. TMRA 2006 was succeeded by a 3-day ISO standardization meeting which emphasized the importance of TMRA.

We would like to thank all those who contributed to this book for their excellent work and great cooperation. Furthermore, we want to thank all members of the Program Committee, and Gerhard Heyer and Miriam Sühnel for their tireless commitment to making TMRA 2006 a true success. TMRA was organized by the Zentrum für Informations-, Wissens- und Dienstleistungsmanagement. We acknowledge the generous support by all sponsors.

We hope all participants enjoyed a successful conference, made many new contacts, gained from fruitful discussions helping to solve current research problems, and had a pleasant stay in Leipzig. Last but not least we hope to see you again at TMRA 2007, which will be held October, 10-12, 2007 in Leipzig.

February 2007

Lutz Maicher
Alexander Sigel
Lars Marius Garshol

Organization

TMRA 2006 was organized by the Zentrum für Informations-, Wissens- und Dienstleistungsmanagement (ZIWD) in Leipzig, Germany.

Program Committee Chairs

Lutz Maicher, University of Leipzig, Germany
Lars Marius Garshol, Ontopia, Norway
Alexander Sigel, University of Cologne, Germany

Program Committee

Kal Ahmed, NetworkedPlanet, UK
Frederic Andres, NII, Japan
Lora Aroyo, Eindhoven University of Technology, The Netherlands
Robert Barta, Bond University, Australia
Michel Biezunski, Infoloom, USA
Dmitry Bogachev, Omega Business Consulting, Canada
Karsten Böhm, FHS Kufstein, Austria
François Bry, University of Munich, Germany
Darina Dicheva, Winston Salem University, USA
Patrick Durusau, Independent Consultant, USA
Eric Freese, LexisNexis, USA
Sung-Kook Han, Won Kwang University, Korea
Gerhard Heyer, University of Leipzig, Germany
Hiroyuki Kato, NII, Japan
Larry Kerschberg, George Mason University, USA
Peter-Paul Kruijsen, Morpheus Software, The Netherlands
Jaeho Lee, University of Seoul, Korea
James David Mason, Y-12 National Security Complex, USA
Graham Moore, NetworkedPlanet, UK
Sung Hyon Myaeng, Information and Communications University, Korea
Steven R. Newcomb, Coolheads Consulting, USA
Jan Nowitzky, Deutsche Börse Systems, Germany
Leo Obrst, MITRE, USA
Jack Park, SRI International, USA
Rani Pinchuk, Space Applications Services, Belgium
Ray Richardson, Bell Laboratories, Ireland
Thomas Schwotzer, neofonie, Germany
Stefan Smolnik, European Business School, Germany
Steffen Staab, University of Koblenz, Germany
Markus Ueberall, University of Frankfurt, Germany
Fabio Vitali, University of Bologna, Italy

Organizing Committee

Lutz Maicher, University of Leipzig, Germany
Steve Pepper, Convenor, ISO/IEC JTC 1/SC 34/WG 3, Norway
Sam Oh, Sungkyunkwan University, Korea

Sponsoring Institutions

Topic Maps 2007, Oslo, Norway
USU Software AG, Möglingen, Germany
Ontopia AS, Oslo, Norway
Networked Planet, Oxford, UK
Media Foundation of the Sparkasse Leipzig, Germany
Alexander Sigel - Semantic Knowledge Services, Cologne, Germany
Space Applications Services, Zaventem, Belgium

Table of Contents

Leveraging the Semantics

Technical Issues of Topic Mapping

Social Software with Topic Maps

Open Space and Poster Sessions

Flat Topic Mapping for a Flat World*

Steven R. Newcomb

Coolheads Consulting, Blacksburg, Virginia, USA
srn@coolheads.com
http://www.coolheads.com/publications.htm

Abstract. Every topic map has something in common with all other topic maps: a commitment to the goal of "one topic per subject", a state in which everything known about each distinct subject will be (apparently) co-located at its unique topic. A side effect of this commitment is that all topic maps, regardless of the diversity of the universes of discourse in which they are expressed, inherently facilitate their combination with other topic maps.

Thus, all topic maps, in all universes of discourse, can be accurately regarded as contributions to the ability of diverse human communities to understand each other. Even though they may use diverse – and even logically incompatible – universes of discourse, all topic mappers are themselves members of a community whose unifying conviction is that subjects exist apart from, and are more important than, any particular ways of identifying them and co-locating information about them.

1 What Unites the Community of Topic Mappers?

One may observe many characteristics that tend to be shared by people who make topic maps. Among these are characteristics common to all scientists and scholars, such as a belief that knowing things – whatsoever they may be – is better than not knowing them, and a certain impatience with the process of finding things out, especially when somebody else has already discovered and expressed them.

Despite the priority of such basic impulses, when topic mappers are asked to articulate why they are so enthusiastic about topic mapping, they tend to focus on the details of some specific way of modeling or processing information, or of interchanging it. This is understandable and, in fact, it's a characteristic of a vibrant community of alert and engaged individuals, but to outsiders (i.e., to all potential *new* members) it can make participation in the topic mapping community appear unattractive by virtue of the community's contentiousness, incoherence and instability.

The question naturally arises: What should be the "marketing message" of the topic mapping community? How can we know when we're "off-message", and get ourselves back on track? What's the right "elevator speech" (the speech

---

* This paper is not an ordinary conference paper, but a paper reflecting the content of the invited opening keynote.

L. Maicher, A. Sigel, and L.M. Garshol (Eds.): TMRA 2006, LNAI 4438, pp. 1–7, 2007.
© Springer-Verlag Berlin Heidelberg 2007

that can be given entirely during a brief elevator ride, and that has a generally *positive* effect on its hearers)? This question has obsessed and often bedeviled the pioneers of the community since the very beginning.

The message that has created the most "traction", by far, was developed by Steve Pepper: the so-called *TAO of Topic Maps* [Pepper02]. The TAO message has all the features of an effective marketing message: it's simple, intuitive, mnemonic, and "catchy." The TAO is the easy on-ramp to topic mapping, and it's easy to explain, too. It gives the potential convert something to think about, at every turn. Each of the thoughts it inspires is beautiful, and each portends yet more elegance and beauty. It comfortingly hides many complexities. It is anchored to notions that are themselves some of the primary pillars of civilization and the Humanities. It is worthy of the highest compliment that can be paid to any meme: *It works!* It has moved the whole idea of topic mapping into the mainstream, and for this the entire community owes Pepper its gratitude, admiration, and, at least arguably, even its existence.

Nobody wants to abandon the TAO, and yet it looks as though it's not, at least by itself, a big enough tent for all the communities that remain to be persuaded that topic mapping:

- – does not (directly) threaten them or their existing practices, investments, identities, or members,
- – is more than a marketing message,
- – is more than just a new vocabulary of catchphrases for talking about existing well-understood concepts,
- – is more than just a data model or database schema,
- – is not technically, philosophically, or politically naive,
- – does not impose prior constraints on the universes of discourse of the communities that choose to use it, and
- – is not obvious (at least not to most information technology practitioners, and at least not until they can see that it's not what their habits of thinking generally lead them to think that it is).

All of the above statements about topic mapping are true. However, the rhetoric of the TAO and of those who use the term "topic mapping" exclusively as an invocation of the Topic Maps Data Model [ISO13250-2], have led people who influence technology adoption decisions to believe that one or more of the above statements about topic mapping is untrue.

Thus, the topic mapping community faces a crisis. Will it seize its opportunity to develop and adopt a marketing message that will identify topic mapping with every community's portion of humanity's *entire* noösphere, and that will also honor and protect the inroads into the public consciousness that the TAO and other efforts have already made? Or will topic mappers be content to say, "If the TAO (or the Topic Map Data Model) doesn't work for you, then seek shelter in another tent. Topic mapping is the TAO (or the Topic Map Data Model), no more and no less." The remainder of this paper argues that the former option is preferable.

The most effective marketing messages direct the attention of potential buyers in ways that persuade them to buy; this truism is demonstrated by the TAO message, for example. It seems reasonable for the community to inventory the things toward which the attention of potential adopters might be directed. To create such an inventory, it seems appropriate to ask, "What unites the topic mapping community? What holds it together? Why do its members insist that topic mapping is a good thing?"

As a step toward such an inventory, here is a list of notions that are central to topic mapping, and that seem unlikely to provoke disagreement within the community. These are things that most if not all topic mappers believe to be virtuous and valuable about topic mapping:

1. **Information interchange requires disclosures of syntaxes, data models, etc.** A recipient of an interchangeable topic map should be able to parse it.

2. **Other ontological commitments must be disclosed.** A recipient of a topic map should be able to understand what it is saying.

3. **One subject per topic.** Topics represent subjects (as in "*subjects* of conversation"). (*Topics* are also called *subject proxies* in the draft Topic Maps Reference Model [ISO13250-5] [Durusau06].) Every topic represents exactly one subject.

4. **One topic per subject.** Topic mapping does not (and, as a practical matter, cannot) *forbid* the existence of multiple topics that all represent the same subject. However, it is the *goal* of all topic mapping activities to produce topic maps in which a certain state has been achieved – a state in which everything known about each subject is available at a *single* virtual "place" (i.e., a single topic), that, at least within the topic map, is the *only* such "place" where information about the subject has been comprehensively co-located.

5. **Subject-sameness must be disclosed.** This is a corollary of the "one topic per subject" principle. Topic mapping does not (and, as a practical matter, cannot) require that the identity of the subject of every topic be disclosed in a fashion that everyone will be forced to admit is well-grounded in any particular sense. Nevertheless, by means of the disclosures of applicable rules and by means of each topic's disclosure of the identity of the subject that it represents, topic mappers generally make it possible for the users of their topic maps to determine whether, under the applicable disclosures, any two topics should be regarded as representing the same subject.

2 What Differentiates the Topic Mapping Community from Other Communities with Avowedly Similar Goals?

Decades ago, a milk truck in New England reportedly bore the following sign: "Brown's Milk. Good as any. Better than some." Such a weak and nebulous claim may have sold dairy commodities in the 20th century, but it will not sell the idea of topic mapping to future adopters in industry and government. Regardless of whether it is true or not, there is a perception, at least in the North American marketplace, that there is an alternative to topic mapping: RDF. Some proponents of RDF feel threatened by topic mapping, and at least one of them misses no opportunity to compare RDF and topic mapping in ways that are very unfavorable to topic mapping, and that sow significant amounts of fear, uncertainty, and doubt in the minds of potential adopters.

For its part, the topic mapping community has no incentive to deprecate, or to promote disinformation about, any other approaches. On the contrary, *all* approaches that meet the needs of the communities that use them are in every way honorable. When properly disclosed, the information resources that they govern can *all* offer opportunities and benefits to their communities of origin, and to other communities, in topic map land, where achievement of the one-topic-per-subject state is always facilitated.

Moreover, topic mapping is simply inevitable, in the long run. Those who need to communicate efficiently, including such diverse entities as aerospace manufac-turers, financial services providers, healthcare providers and government agen-cies, are eventually going to adopt the practices of topic mapping, regardless of whether they do so under the explicit rubric of "Topic Maps". (The same cannot be said of RDF, which demands of its adopters that all their subject identifiers shall always be URIs. There is nothing wrong with URIs; they are ideal subject identifiers for the information spigots that can be addressed on the Web. However, it is hard to see a significant benefit for society at large in the constraint that all other things, such as gender, Hamlet, middle C, and the class-instance relationship class, must also be identified just as if they were such spigots. Subject identification is necessarily an unboundedly subtle thing.)

Anyway, for the sake of potential adopters, and for the sake of the existing and future members of the topic mapping community, it is vital that the features of topic mapping that make it "better than some" be articulated clearly and compellingly. With that goal in mind, let us return to our list of things that presumably all topic mappers believe to be virtuous and valuable. Are there any of them that are not also believed to be virtuous and valuable by, for example, the RDF community?

1. **Standard syntaxes and data models.** Every community that is seri-ous about digital information interchange has some of these. There is nothing unique about the fact that the topic mapping community has its own. True, these syntaxes and models are unique to the community, but the same can be truthfully said about every comparable community. If the syntaxes and data models of topic mapping are better than RDF's, *how* are they better? And, even if it's true that they are better, why does it matter? This is a losing ar-gument for topic maps, if for no other reason than the fact that RDF already has more adopters, and RDF emanates from an alliance of major IT industry players whose combined economic clout cannot be overmatched. Few people really care very much if there is a better syntax, or a better data model.

Moreover, topic mapping is a grassroots phenomenon. It is a response by information managers to their problems, and, at least at its roots, it is not part of anyone's strategy to dominate some IT or media arena. Among other things, this means that no market leaders are saying to potential adopters of topic mapping, "We will stand behind your commitment to topic mapping, and we will not let your project fail." (Few if any companies are saying that about RDF, either, but the name of the Microsoft, IBM, and Sun alliance – "The World Wide Web Consortium" – is frequently mentioned by those who wish to promote uncertainty about topic mapping by implying that Microsoft, IBM, Sun, and all the other WWW members are standing behind RDF, so topic mapping should therefore be regarded as an technological orphan to be avoided by the risk-averse.)

2. **Ontological commitments must be disclosed.** All information interchange communities at least pay lip-service to the idea that people should say what they mean, and mean what they say. There is nothing special here about topic maps, and, worse, some of the disclosure and grounding of even the flagship Topic Maps Data Model is explained as a raw procedure, rather than in terms that emphasize the semantics that are being preserved and supported by the procedure. Thus the TMDM is still vulnerable to unfavorable comparison to the (at least arguably) more declarative apparatus already widely available in the RDF world. Topic mappers would be well-advised to avoid making broad claims of superiority for disclosures of the ontological commitments of topic maps, at least until the TMDM's semantics have been disclosed more declaratively.

   The best that can be said about this (non-)differentiator is that the disclosure intentions of the topic mapping community are good, as evidenced by the fact that the Topic Maps Reference Model explicitly demands that such disclosures be made.

3. **One subject per topic.** Again, there's nothing here that compellingly differentiates topic mapping from RDF. It can be justifiably argued that every RDF "node" represents *something*, and much of the literature on RDF can be read in such a way that every "resource" is, in fact, the same thing that is called a "subject" in the parlance of topic mapping. While there are significant "impedance mismatches" between RDF and the radical subject-centricism of topic mapping, it would be hard to argue that the principle of "one subject per topic" is not, in fact, just as fundamental to RDF as it is to topic mapping.

4. **One topic per subject and subject-sameness must be disclosed.** Topic mapping appears to be genuinely different from anything else in that it is all about the goal of co-location. Topic mapping does not require conformance to much of anything, really, other than that there must be sufficient disclosure to allow subject sameness to be detected. Topic mapping neither requires nor interferes with any of the features of any particular universe of discourse, and therefore it is compatible with all of them. RDF's syntaxes, semantics, and logics are not excluded, but in order to regard RDF resources as topic maps, commitments as to what they are talking about

are required. In combination with disclosures of these commitments, RDF resources in fact become topic maps, and, at least theoretically, they are as combinable with all other topic maps as any other topic maps. The benefit offered by topic mapping – facilitation of the "one topic per subject" state – is available even when combining RDF resources with arbitrary non-RDF resources. There are no prior constraints on what can be said in a topic map, because there are no prior constraints on how to say it. Communities need not sacrifice any of their independence with respect to how they will think, communicate and work, before they can participate in an open market of integrations of their information with the information of other independent communities.

3   Natural Selection of Universes of Discourse

The scientific reality – the ontology of reality – in which we human beings currently find ourselves is one in which natural selection is an ontological commitment. Just as the genes of organisms are competing for survival via the organisms they govern, so too are the universes of discourse of communities competing via the communities they govern. All systems of every kind, including all human cultures, are participating in a process in which natural selection is always and everywhere ongoing. It is important to understand this in order to gain a broad perspective of the opportunities for public benefit that topic mapping can create.

In human affairs, wars and other atrocities are sometimes committed as sideeffects of competitions between systems of thinking – between cultures. Human individuals, and even humanity itself, are also competing for survival. All of these systems (individuals, species, cultures, etc.) need to adapt to each other's existence, and to find ways to be comfortable with each other. All the other alternatives, including genocide and monoculture, are ultimately deadly. It is simply not in the best interests of human beings that they adopts a single dominant universe of discourse. For one thing, no person and no community is wise enough to design or maintain it.

4   Topic Mapping as a Survival Skill

Humanity's knowledge management professionals would be wise to face the reality that the development of ways of thinking and being cannot realistically be controlled or planned. Universes of discourse must be invented as they are needed, and they must be abandoned as they are found wanting. No single universe of discourse can provide for the expression of everything that may ever need to be expressed. Individual human beings cannot all live in the same universe of discourse – they are just too limited, and in the aggregate they are just too diverse. Nevertheless, all human individuals must live on the same planet. If we are ever going to be comfortable with each other, we are going to have to find a way to adapt to the diversity and constant independent evolution of our various communities and their universes of discourse. Even if we could trade the ontological independence of the various human communities responsible for the maintenance of our cultures and civilizations, in exchange for the ability to communicate accurately and reliably about any given set of issues, we would only defeat ourselves by making such a trade. We need our communities to maintain their ontological independence in order to preserve our overall ability to adapt to changing conditions.

Natural Selection can be brutally extinctive when there is too little diversity for Nature to make Selections from.

References

[Pepper02]   Pepper, S.: *The TAO of Topic Maps*. Ontopia, April 2002.
               http://www.ontopia.net/topicmaps/materials/tao.html
[ISO13250-2]   ISO/IEC 13250-3:2007: *Topic Maps – Data Model*; International
               Organization for Standardization; Geneva.
               http://www.isotopicmaps.org/sam/sam-model/
[ISO13250-5]   ISO/IEC 13250-5: *Topic Maps – Reference Model*; International Or-
               ganization for Standardization; Geneva; Committee Draft 2006-03-01.
               http://www.isotopicmaps.org/TMRM/TMRM-6.0/TMRM-6.0.pdf
[Durusau06]   Durusau, P.; Newcomb, S. R.: *The Essentials of the Topic Maps Refer-
               ence Model (TMRM)*. In: Procs. of TMRA 2006, this volume (2007).

On Topic Map Templates and Traceability

Markus Ueberall and Oswald Drobnik

Telematics Group, Institute of Computer Science, Johann-Wolfgang-Goethe
University, D-60054 Frankfurt/Main, Germany
{ueberall, drobnik}@tm.informatik.uni-frankfurt.de

Abstract. A major challenge regarding project management is traceability, i.e., to ensure the completeness of information about every step within a process chain. This paper outlines an approach based on Topic Map Templates, augmented with query and constraint definitions, to systematically address traceability aspects in the context of software development processes, in particular for requirements engineering and transitions to subsequent development phases. Furthermore, it is shown that Templates, when expressed in a uniform way, are an important means to enhance the functionality of, e.g., editors and viewers for Topic Maps. In order to illustrate the proposed approach, individual development steps regarding the realisation of a simple flight reservation system, particularly highlighting then-supported interactions between participants, serve as an example.

1 Introduction

Particularly in collaborative project management scenarios, a major challenge during the entire lifecycle is *traceability*, i.e., the ability to chronologically interelate the uniquely identifiable entities to ensure the completeness of information about every step within a process chain [11,20].

In software development, the term traceability refers to the ability to link the requirements set forth at the beginning of a project to the corresponding design artefacts, the resulting software, and associated test cases.[1] This allows for improved software quality, enhanced productivity, efficient change impact analysis, and, moreover, for timely and consistent documentation. As far as timely documentation is concerned, Wiki engines [2] are appropriate tools and are gaining in importance even in industrial software development. However, Wikis lack possibilities for typing and validating concepts and relationships between them, needed to efficiently support consistent linking of requirements etc. [23]. Therefore, more extensive approaches have to be developed to express well-structured conceptualisations for application domains and process chain support.

In the following, we show how the expressiveness of Topic Maps offers a suitable basis to systematically address traceability aspects in the context of software development phases, in particular for requirements engineering. To illustrate

---

[1] cf. http://en.wikipedia.org/wiki/Traceability

L. Maicher, A. Sigel, and L.M. Garshol (Eds.): TMRA 2006, LNAI 4438, pp. 8–19, 2007.

our approach, we use a flight reservation scenario as example application. Section two introduces a conceptualisation of requirements in terms of Topic Map Templates. Sections three and four describe necessary refinements to support computer-supported generation and validation of requirement definitions. The phase transition from requirements analysis to design is discussed in section five. Finally, navigation and phase-related views are presented in section six.

2   Use Case Descriptions and Templates

Requirements engineering is the starting point of the system development process and identifies the needs and objectives of the stakeholders. Stakeholders define requirements in terms of use cases, which are the basis for designers to propose adequate system components and their interactions.

For specifying use cases, we adopt the definitions from the UML Superstructure [13], in particular:

- a *use case* is the specification of a set of actions performed by a system, which yields an observable result [...] of value for one or more actors
- an *actor* specifies a role played by a user or any other system that interacts with the subject
- the *extend* relationship specifies that the behaviour of a use case may be extended by the behaviour of another use case
- an *include* relationship defines that a use case contains the behaviour defined in another use case

Additional UML concepts address behaviour, i.e., actions with preconditions and postconditions. All these UML concepts form the basis of an ontology which is independent of the application domain [8].

In LTM notation [5], excerpts of this ontology may be expressed as follows:

```
// topic types
[Actor = "Actor" @"http://.../UML_Sstrct/UseCases/#Actor"]
[UseCase = "UseCase" @"http://.../UML_Sstrct/UseCases/#UseCase"]

// role definitions
[placeholder = "placeholder" @"http://.../Templates/#Placeholder"]
[ExtendingUseCase : UseCase = "ExtendingUseCase" @"http://..."]
[ExtendedUseCase : UseCase = "ExtendedUseCase" @"http://..."]
[IncludingUseCase : UseCase = "IncludingUseCase" @"http://..."]
[IncludedUseCase : UseCase = "IncludedUseCase" @"http://..."]

// association types
[extends = "extends" @"http://.../UML_Sstrct/UseCases/#Extend"]
[includes = "includes" @"http://.../UML_Sstrct/UseCases/#Include"]
```

```
// "examples" of associations
extends(placeholder : ExtendedUseCase,
  placeholder : ExtendingUseCase)
includes(placeholder : IncludingUseCase,
  placeholder : IncludedUseCase)
```

Apart from the placeholder topic discussed in the next section, these basic definitions are fairly straightforward. Each definition is to be associated with a Published Subject Identifier (PSI), which refers to a Subject Indicator that is supposed to unambiguously identify its subject and to provide all needed semantics–at least to human beings [16].

In particular, the definitions given above represent a *Topic Map Template* as coined by the ISO working group [17], i.e., it is a Topic Map "that only consists of topics that are declared in order to be used as types in a class of Topic Maps". Accordingly, Vatant [22] defines a single *Template* as "the formal declaration of a required *Pattern* for a given [Topic Map construct] type", whereas a Pattern in turn is defined as "the structure of an individual [Topic Map construct]". Note that Vatant as well as Biezunski and Newcomb [4] focus on associations, because a lack of association templates is likely to trigger the biggest interoperability issues, but the definitions hold for all kinds of topic templates.

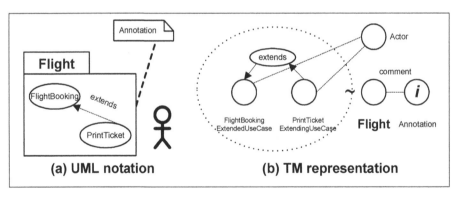

Fig. 1. Example of a template which is based on other templates: (a) UML notation, (b) visualisation of the Topic Map based representation as given in the text

To support a concrete application such as a flight reservation system, additional definitions are needed to express application domain specifics:

```
// initial use case with actor
[FlightBooking : UseCase = "FlightBooking"
  @"http://.../#FlightBooking"]
[Customer = "Customer" @"http://.../#Customer"]
tmdm:supertype-subtype(Actor, Customer)
```

```
// a complete use case description links use cases and actors
[UseCaseDescription]
exmpltm:is-part-of(placeholder: UseCaseDescription,
  placeholder: UseCase)
exmpltm:is-part-of(placeholder: UseCaseDescription,
  placeholder: Actor)

// a customer is an individual person with certain attributes
[Person = "Person" @"http://.../#Person"]
[Address = "Address" @"http://.../#Person_Address"]
[Age = "Age" @"http://.../#Person_Age"]
[BankingAccount = "BankingAccount"
  @"http://.../#Person_BankingAccount"]
exmpltm:has-attribute(placeholder: Person, placeholder: Address)
exmpltm:has-attribute(placeholder: Person, placeholder: Age)
exmpltm:has-attribute(placeholder: Person,
  placeholder: BankingAccount)
...
tmdm:supertype-subtype(Customer, Person)

// use case refinement
[RegisterCustomer : UseCase = "RegisterCustomer" @"http://..."]
[DeliverTicket : UseCase = "DeliverTicket" @"http://..."]
includes(FlightBooking: IncludingUseCase,
  RegisterCustomer: IncludedUseCase) ~ reificatedINCL
extends(FlightBooking: ExtendedUseCase,
  DeliverTicket: ExtendingUseCase) ~ reificatedEXTD
```

The tmdm: prefix denotes associations defined in the Topic Maps Data Model [9], whereas other prefixes such as exmpltm: denote associations/templates which serve as illustrations only and would have to be defined in a separate ontology.

Aside from the previous application domain-specific concepts, a predetermined set of generic basic concepts and relationships as depicted in fig. 2 should allow all participants in the software development process to quickly bring in, e.g., personal records of thought processes or references to external documents into the Topic Map, which are not subject to formal guidelines [15].

3   Nested Templates

The includes/extends templates in the previous section obviously refer to other templates. In order to instantiate such kind of *nested template*, we have to provide instantiations of all templates representing "mandatory attributes/parts" as well. Though such a construct is identical to a hierarchy of topic/association types, the term "nested template" seems more convenient to emblematise that

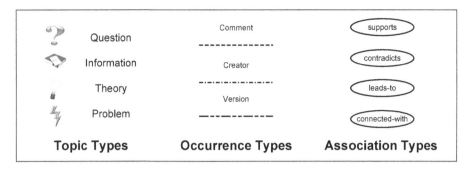

Fig. 2. A set of generic basic types (i.e., templates) should be used to quickly and easily express fundamental statements

we are talking about "[related] patterns used for making multiple copies of a single object", which is the common definition of a template.[2]

Provided that all templates and their associations are expressed in a uniform way, i.e., they can be identified unambiguously, tools like editors and viewers for Topic Maps can be enriched with corresponding support functionality.

An editor can support the input of use case descriptions by generating forms from templates. These forms can then be filled in by, e.g., a stakeholder, who should be familiar with use case descriptions (at least to some extent), but not with Topic Maps. If he encounters problems expressing requirements by means of existing concepts, he can use the generic basic set of concepts and relationships to attach a free-form comment containing a problem description. Then, another participant could modify/extend the underlying set of concepts in order to meet the needs of the stakeholder. Contrariwise, if a stakeholder is able to further formalise, e.g., preconditions for actions, he can enter hints concerning related concepts in terms of annotations as well.

In addition, the editor should support users with help functions, e.g., by providing information about the semantics of use case attributes by accessing the metadata associated with corresponding subject indicators.

Technically, when constructing the forms starting from the template to be instantiated in the first place, e.g., `UseCaseDescription`, the `placeholder` topic introduced in the preceding section can be used to identify all underlying templates by recursively following all associations that contain this topic. Of course, precautions have to be taken to detect possible circular references. Furthermore, in practice it should be possible to specify those parts of the resulting hierarchy which are not mandatory.

4   Requirements Engineering and Traceability

One objective of requirements engineering is to ensure consistency of requirements. A simple example for an incorrect usage of concepts would be trying to

---

[2] cf. `http://en.wiktionary.org/wiki/template`

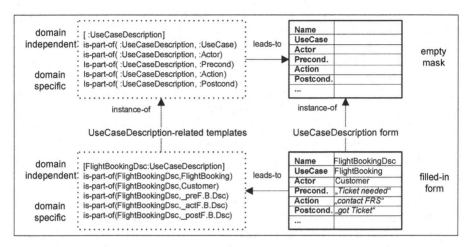

Fig. 3. Exploiting properties of nested templates using a forms-based editor to generate instances of, e.g., use case descriptions without knowledge about Topic Map internals

relate two actors by means of an `extends` association which is defined for use cases only. To avoid such problems, templates have to be augmented by usage restrictions. This can be achieved by introducing constraints (cf. [10,12] for the forthcoming TMCL) and/or queries and predicates, i.e., boolean functions, all of which can be conveniently associated by means of occurrences.

Using OSL notation [14], the appropriate usage of `extends` could be enforced as follows:

```
[Constraint = "Constraint" @"http://.../Restrictions/#Constraint"]
{extends, Constraint, [[<association>
  <instanceOf><internalTopicRef href="#extends"/>
    </instanceOf>
  <role min="1" max="1">
    <instanceOf><internalTopicRef href="#ExtendingUseCase"/>
      </instanceOf>
    <player><internalTopicRef href="#UseCase"/></player>
  </role>
  <role min="1" max="1">
    <instanceOf><internalTopicRef href="#ExtendedUseCase"/>
      </instanceOf>
    <player><internalTopicRef href="#UseCase"/></player></role>
  </association>
]]}
```

The given constraint states that associations of this type must contain exactly two roles of type `ExtendingUseCase` and `ExtendedUseCase`, respectively, whereas both role players must be `UseCase` instances.

As mentioned above, validation rules can also be expressed in terms of either (boolean) predicates or queries. The advantage of devising queries in this context lies in the possible reuse for other tasks, cf. section 6–obviously, if a boolean value is needed, it is sufficient to evaluate whether the query yields any results or not. However, predicates (or, for that matter, functions in general), are an important means to simplify queries, and should be predefined in a timely manner, possibly directly accompanying new template definitions.

The following example in TMQL/AsTMa= notation adopted from [3] states that use cases are only considered valid as long as they don't include or extend invalid use-cases (though TMQL itself is still being drafted [6], available query languages such as tolog [7] can be used instead):

```
[Predicate = "Predicate" @"http://..."]
{UseCase, Predicate, [[is-valid-indirect isa tmql_predicate where:
  """ is-valid (UseCase: $usecase) &
  not(extends(
    ExtendedUseCase: $usecase', ExtendingUseCase: $usecase) &
  not(is-valid-indirect(UseCase: $usecase'))) &
  not(includes(
    IncludedUseCase: $usecase'', IncludingUseCase: $usecase) &
  not(is-valid-indirect(UseCase: $usecase''))) """
]]}
```

Restrictions on Templates are a prerequisite for validating the correctness of attribute values immediately during the instantiation of the corresponding Templates.

However, consistency problems may also arise due to evolutionary changes of Templates, e.g., triggered by the needs of stakeholders to introduce new use case scenarios, by correcting incorrect templates, or by requirements of subsequent development phases. To deal with such problems, traceability of modifications and their impact on artefacts has to be established, e.g., on the basis of a versioning system on conceptual level, as described in [21]. Additionally, inconsistency management techniques [19] are needed.

5   Consistency-Preserving Phase Transitions

The transition from the requirements analysis phase to the design phase has to preserve the consistent mapping of requirements to corresponding artefacts, e.g., design patterns, also defined as Templates. Such a mapping can be supported by additional restrictions, or rather regulations, concerning Templates from both phases. E.g., a regulation may state that any use case instance has to be associated with at least one design pattern instance.

In order to implement this exemplary regulation, basically it is again sufficient to specify a query as follows:

```
[Query = "Query" @"http://..."]
[DesignPattern = "DesignPattern" @"http://..."]
{UseCase, Query, [[
  SELECT $usecase WHERE
  applies-to($usecase: UseCase, $dpattern: DesignPattern)
]]}
```

Obviously, the restrictions introduced in section 4 have to be handled in a different way than the regulations concerning phase transitions. The former may prevent instantiations, but it may not feasible to, e.g., reject use case descriptions because no suitable design pattern has been assigned (yet)–recall that normally, different participants would be involved. Rather, unmapped artefacts in question should be marked as "to-be-reviewed", and participants from other phases should be notified about this incident in order to provide missing mappings, e.g., appropriate design patterns. However, except from the handling, the query is evaluated in the same way as those from the preceding section.

In practice, the notification could be realised by adding occurrences, e.g., utilising the generic basic set from section 3. Using FLWR[3] expressions, TMQL will allow to encapsulate the query and construct occurrences by means of RE-TURN clauses [6,3]–in the meantime, this has to be realised in terms of application logics. Apart from enforcing regulations, the same mechanisms can also be used to annotate related instances with hints (cf. the stakeholder example above).

Interestingly, additional regulations can be introduced, which, while easy to specify, can have strong impact on the entire development process. E.g., the following variation of the query covers transitions between several subsequent development phases:

```
[Component = "SoftwareComponent" @"http://..."]
{UseCase, Query, [[
  SELECT $usecase WHERE
  applies-to($usecase: UseCase, $dpattern: DesignPattern) AND
  is-implemented-by($dpattern: DesignPattern, $comp: Component)
]]}
```

The corresponding activities of the participants–in particular when concerning phase transitions–have to be coordinated, possibly by means of an explicit process model which not only could support inconsistency management [19], but organise collaboration in general. As shown in [21], needed subprocesses could then be specified by means of Topic Maps as well; associated application-specific logics could be added using dynamic loadable classes as supported by, e.g., the Java programming language.

---

[3] cf. http://en.wikipedia.org/wiki/FLWR

6   Navigation and Views

All instances of use cases, design patterns, etc. from our example have to be accessible in an efficient way in the resulting Topic Map. Obviously, participants should be supported in specifying the required level of details by means of filters.

Filtering is achieved by means of queries that can be attached to templates in the same way as constraints and predicate definitions in the preceeding sections. Actually, like with constraints and predicates, it seems advisable that participants who introduce new templates at the same time also provide a set of associated–and commented–queries, if possible. In this way, other participants, possibly without the same level of domain knowledge, could be supported in acquiring information about artefacts from different development phases by simply building upon predefined queries.

E.g., project managers are interested in getting a status report about the project, which includes the highlighting of use cases which are not implemented yet–cf. the example in section 5 and fig. 4.

In order to present the results, it is possible to define suitable *views*. A view consists of filters, representation artefacts (e.g., symbols as depicted in fig. 2), and associated application logics (e.g., dynamically loadable Java classes containing layout algorithms). By linking views related to artefacts from different development phases, it is possible to, e.g., navigate between initial use case descriptions, corresponding design patterns, and resulting software components.

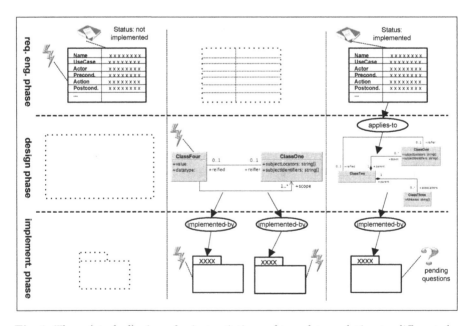

Fig. 4. Three (stacked) views for instantiations of templates relating to different development phases, grouped with respect to markings

View definitions can be stored in Topic Maps as well. Hence, when introducing new templates that require, e.g., different visualisation or editing facilities, it is possible to add them on-the-fly:

```
[View = "View" @"http://..."]
[JAR = "JavaArchive" @"http://.../App/#JavaArchive"]
[Filter : JAR = "FilterLogics" @"http://.../App/#FilterLogics"]
[Display : JAR = "DisplayLogics" @"http://.../App/#DisplayLogics"]
[Editor : JAR = "EditorLogics" @"http://.../App/#EditorLogics"]


uses-layouter(placeholder: View, placeholder: Layouter)
has-filter(placeholder: View, placeholder: Filter)
has-display(placeholder: View, placeholder: Template,
  placeholder: Display)
has-editor(placeholder: View, placeholder:Template,
  placeholder:Editor)
is-connected(placeholder: View, placeholder: View)
...


[FormsEditor:Editor = %"http://.../App/FormsEditor.jar"]
[UseCaseDescView:View = @"http://.../App/#UseCaseDescriptionView"]
[DesignPatternView:View = @"http://.../App/#DesignPatternView"]


has-editor(UseCaseDescView, UseCaseDescription, FormsEditor)
is-connected(UseCaseDescView, DesignPatternView)
...
```

Furthermore, additional zooming capabilities are provided by exploiting the identification of nested templates in the same way as the editor works. However, while the forms-based editor mentioned in section 3 should illustrate the hierarchy of templates, e.g., by visually nesting all associated input fields within a single form accordingly, the views should restrict the visualisation to the specified level of detail.

7   Conclusion

In this contribution, an approach has been outlined how to use Topic Map Templates for requirements engineering and transitions to subsequent development phases. The approach supports editing, validation and participant-specific presentation of Template instantiations. In particular, consistency-preserving phase transitions and versioning mechanisms lead to well-structured conceptualisations for applications and systematic software development processes and therefore to efficient traceability management.

As proof-of-concept, an Eclipse-plugin is currently being implemented, which also provides support for consistency checks between use cases and design patterns stored in a Topic Map and annotated Java code, thereby addressing round-trip engineering [18].

It may be interesting to examine whether our approach for traceability support may be transferred to business process management as well.

References

1. Ahmed, Khalil: Beyond PSIs: Topic Map design patterns. Proc. Extreme Markup Languages (2003), `http://www.idealliance.org/papers/extreme03/html/2003/Ahmed01/EML2003Ahmed01.html`
2. Ebersbach, A., Glaser, M., Heigl, R.: Wiki Web Collaboration, Springer (2006), ISBN 3-540-25995-3
3. Barta, R.: TMQL Introduction. Presentation, ISO/IEC JTC1/SC34 Meeting (2006), `http://topicmaps.it.bond.edu.au/docs/41?style=printable`
4. Biezunski, M., Newcomb, S.: Specializing Occurrences in Topic Maps by Association Template Subclassing. Proc. Extreme Markup Languages (2001), `http://www.idealliance.org/papers/extreme02/html/2001/Biezunski01/EML2001Biezunski01.html`
5. Garshol, L. M.: The Linear Topic Map Notation: Definition and introduction, version 1.3 (rev. 1.22, 2006/01/07), `http://www.ontopia.net/download/ltm.html`
6. Garshol, L. M., Barta, R.: Topic Maps Query Language. SIO/IEC JTC1/SC34 Working draft, last updated 2005/02/18, `http://www.isotopicmaps.org/tmql/spec.html`
7. Garshol, L. M.: tolog – A Topic Maps Query Language. First International Workshop on Topic Maps Research and Applications (TMRA). Springer Lecture Notes in Artificial Intelligence (LNAI) 3873 (2005) 183–196, `http://dx.doi.org/10.1007/11676904_17`
8. Gómez-Pérez, A., Fernández-López, M., Corcho, O.: Ontological Engineering, Springer 2004, ISBN 1852335513
9. ISO: Topic Maps Data Model. Final Draft International Standard, last updated 2005/12/16, `http://www.isotopicmaps.org/sam/sam-model/`
10. ISO: Topic Maps Constraint Language. Draft International Standard, last updated 2005/10/20, `http://www.jtc1sc34.org/repository/0668.pdf`
11. Kelleher, J.: A Reusable Traceability Framework using Patterns. Third international workshop on Traceability in emerging forms of software engineering (2005), `http://doi.acm.org/10.1145/1107656.1107668`
12. Moore, G., Nishikawa, M, Bogachev, D.: Topic Map Constraint Language (TMCL) Requirements and Use Cases. Editor's Draft (2004/10/16), `http://www.isotopicmaps.org/tmcl/`
13. OMG: UML Superstructure Specification v2.0, OMG (2004), `http://www.omg.org/cgi-bin/doc?formal/05-07-04`
14. Ontopia: The Ontopia Schema Language. Reference Specification, version 3.0 (rev. 1.1.6, 2006/01/12), `http://www.ontopia.net/omnigator/docs/schema/spec.html`
15. Park, J., Cheyer, A.: Just For Me: Topic Maps and Ontologies, First International Workshop on Topic Maps Research and Applications (TMRA 2005). Springer Lecture Notes in Artificial Intelligence (LNAI) 3873 145–159 `http://www.adam.cheyer.com/papers/Just_For_Me-Final.pdf`
16. Pepper, S.: Curing the Web's Identity Crisis. Technical Report, Ontopia (2003). `http://www.ontopia.net/topicmaps/materials/identitycrisis.html`

17. Rath, H.H., Pepper, S.: Topic Maps: Introduction and Allegro. Proc. Markup Technologies (1999), http://www.ontopia.net/topicmaps/materials/allegro.pdf
18. Sendall, S., Küster, J.: Taming Model Round-Trip Engineering. Position Paper, Model-Driven Software Development Workshop, OOPSLA (2004), http://www.softmetaware.com/oopsla2004/sendall.pdf
19. Spanoudakis, G., Zisman, A.: Inconsistency Management in Software Engineering: Survey and Open Research Issues. In: Chang, S. (ed.), Handbook of Software Engineering and Knowledge Engineering. World Scientific (2001), ISBN 981-02-4973, http://www.soi.city.ac.uk/~gespan/hseke01.pdf
20. Strašunskas, D.: Traceability in Collaborative Systems Development from Lifecyce Perspective. Position Paper, Proceedings of the 1st International Workshop on Traceability (2002), http://www.idi.ntnu.no/~dstrasun/papers/strasunskas2002.pdf
21. Ueberall, M., Drobnik, O.: Collaborative Software Development and Topic Maps. First International Workshop on Topic Maps Research and Applications (TMRA). Springer Lecture Notes in Artificial Intelligence (LNAI) 3873 (2005) 169–176, http://dx.doi.org/10.1007/11676904_15
22. Vatant, B.: From Implicit Patterns to Explicit Templates: Next Step for Topic Maps Interoperability. Proc. XML (2002), http://www.idealliance.org/papers/xml02/dx_xml02/papers/05-03-06/05-03-06.html
23. Yin, M.: Organizational Paradigms. Draft, last accessed 2006/05/02, http://wiki.osafoundation.org/bin/view/Journal/ClassificationPaperOutline2

Towards a Methodology for Developing Topic Maps Ontologies

Lars Marius Garshol

Ontopia AS, Oslo, Norway
larsga@ontopia.net
http://www.ontopia.net

Abstract. This paper describes a proposed methodology for developing Topic Maps ontologies. The methodology is explicitly designed for the development of an initial ontology for a web portal, but can be adapted for other purposes. A procedure for producing a complete ontology is described, as are guidelines for how to produce an ontology.

1 Introduction

Every Topic Maps project needs an ontology, and most projects need to develop an ontology of their own. For many potential adopters of Topic Maps this is the greatest obstacle to overcome, in part because they do not know how to approach it. Part of the problem is that hardly any published information exists on how to create a Topic Maps ontology, and so adopters today have few options but to dive in and figure it out as best they can.

This paper presents a proposed methodology that organizations can follow in order to produce an ontology for their web portal. It aims at clarifying the overall process, the roles involved, and the main issues that need to be considered when creating an ontology.

The methodology explicitly only covers the initial phase from the project is conceived until it goes into production. An in many ways equally challenging aspect of ontology development is maintenance of the ontology after the application has gone into production. The methodology currently does not cover this aspect, and more work is necessary in order to create an methodology that covers the full lifecycle of a portal.

1.1 The Role of the Ontology

The term "ontology" has been used and abused in many different contexts for a large variety of purposes, and so it is necessary to define its use in this paper. For our purposes the ontology is the set of topic, name, occurrence, association, and role types used in a particular topic map (or a set of similarly-structured topic maps). In some cases, sets of particularly prominent instances are also considered to be part of the ontology.

It should be noted that we do not here mean an ontology in the sense of a logical knowledge base of some domain, intended to support logical inferencing.

L. Maicher, A. Sigel, and L.M. Garshol (Eds.): TMRA 2006, LNAI 4438, pp. 20–31, 2007.
© Springer-Verlag Berlin Heidelberg 2007

The kind of ontology used for Topic Maps portal projects is more of a conceptual model of the domain, which should use a structure and terminology that is intuitively familiar for the end-users.

The ontology is crucial to the development of a Topic Maps-driven portal, for several different reasons:

- It defines the structure of the topic map used, in much the same way that a database schema defines the structure of a relational database. The ontology thus determines what the topic map contains.
- The structure of the web portal necessarily follows the structure of the ontology quite closely, and so the ontology is effectively the blueprint for the information architecture of the web portal.
- All application code will be written against the ontology. This includes the presentation layer, any administrative interface and tools, as well as data integration code.

In short, the ontology determines how everything in the portal hangs together.

1.2   What's in the Methodology

Developing an ontology is a complex task that requires a high degree of analytical and abstract thinking, as well as interfacing against many different participants in a project to extract requirements, and ensure consensus on decisions. It is in other words a highly complex task, and one in which guidance of several different kinds may be useful.

The envisioned methodology consists of three parts:

Ontology Development Process. A procedure detailing how to approach the task of developing the ontology. The procedure is intended to help the modeller ensure that the ontology developed actually matches the requirements of the project, that there is general agreement on the ontology once produced, and to keep the process short.

Ontology Development Guidelines. A set of guidelines for the correct construction of ontologies. The purpose of the guidelines is to help the modeller use the constructs in Topic Maps correctly, and to avoid common modelling mistakes. The guidelines are outlined in 3 on page 25.

Pattern Library. A pattern library consisting of common solutions to common problems in ontology design. The purpose of these patterns is to help the modeller deal with complicated design issues in a way that is consistent with known best practices. So far only the procedure and the guidelines have been developed; the pattern library remains as future work.

2   The Ontology Development Process

This section describes the ontology development process as defined by the methodology. The process is defined in terms of a set of roles, and a set of phases that specify the interaction between the roles and a set of deliverables for each step in the development process.

2.1   Roles

Portal projects are generally run by complex project organizations fulfilling a large set of different roles. The participants playing the different roles all contribute to the ontology in their own ways, and so understanding the interplay between roles and the ontology is necessary in order to understand the methodology.

The roles defined by this methodology are:

Project manager. The person or persons responsible for the direction and management of the project.

Site owners. The group of people who have the last word in business decisions regarding the portal, and who have have the right to hire and dismiss the people in all other roles (usually except the data source owners).

Editors. The people responsible for all aspects of the communication between the portal and its end users, including layout, terminology, information architecture, and the actual content.

Ontology modeller. The person who creates the Topic Maps ontology for the portal.

Developers. The people who implement the actual portal, including the presentation layer, the editorial system, and the data integration.

Data source owners. The people responsible for the systems which provide input to the portal via data integration.

Interaction designer. Person(s) responsible for the definition of the page structure and the visual profile and communication of the portal.

End-user. The people who use the completed portal to get information.

Authors. The people who write text for the portal, or who write content for the topic map. Editors are usually also authors.

Domain expert. Someone who knows the domain being modelled. This could be an editor or a data source owner, but it need not be.

It is of course possible for some of the project participants to play more than one of the above roles in the same project. All roles except "site owner" and "editorial staff" may be filled by people external to the organization owning the portal.

2.2   The Process

The process is defined by a sequence of phases, each of which involves some defined subset of the roles, and which delivers a specified set of deliverables. The process does not aim to cover the development of the portal itself, only the ontology, and so many steps necessary for the creation of the portal have been left out.

The startup phase. The *purpose* of the startup phase is to help the modeller understand the project. Specifically, the modeller should seek to learn the vision of the project, the project team, the target audience, and any outside players with which the portal has a relationship. Getting an overview of data sources

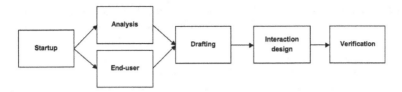

Fig. 1. Overview of the phases

and related information systems is crucial. This phase should involve the project manager, the site owners, and the editors.

The exact *format* of this phase often varies with the level of preparedness of the project. Very often it takes the form of a workshop, where project members present the project, followed by interviews with the project team, and members of other relevant teams.

The *output* of this phase should be personal notes for the developer describing the vision, the project team, outside players, and a list of the data sources the portal is going to use.

The end-user phase. The *purpose* of this phase is for the modeller to learn what information end-users want from the portal, and, if possible, what terminology (or terminologies) they use. This will help ensure that the ontology used in the portal communicates well with the end users, and that it provides the information wanted by the users.

This phase can take many *formats*, depending on the needs and preferences of the project. Essentially, this is a well-known information architecture (IA) exercise, and will often use established IA techniques like competency questions, personas, card sorting, or even end-user interviews.

The *output* of this phase will vary with the methods used, but the modeller should aim to produce notes which can be used in the verification phase.

The analysis phase. The *purpose* of this phase is for the modeller to get an in-depth understanding of the data from the data sources identified in the previous phase. For already existing data sources the modeller must attempt to get documentation, schema information, and, if possible, exports of the data and study these. For data sources not yet established, the modeller must be content with any information which can be obtained. This phase primarily involves interacting with the data source owners.

The *format* of this phase is generally a workshop with the editors, the project manager, and some domain experts. There may also be interviews with the owners of each data source followed by analysis of the material received from that data source. Quite often there are follow-up exchanges via email and phone to answer questions arising from the study of the material.

The *output* of this phase should be a draft of the portal's data flow from the various data sources through any intermediate steps and into the portal. There should also be notes towards the ontology showing the main topic and association types from each data source.

The drafting phase. The *purpose* of this phase is to create an initial picture of what the ontology might look like, to establish a shared vision of the content of the portal between the modeller and the portal stakeholders. The draft ontology need not necessarily be correct or complete at this stage; the main thing is for the stakeholders to be able to judge whether or not there are any major omissions or misunderstandings in the draft. This phase generally involves the modeller, the project manager, the developers, and the editors.

This phase generally takes the *form* of the modeller creating a draft document, which is then sent to the relevant stakeholders for review. This work may reveal gaps between the information available for the portal and either the requirements or the needs of end-users. In this case it may be necessary to revisit work from earlier phases, or to extend the scope of the project. There may be several drafting-review cycles before the draft is approved, and in the worst case parts of the earlier two phases may need to be repeated. It is recommended to also present the draft to the stakeholders in person.

The *output* from this phase is a document describing the ontology. Guidelines for the documentation are given in 2.3 on the next page.

The interaction design phase. The *purpose* of this phase is to agree on the user interface of the portal, and to ensure that the ontology can actually support that user interface. The interaction design of the portal and the ontology are intimately related, and so this phase is likely to cause substantial refinements to the ontology. This phase generally involves the project manager, the modeller, the interaction designer, the editorial staff, and the developers.

The *format* of this phase is a workshop involving the project manager, the editorial staff, the ontology modeller, and the interaction designer. In the workshop a set of screen sketches documenting the various parts of the portal are created. The ontology modeller participates in the workshop to ensure that the interaction design is consistent with the ontology, and will modify the draft ontology where necessary. After the workshop the modeller updates the ontology documentation (which is then reviewed), and produces an actual topic map containing the ontology.

The *output* of this phase is the documentation of the interaction design, an updated version of the ontology documentation, plus the topic map. The topic map can be in some format (XTM or LTM or something else), or stored in a database.

The verification phase. The *purpose* of this phase is to verify that the ontology actually matches the data in external sources, satisfies the needs of end-users, and meets the requirements of the site owners. It also includes verifying that the quality of data in external sources is sufficient for the purposes of the portal. This phase is likely to result in minor modifications in the ontology, which may again affect the interaction design. This phase generally involves the modeller, the data source owners, the project manager, and the editors.

This phase takes the *form* of the modeller working with output from the data providers and consulting them on modifications to the source data and the interpretation of the source data. It also involves the editor verifying the ontology against the output of the end-user phase, and against any requirements documentation.

The *output* of this phase is updated versions of the documentation (ontology and interaction design) as well as an updated version of the topic map. The output also includes an initial version of the conversion code, and a draft topic map with converted data.

After the verification phase is completed development of the portal can begin.

2.3 The Ontology Documentation

The topic map containing the ontology is the only output from the ontology modelling on which there is a physical dependence, but the ontology documentation is in many ways equally important. The ontology documentation is what communicates the intention behind the ontology to its users (the developers, the authors, and the editors), as well as to its owners (the portal owners), and it is therefore a crucial deliverable from the ontology development.

The documentation should consist of a single document that serves as both an introduction and a reference. It should begin with a general introduction outlining the structure of the ontology, and then follow with detailed sections defining each part of the ontology in detail. It is recommended to break the ontology into "modules" or parts which can be explained separately. The PSI namespaces used in the ontology and their QName prefixes should also be defined for reference.

The detail documentation should use UML class diagrams [ISO19501] to document the ontology[1]. It is recommended to break the diagrams into parts to keep them visually manageable, but they should be complete for the parts of the ontology that they do cover, and they should include cardinality information.

The detail documentation should also for each ontology construct include its PSI (in the form of a QName), a definition, and a description of where the construct originates. That is, it should be clear which data source the instances of the construct come from, or whether this is maintained manually. If the information is maintained manually it should be described who is responsible for it, and which tool will be used for the maintenance.

If possible, the detail documentation should also describe which code has dependencies on each part of the ontology. This may be presentation logic, the editorial system, data integration code, or even, if web services are used, external systems and partners. This information is crucial for enabling later impact analysis on proposed ontology changes.

3   Guidelines for Ontology Development

The guidelines are used by the during the modelling of the ontology to ensure that correct design decisions are made. In general, the guidelines assume that

---

[1] ISO is working on a graphical notation for Topic Maps known as GTM, and when this is ready it will replace UML. For now UML is the best alternative, however.

the reader is familiar with the basics of data modelling, and so the discussion for the most part confines itself to aspects of modelling that are peculiar to creating Topic Maps ontologies. Note that the guidelines as given in this paper are only a summary of the full set of guidelines, which are given in [Garshol07].

3.1   General Principles

This section gives a large number of specific guidelines and rules, but the modeller should always remember that very few, if any, rules are absolute. Sometimes the correct decision is to deviate from a rule, and one of the skills required of an ontology modeller is to know when to break the rules.

A goal for the design process is to make the ontology as close to the domain as possible. That is, for each topic and association type there really should be some class of things in the domain to which these correspond, and the correspondence should be as close as possible.

In general, redundancy is to be avoided. That is, the ontology should not be constructed in such a way as to include information that can be derived from other information in the ontology. The process of removing redundant constructs in an ontology is at heart the same as that of normalizing a relational data model, and the trade-offs are in many cases the same.

In general, constructs that have context assumptions built into them are to be avoided. For example, a topic type `employee` which implies that instances are employed in a particular organization should be avoided. The topic type implies an association to a specific organization, and in general it is better to state this explicitly.

In many cases many different alternatives for modelling the same information will present themselves, and it may not be obvious which to prefer. In these cases taking the needs of the application being built into consideration will often make it clear what is the best alternative in the given situation.

3.2   Topic Types

Topic types are the cornerstone of any ontology, and usually the starting point for any modelling effort. The question, of course, is what really constitutes a topic type. Generally, a topic type is the name for an abstract concept, a class or template of things in the universe of which are said to be instances of that type. A topic type is like a category, in the sense that both subdivide the universe into named subset. The difference lies in the fact that categories do not have instances. "Geography", for example, is a category, but not a topic type, because it has no instances; that is, there are no things which *are* geographies. "Country", on the other hand, is a topic type, because there really are things which are countries.

The characteristics of a good topic type are best approached through the relationship between the topic type and its instances. For one thing, a good topic type is clearly defined, so doubt about which things qualify as instances is minimized[2]. Generally, an instance should inherently, by its very nature, be an

---

[2] Removing doubt entirely is in most cases difficult, if not impossible.

instance of the given type. It follows from this that each instance should remain an instance of the same type throughout its entire lifetime. It should also be immediately obvious, given an instance, which topic type it is an instance of.

As an examples consider the topic type "lawyer". Is this a good topic type? Well, it is relatively clearly defined. However, is it inherent in the very nature of lawyers that they are lawyers? That is, if a lawyer were to share an elevator ride with you, could you tell at a glance that you were sharing the elevator with a lawyer? Obviously not. Are they lawyers from birth to death? Again, obviously not. Lawyer is a profession, something the lawyer is at work, but not at home, not in retirement, and not in childhood. The lawyer is, by his or her nature, definitely a person, however, and a person from birth to death, and in all situations. And of course there would be no doubt that you were sharing the elevator with another person. The correct topic type is therefore "person", and not "lawyer".

3.3   Class Hierarchy

The Topic Maps standard defines a supertype-subtype association type which can be used to build class hierarchies. The class hierarchies work as in other modelling paradigms, so the basic concept should be familiar, and need no introduction.

It is always possible to create a class hierarchy that encompasses all the topic types in the ontology[3], and which is elaborated downwards into a very large number of more specific subtypes. In general, however, it is not recommended to introduce more types in the class hierarchy unless there is some specific need for these.

Common, and legitimate, reasons to introduce new types into the basic set of topic types are:

- In order to make the relationship between existing topic types clearer, or to capture commonalities between them. For example, in an ontology that has the topic types "company" and "research institute" the introduction of a common supertype "organization" for these two topic types is almost inevitable. The supertype captures the fact that the two topic types are nearly the same, and gives a name to the commonality.
- In order to simplify the expression of the constraints on the ontology. Generally this means creating a common supertype that captures the set of constraints shared between its subtypes. The "organization" example above illustrates this, as most likely the two subclasses will have nearly identical constraints, and creating the superclass saves having to repeat these twice.
- In order to simplify searching in the application. It is very likely that users will want to search simply for "organizations" rather than for "company" *and* "research institute", and having the supertype makes this easier.
- In order to simplify communication with the users of the application. The users may find the subclasses too detailed or not even understand them, while the superclasses may be the terms that they are used to. (This can also apply to subclasses.)

---

[3] All topic types are subclasses of "subject".

3.4 Names

Names are most easily understood as a special kind of field on a topic type, and the difficulty is knowing when a field should be a name, and when it should not. A simple rule of thumb is that if one would ever want to show the contents of the field in a user interface as a label for the topic, then it is a name, and if not it is not a name.

Generally, every topic type should have exactly one name of the default name type[4], which should serve as the name under which the topic is displayed except in special circumstances. The cardinality should be exactly one, because if there is more than one software has no way to choose between the names (in the absence of scope), and if there is no default name the topic is without a default name that can be used to show it.

Additional name types can of course be added as desired, and these generally follow the guidelines for internal occurrence types.

3.5 Internal Occurrence Types

Internal occurrence types are effectively equivalent to properties or attributes in other modelling paradigms, and so do not present any modelling challenges specific to Topic Maps. Typical internal occurrence types for the topic type "person" in a topic map might be "date of birth", "height", "email address", etc. As in other modelling paradigms, for each occurrence type the datatype and cardinality should be defined.

3.6 External Occurrence Types

Formally speaking, external occurrence types are just occurrence types with the datatype URI. In practice, however, they are conceptually special, and present additional challenges. Part of this follows from the fact that the URI that is stored in the topic map references an external information resource, which is an entity in its own right, but one that (when modelled as an occurrence) does not get a topic in the topic map.

There are two ways to represent information resources in a topic map:

- Use external occurrences. In this case, no other information about the resource can be captured than the type and scope of its relationship with one (or more) of the topics in the topic map.
- Create a topic for the resource and use associations instead of external occurrences. In this case there are no limitations on what can be said about the resource.

The above also provides a simple rule of thumb for choosing between the two approaches: if you want to say something about the resource create a topic for it. If not, use an external occurrence.

---

[4] This is the type of topic names which do not have a `type` element in the XTM 2.0 syntax.

In many cases there are additional concerns about external occurrences, such as limitations on where they can be stored, what formats they may be in, etc. These need to be documented in the ontology documentation, as they cannot be captured in a formal schema.

3.7 Association Types

In Topic Maps there is only one way to express relationships between topics: with associations. This makes modelling these relatively simple, and defining the types of the associations is generally the same as in ER or UML modelling (see [Chen76] and [ISO19501]. There is again the difference that the same association type may recur in different places in the model, something that doesn't happen in ER and UML, but again this does not represent a problem in practice.

The main difficulty in modelling association types lies in the handling of the roles. Topic Maps support associations of arbitrary non-zero arity, something which has led many modellers astray. Some simple rules of thumb may help:

– All associations of the same type should have the same set of role types. In some cases it may be permissible for some of the role types to be optional, but their omission should then indicate missing information.
– A single association should represent a single real-world relationship.
– Association types should generally have the lowest possible arity that does not lose information.
– Each role type should not occur more than once in each association[5].

A special case that sometimes occurs is the symmetrical relationship, where both topics in the association participate in the same way. A simple example is a friendship between two people. This relationship is the same from both sides, meaning that is A is a friend of B, then B must necessarily be a friend of A. In Topic Maps this is represented as an association of type "friendship" with two roles both of type "friend".

For association types the following should be defined:

– The role types in associations of this type. For each role type the topic types which may play the role must be defined and the cardinality of the role type within the association. The cardinality should as a rule be `1..1`, although `0..1` may sometimes occur.
– The cardinality of each role type/association type combination for each topic type which can play the given role type in the given association type. All cardinalities are permissible here.

3.8 Identifiers

In general, all types in the ontology should have PSIs defined, as this greatly simplifies identifying the types in application code and configuration files of various kinds. It also greatly simplifies data integration in the future. Further, creating a subject indicator for each type is generally a useful activitiy in its own

---

[5] Symmetrical relations are an exception.

right, as it serves as human-readable documentation of the type, and requires the modeller to consider the semantics of the type in more detail. Such reflection can often lead to insights which improve the ontology.

As a general rule it is considered to advisable to reuse types defined elsewhere where the semantics of the types really do match. It is further recommended to define all the remaining types in a single PSI namespace. This would generally mean an HTTP URI ending in a slash (/), where the PSIs of the individual types in the namespace each have URIs that share this common prefix and only differ in the last part of the URI, which should contain no slahes or hashes.

4   Related Work

There already exists a vast body of literature on the general subject of data modelling, most of which is also to some degree relevant to the development of Topic Maps ontologies. Obviously relevant are modelling formalisms such as ER, UML, and ORM [Halpin01], and the methodologies for using these. A good study of the applicability of UML and ORM to the modelling of Topic Maps is [Gulbrandsen05].

However, ontology modelling is different from normal data modelling, and has concerns of its own. There is also much existing work on ontology modelling, but very little of this is actually dedicated to Topic Maps, and so much of it is not directly applicable. A good survey of methodologies for ontology development is [Visser98].

None of the existing ontology development methodologies were found to be applicable directly to the development of ontologies for Topic Maps portals. However, several were used as input for the present methodology, both for the process and the guidelines. The most important of these were the DILIGENT methodology [DILIGENT], and the ontology modelling tutorial by Noy and McGuinness [McGuinness01].

Within the space of Topic Maps, the most relevant work has been done by Kal Ahmed, most notably his work on patterns for ontology design [Ahmed03], and his paper on the creation of an ontology for the Samuel Pepys diaries [Ahmed05]. The basis for the present methodology, however, has been the (unpublished) Ontopia ontology modelling course.

References

[Gulbrandsen05]   Are D. Gulbrandsen, *Conceptual Modeling of Topic Maps with ORM Versus UML*, TMRA 2005, Lecture Notes in Computer Science, Volume 3873, Springer, Feb 2006, Page 93, DOI 10.1007/11676904_8, URL http://dx.doi.org/10.1007/11676904_8

[Visser98]   Jones, D.M., Bench-Capon, T.J.M. and Visser, P.R.S. (1998b) *Methodologies for Ontology Development*, in Proc. IT&KNOWS Conference, XV IFIP World Computer Congress, Budapest, August. URL http://www.iet.com/Projects/RKF/SME/methodologies-for-ontology-development.pdf

[McGuinness01]   N. F. Noy and D.L. McGuiness. *Ontology Development 101: A Guide to Creating Your First Ontology.* Stanford University, 2001. URL http://protege.stanford.edu/publications/ontology_development/ ontology101-noy-mcguinness.html

[DILIGENT]   D. Vrandecic, S. Pinto, C. Tempich, Y. Sure, *The DILIGENT knowledge processes*, Journal of Knowledge Management, Volume 9, Issue 5, 2005, pp 85-96, ISSN 1367-3270. URL http://www.aifb.uni-karlsruhe.de/WBS/ysu/publications/2005_kmjournal_diligent.pdf

[Ahmed03]   K. Ahmed, *Topic Map Design Patterns For Information Architecture*, XML 2003, IDEAlliance, December 2003, URL http://www.techquila.com/tmsinia.html

[Ahmed05]   K. Ahmed, *Topic Mapping the Restoration*, XTech 2005, May 2005 Amsterdam, IDEAlliance, URL http://www.idealliance.org/ proceedings/xtech05/papers/03-08-02/

[Garshol07]   L. M. Garshol, *The Ontopia Ontology Development Guidelines*, Ontopia Technical Report, in publication.

[Halpin01]   T. Halpin, *Information Model ling and Relational Databases – From Conceptual Analysis to Logical Design*, Morgan Kaufman, San Francisco, USA, 2001. ISBN 15586606726.

[ISO19501]   ISO/IEC 19501:2005 *Information technology – Open Distributed Processing – Unified Modeling Language (UML) Version 1.4.2*, International Organization for Standardization (ISO), Geneva, Switzerland, 2005.

[Chen76]   P. P. Chen, *The Entity-Relationship Model – Toward a Unified View of Data.* ACM Transactions on Database Systems 1 (1): 9-36, 1976. ISSN 0362-5915. DOI http://doi.acm.org/10.1145/320434.320440

TopiMaker -
An Implementation of a Novel Topic Maps Visualization

David De Weerdt, Rani Pinchuk, Richard Aked,
Juan-Jose de Orus, and Bernard Fontaine

Space Applications Services, Leuvensesteenweg 325, B-1932 Zaventem, Belgium
{david.deweerdt, rani.pinchuk, richard.aked, juan.jose.de.orus,
bernard.fontaine}@spaceapplications.com
http://www.topiwriter.com/

Abstract. As Topic Maps allow a structural representation of knowledge, this structure often needs to be visually presented to end-users. Issues, often contradictory, such as representation and navigation requirements, arise.

TopiMaker addresses most of these issues by putting the Topic Map as a graph on a 2D ground plane in an interactive 3D world. Topics can be elevated to planes that are parallel to the ground plane. This results in some unique qualities. Furthermore, the notion of *ghost topics* is introduced to alleviate information overload and occlusion problems. A separate window exploits tree-like features of certain association types. Features such as filtering, searching, selecting, modifying, importing, exporting, merging, querying and constraining the Topic Map are integrated with this visualization technique to make of TopiMaker a novel Topic Map authoring environment.

1 Introduction

As a Topic Map is a network of concepts, at some point or another, one will want to visualize and use this network. A Topic Map representation should be chosen in such a way that it offers a good trade-off between the sometimes conflicting requirements of representation and navigability [1].

Representation requirements include:

- clustering of semantically close topics;
- clarity of 'more important' topics such as topic types;
- a certain level of detail (e.g. including baseNames but not variants);
- minimal change in the representation when modifying the Topic Map.

On the other hand, some navigation requirements are:

- information should be accessible, explorable and searchable quickly and intuitively;

L. Maicher, A. Sigel, and L.M. Garshol (Eds.): TMRA 2006, LNAI 4438, pp. 32–43, 2007.

- information overload or information occlusion should be avoided;
- facilities for both novice and knowledgeable users of the Topic Map should be provided.

Most Topic Maps contain a vast amount of topics and associations. When focussing on a specific part of the Topic Map, one of at least three approaches can be taken to minimize this possible information overload:

1. Only the relevant part is shown, everything else is hidden.
2. The relevant part is highlighted, everything else is unchanged and remains visible.
3. The Topic Map is constantly reordered for maximum clarity and visibility of the whole, with a special care to clarity of the relevant part.

Clearly, with the first approach, it is more likely that the overview of the Topic Map is lost. The last approach is the most sophisticated and clearly has some unique qualities but it lacks in one major area: building a mental image of the Topic Map. As the human memory is heavily based on graphical recall, a representation that constantly changes looses a significant edge on this point.

As we consider the ability to build a mental image of the Topic Map to be a very crucial issue, we have chosen for the approach where the complete Topic Map remains visible and relevant parts are highlighted (i.e. the second approach).

In the following sections, TopiMaker, the Topic Maps authoring environment developed by Space Applications Services, and its design issues are elaborated upon. First, the choice of placing the Topic Map on a 2D plane in a 3D world is explained. The following section discusses how the topics and associations are placed on that 2D plane. Next, the techniques to browse and query the Topic Map and how these techniques actively help understand the Topic Map, are detailed. After that, the concept of *ghost topics* is introduced as a means to overcome the inherent problem of the 3D representation that not necessarily all neighboring topics of a selected topic are visible in the viewport. Afterwards, the reasoning around the how and why of the possibility to elevate topics and associations to a plane, parallel to the Topic Map 2D plane, is exposed. Manually manipulating the Topic Map and its representation is the next item of discussion while another complete section is dedicated to solving information overload issues. The second to last section deals with the fact that the representation of the Topic Map can be saved and loaded again. Finally, a conclusion and some further ideas are formulated.

1.1 Related Work

A lot of work in this area has been done in [1] and [3] which elaborate on the different visualization requirements and also list approaches and implementations in handling these requirements.

2   A 2D Plane in a 3D World

In TopiMaker, all topics and associations are by default shown in a fixed 2D layout on a plane in a 3D world. More concretely, during the initialization phase, when the Topic Map is loaded, a 2D graph [2] [3] of the Topic Map is created that contains all topics and all associations. The nodes (topics) of the graph are shown as cylinders while the edges (associations) are displayed as lines between the nodes. Associations with more than two members can be represented. Such associations are split into multiple edges, each with exactly two nodes (members). Hoovering over or selecting one edge will clearly highlight the other edges of the same association. After the initialization phase, this layout is not automatically changed anymore. This means that, if the user does not modify the layout on purpose, the Topic Map can be browsed and inspected indefinitely without this layout changing. Hence, once some cognitive familiarity with the graph has been built, the user will be able to orient himself very quickly.

To be actually useful however, any non-trivial Topic Map requires a non-random arrangement of its topics and associations on this 2D plane. Conveniently placing nodes (topics) and edges (associations) on a 2D plane is a whole subject in itself and is discussed in greater detail in section 3 below.

The decision to use a 2D graph instead of a three dimensional one is based on several ideas. First of all, in our opinion, a fully fledged three dimensional graph is not necessarily better for giving an overview of the structure of the Topic Map. Indeed, for having a complete view of the Topic Map that is shown as a 3D cloud, one has to zoom out until the complete cloud is visible, at which point, the cloud looks like a 2D representation. An advantage of the 3D cloud however, is that it is possible to rotate it to look at it from different angles and thus to obtain a different 2D look. When zoomed in to a level that the viewpoint is close to (or inside) the Topic Map, a 3D cloud representation suffers from the fact that now Topic Map objects can be hidden behind the virtual eye. Furthermore, in a 3D cloud, it is more likely that nearby topics hide other topics or associations. Also, the fact that one can orient himself in any direction in a 3D Topic Map cloud can form an obstruction for the construction of the mental image of the Topic Map.

The previous reasons made us opt for putting the Topic Map on a 2D plane. However, this 2D plane is placed in a 3D world, to not loose some of the qualities of a 3D representation. These include —but are certainly not limited to, as will be discussed in sections 4 and 6 below — the fact that not only it allows to take advantage of the perspective (if the plane is tilted) to determine whether topics are far away or not, but also that it just looks nice to have 3D objects on a 2D plane in a 3D world.

3   Placement Algorithm

As all topics and associations are placed on a 2D plane, an important aspect of its development is the algorithm that decides the location of the topics on this plane. A number of, mostly aesthetic, issues need to be considered. For example, one will want to avoid overlapping nodes and crossing edges as much as possible while still maintaining properties such as symmetry or even distribution of the nodes and edges. Additional qualities such as performance and ease to add or delete topics and associations are also important. A multitude of algorithms have been developed and tested, each with their own advantages and disadvantages.

As the graphs that need to be produced in TopiMaker can have a substantial amount of nodes and edges, the algorithm that is used focusses a lot on speed. Especially a $O(n^2)$ algorithm or worse is quite unacceptable. This issue is mitigated though by the fact that runtime generation of the graph is not required. Also, because different Topic Maps can have different characteristics (small or large, sparse or dense, etc.), it needs to be possible to, at least to some degree, tune up the algorithm to the users preferences.

The algorithm chosen for TopiMaker is based on the force-directed placement method [4][5], but with the nodes placed on a grid with at most one node per square of the grid. If the width of the squares of the grid is equal to the minimum distance between two nodes, calculating repulsive forces becomes unnecessary. This comes with a cost though, under the form of instabilities. In figure 1, this is shown for three nodes, all associated with each other and with a desired edge length that is equal to the width of a square. In the leftmost frame, the resulting attractive forces between the nodes are drawn. In the second frame, the bottom node is moved one square up and again the resulting forces are drawn. In the third frame, the node moved again due to the forces, now to the left. In the fourth picture, the node moves back to the right and so on.

In the algorithm, the desired edge length is equal for each edge. The algorithm can be broken down into two parts. The first part relaxes edge lengths while the second part relaxes edge crossings. The relative amount of computation can be shifted between the two parts to accomplish either an average edge length that is closer to the desired edge length, or to minimize the number of edge crossings. As it is in most cases impossible (i.e. for example if the Topic Map does not satisfy $e \leq 3v - 6$ with e the number of edges and v the number of nodes) to get to an ideal planar graph (a graph without edge crossings) wherein each edge length is

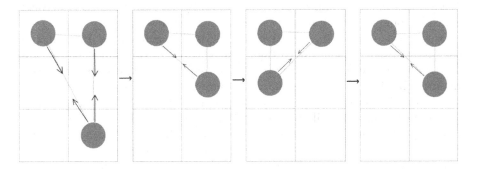

Fig. 1. Instability caused by the grid

equal to the desired length, a trade-off is necessary. Furthermore, during each iteration, a node can only move one square in any direction. If a node is to be moved to a square that is already occupied, the node on the latter square is also moved in the same direction and so on. The square whereto a node is supposed to be moved to is determined by the combined forces of both the edge length stress and the edge crossings resolution force.

Extensions. Some additions to the base algorithm can be made to improve its overall performance. As a first improvement, a starting placement of the nodes that has been given more thought than a random placement can increase the efficiency of the algorithm. For example, in case of a relatively sparse Topic Map with only a limited number of topics that have a lot of associations, an initial placement where those topics are placed far away from each other will cause a quicker convergence than a random arrangement. Also, the desired length of an edge can be adjusted using some heuristics to get some positive effect. As an example, consider the case where the desired edge length is equal to the minimum distance (and thus the width of a square of the grid) between the two nodes. If a node has four or less associated nodes, a stable state can be reached. In case of five or more associated nodes however, this is not possible. Extending the desired edge length for these latter edges would make it possible to get to a stable state. This observation leads to the simple deduction that it can be profitable to let the desired edge lengths be a function of the number of associated nodes of a node.

Doing some more iterations after the base algorithm has been executed, but now with a smaller or even no grid, more aesthetically pleasant results are obtained.

4   The Viewport, Its Controls and Camera Movements

Clicking on a topic or association in the 3D window will select it. This means that the topic or association becomes highlighted and also selected in the editor part of TopiMaker. In this editor, the topic or association can be modified. Changes are automatically and immediately propagated to the 3D window. If deemed necessary, topics can be dragged to a new, more suitable location.

Using mouse and keyboard controls, the virtual camera can be manipulated to zoom, translate and rotate in the Topic Map. Also, the camera moves automatically when changing the viewport in TopiMaker. This is not only visually appealing but it serves an important purpose too. If a topic is selected in a viewport, the camera first zooms out and then 'catches' the selected topic. This animation aids in building a mental image of the Topic Map. Even when drastically changing the viewport from one side of the Topic Map to the other —possibly unknown— side, this fluent motion between the two viewports will make it easier to understand what exactly is happening. The user will have less difficulty in understanding how the Topic Map is structured, where he is going to, relative to the original location, and how to go back.

Often, a user will want to have multiple views of the same Topic Map, and obviously he will not want to constantly change his viewport between two or more views of the Topic Map graph. Therefore, it is possible in TopiMaker to duplicate a certain viewport, together with the current state of the editor. From this moment on, the two duplicate representations are independent of each other and can be used for example for selecting two different topics for comparing them. This cloning process can be done multiple times. Apart from this, views can also be given bookmarks. This way, users can, in the same viewport, return to previous views.

5   Ghost Topics are Surrogates for Far Topics

So far, no solution has been given for the problem of topics not in the viewport of interest. Even a perfect placement algorithm will not always be able to place all neighboring topics next to or even close to each other. An example of this is a Topic Map with fifty topics that are all associated with all other topics. In this case, it is possible that the placement algorithm will (have to) place some neighboring topics on opposite sides of the Topic Map plane. Those topics would never be visible at the same time, except if one zooms out until the complete Topic Map is shown, at which point the two topics would have become useless dots. To overcome this obstacle, the concept of *ghost topics* has been devised. Basically, a ghost topic makes an invisible (i.e. out of viewport) neighbor of a

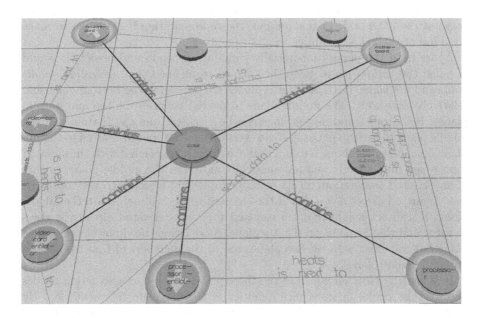

Fig. 2. One topic selected with four of its neighbors visible as ghosts (with arrows)

topic of interest visible. This is done by drawing the neighboring topic inside and at the border of the viewport and on the association edge between the topic of interest and the neighboring, out-of-viewport, topic, as is shown in figure 2. This way, except for a distinctive mark on the ghost topic, it looks as if the neighboring topic is inside the viewport. The location of the ghost topics is automatically and constantly updated when the user changes the viewport in some manner (translating, zooming, rotating) to give a consistent look and feel. Apart from the fact that there is a visual difference between ghost topics and ordinary topics, ghost topics behave very similar to topics: they can be elevated to the top or middle plane, as discussed in section 6. Also, ghost topics too can be manually dragged by the user to a new location. Note that when dragging a ghost topic, the user is actually dragging the topic itself. This means that once a user drags a ghost topic to a different location in the viewport, the topic itself is dragged to that new, visible location and thus the ghost topic becomes the topic it surrogated. This technique can actually be used to quickly put all neighboring topics in the vicinity of the selected topic, even those that are in a complete different area of the Topic Map plane.

6   Exploiting the Third Dimension — Elevation of Topics and Associations

Up until now, the Topic Map representation is limited to a 2D plane, floating in a 3D world. Apart from the added perspective and the ability to move the virtual camera around more freely than in a 2D world, no real use is made of the space of the 3D world. In this section, the representation is extended to make good use of the 3D possibilities.

Apart from the plane that initially contains all topics and associations and is called the *bottom plane*, two other planes are defined that are called *middle plane* and *top plane*. Both additional planes are parallel to the bottom plane and relatively close to it. The middle plane is located between the top and bottom planes. Both topics and associations can be *elevated* from the bottom and the middle plane to the top plane, and vice versa. When a topic is elevated to the top plane, its direct neighbors —topics that are directly associated with the elevated topic— are immediately and automatically moved to the middle plane. In case of an elevated association, all its member topics are elevated to the top plane too. Again, all direct neighbors of the elevated topics will be put on the middle plane. If a direct neighbor of an elevated topic was elevated already, it stays elevated and thus remains on the top plane. Associations need not be on a single plane but can exist between two planes too, if the members of that association are on different planes.

It is visually clear on which of the three planes a topic or association resides and all this results in some nice qualities of the complete representation. By elevating a topic, this topic and its neighbors are clearly highlighted. This is accomplished by their distinctive colors and the fact that they are not located on the same plane as all the other topics. Moreover, the default-on option to

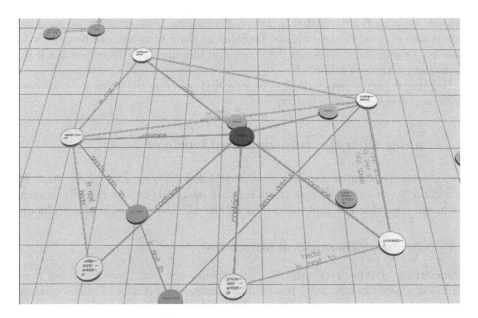

Fig. 3. A small Topic Map view with one topic elevated to the top plane and its six direct neighbors lifted to the middle plane

animate movements of topics and associations between planes, further clarifies to the user what exactly is happening.

Multiple topics and associations can be elevated at the same time. This gives a great navigational tool: when elevating a single topic, all its direct neighboring topics are shown in the middle plane and are thus highlighted. This way, the user can easily focus on any topic that is directly associated with the topic of interest. If the user then elevates one of these direct neighbors, a path is being formed in the top plane of elevated topics. By continuing like this, one can for example clarify how (i.e. through which topics and associations) two topics are related.

7   Manipulating the Topic Map

The graphical representation of the Topic Map is also used for doing structural modifications to the Topic Map. These structural modifications are: adding and removing topics, and adding and removing associations. Modifying the content of topics and associations is done in the editor part of TopiMaker and has already been mentioned in section 4 on page 36.

When adding a topic, which is done by simply pressing a button, an empty topic is generated and put on the bottom plane in the center of the screen, wherever this may be in the Topic Map view. The topic is **not** placed in a location that is calculated by TopiMaker, but can be dragged to its final destination.

To create an association, first at least one member of the future association needs to be marked because an association can never have zero members. The association is then also created by pressing a button. Once created, the association is also selected in the editor of TopiMaker where members can be modified, removed or added. At all times, both the graphics and the editor part are kept up to date with each other.

Deleting topics or associations is done by first selecting the items to be deleted and then pressing a delete button.

8 Coping with the Information Overload

An inherent problem to the way that TopiMaker represents the Topic Map is that there is a constant danger of information overload. This section discusses a few techniques that are implemented to aid the user in overcoming this problem.

8.1 Visualizing Hierarchical Structures

Associations of type 'type-instance' lend themselves quite well for being presented in a tree-like structure. It would be convenient if it were possible, given a starting topic, to show all topics that are directly or indirectly associated to that topic through (an) association(s) of the 'type-instance' type. This would create a hierarchy with the starting topic at the top (level 0), topics that are instances of the starting topic are below the top (level 1), topics that are instances of the topics at level 1 are at level 2, and so on.

As this kind of view is not possible with what is presented until now, Topi-Maker uses a separate window in which this kind of tree can be shown. In fact, because some other types of associations are also suited to be shown in a hierarchical view, this window can also be configured to show these other types of associations. Some examples include 'subclass-superclass', 'part-whole' or 'parent-child'. Also, a strict top-down structure with the given topic at the top is not a necessity. Indeed, nothing prohibits us from fanning out in the opposite direction too and creating an inverted tree. For a 'parent-child' association type for example, a starting topic would be placed in the middle of the window. Its children, grandchildren and so on would be placed in the tree below the starting topic at respectively levels 1 and 2, and its parents, grandparents and so on are placed in the inverted tree above the starting topic at respectively levels -1 and -2. Obviously, the more topics and associations that are shown in this window, the greater the risk that its actual usefulness becomes more and more limited because of information overload. If too many topics need to be shown in this topic, they will overlap and be accessible/selectable using a dropdown list.

8.2 Searching and Filtering

When one does not know exactly where to find a topic or association in the 3D window, it can be searched for using a advanced searching mechanism. A normal full text search was deemed insufficient as this does not exploit any of the powers of Topic Map technology.

Basically, a search consists of selecting a plain text query from a list, filling in some parameters of this query and executing it. This will result in a list with possible answers (topics or associations) to the query. After choosing one of the possible answers (presumably the topic or association that the user was looking for), this topic/association is selected and shown in both the 3D window and the editor. TopiMaker comes with a broad range of pre-defined queries and it is possible, for a more advanced user, to construct user-defined queries by linking a new plain text query to a Toma query [6]. Two out of the box queries are given as an example:

- Show all topics that have a baseName that has a scope *fill_in*
- Show all topics that take part in at least *fill_in* association(s) of type *fill_in* where they play the role of *fill_in*

The ability to filter topics and associations in a Topic Map can be a great asset. Indeed, if the filtering mechanism is able to hide, show or recolor topics and associations, this can be used for fulfilling several wishes.

First of all, by hiding information of little interest, the information overload problem is solved. As an unlimited number of filters can be created and combined, it is possible to create a view of the Topic Map that only shows those parts of the Topic Map that are of interest. A very simple, almost self-explaining example with two filters will clarify the power of filters.

1. Hide all topics and associations
2. Show all associations of type 'part-whole' and all topics that take part in an association of type 'part-whole'

These two filters are applied in order (which can be changed at run-time) and will result in a Topic Map view that only shows topics and associations that are players in the 'part-whole' association type. It is important to note here that although the view of the Topic Map changes as topics and associations are hidden or shown, the arrangement of topics and associations will not change. In fact, by enabling and disabling filters, it is easy and visually attractive to see at a glance which topics are hidden or shown. Taking this a step further, we can next to just hiding or showing topics and associations, also provide the ability to color topics and associations. Naturally, when using an excessive amount of different colors, the view may become so chaotic that all benefits are overshadowed by the chaos. It is up to the user to find a suitable compromise. Using colors, it can be nice to rephrase the filter example, given above, to the following.

1. Hide all topics and associations
2. Show all associations of type 'part-whole' in orange, all topics that take part as the role 'part' in yellow and all topics that take part as the role 'whole' in red

The actual process of defining filters is very similar to searching process.

9   Constraining the Topic Map

It is possible to define constraints on the Topic Map. These constraints are not truly enforced in the sense that TopiMaker will not prevent users to continue without fixing broken constraints. Instead, warnings are clearly displayed when there are broken constraints. Also, the offending topics and/or associations are marked in the 3D window. The reason for this choice is that if it were made impossible to continue with broken constraints, a possible deadlock can occur when multiple constraints have been broken at the same time. Again, the user can both use built-in parameterized constraints or he can define his own using a mechanism that is extremely similar as the filtering and searching mechanism. Some examples of the constraints that are by default supported by TopiMaker are:

- all topics of type *fill_in* must have at least one occurrence of type *fill_in*
- all associations of type *fill_in* must have at least *fill_in* members

The possibilities for creating user defined constraints are endless. The following constraint possible to define and configure with actual parameters.

- the sum of the contents of each occurrence of type **weight** of all topics that take part in an association of type **part-whole** where the topics take the role **part** and the topic **International Space Station** takes the role **whole** must not exceed **184000** kg.

10   Saving the State of the Virtual World

In TopiMaker, the representations of a Topic Map are always saved together with the Topic Map, so closing and opening the Topic Map again will result in the same representations, without the need to wait for a recomputation of the layout. This also helps the user to continue his work on the Topic Map, starting from the point it was left the day before.

11   Conclusion

The main strength of the visualization part of TopiMaker is that the 3D visualization of the Topic Map is quite new and finds a nice balance between representation quality and navigability. The static graph on the 2D plane in the 3D world, together with the ability to elevate topic map objects and the concept of the ghost topics, make the topic map representation easy to understand and to use. From this base design of TopiMaker, new ideas for enhancing the representation raise, yet these have to be balanced with the problem of information overload.

- Instead of three planes with respectively elevated topics, neighboring topics of elevated topics and all the other topics, additional planes can be added.

If, for example, one also wants to highlight second degree neighboring topics of an elevated topic, a fourth plane can be added between the bottom and the middle plane. This idea can be further extended to even more planes;
– Currently, only topics and associations are shown in the 3D window. It can be imagined, when zoomed in to a sufficient level, to also show topic characteristics (baseNames, occurrences and so on) as nodes in the graph, connected with the centered topic.

Except for section 8.1, which is still under development, TopiMaker, as described in this paper, has been implemented both in a linux and in a MS Windows version.

References

1. Le Grand, B., Soto M., Visualisation of the Semantic Web: Topic Maps Visualisation, IEEE IV 2002, London, July, 2002
2. Harary, F., Graph Theory., Addison-Wesley, 1969
3. Amende, N., Groschupf, S.: Visualizing an Auto-Generated Topic Map
4. Fruchterman, T. M. J., Reingold, E. M.: Graph Drawing by Force-directed Placement, Software—Practice and Experience, Vol 21(11), 1129–1164 (November 1991)
5. Kamada, T., Kawai, S.: An algorithm for drawing general undirected graphs, Information Processing Letters, 31, pp 7–15, 1989
6. Pinchuk R. et al., Toma - TMQL, TMCL, TMML, (hopefully) TMRA 06, 2006

Visual Browsing and Editing of Topic Map-Based Learning Repositories

Boriana Ditcheva[1] and Darina Dicheva[2]

[1] Columbia University, Department of Computer Science
450 Computer Science Building
1214 Amsterdam Avenue, New York 10027
bhd2105@columbia.edu
[2] Winston-Salem State University, Department of Computer Science
3206 E J Jones Computer Science Building
Winston Salem, NC 27110, USA
dichevad@wssu.edu

Abstract. Topic Maps For e-Learning (TM4L) is an environment for building, maintaining, and using standards-based, ontology-aware e-learning repositories. This paper discusses the intuitive, visual interface of the system in the context of TM4L evolution. The focus is on our work on extending TM4L with visual editing functionality. The integration of the editing and visualization supports authoring by providing browsing and editing "in one view."

Keywords: Topic maps, visualization, editing ontology-based collections.

1 Introduction

The success of e-learning ultimately depends on the availability of efficient authoring tools that support authors and learners in creating and browsing online learning materials, and availability of tools with intuitive interfaces and uniformity in their appearance and operation. Using knowledge standards, such as Topic Maps [2], it is possible to incorporate learning content in semantically rich data models.

Topic Maps (TM) are among the most promising Semantic Web technologies for organizing and navigating through large information pools. They can provide a "bridge" between the domains of knowledge representation and information management [17] and serve as the skeleton of ontology-aware applications, such as digital learning repositories. Despite some successes, however, the lack of convenient tools that allow authors to directly enter, modify, index, and query resources in ontology-aware digital repositories remains a major obstacle to their deployment. Among the main reasons for this bottleneck is that resource authors typically lack ontology engineering skills to build them, and ontology engineers lack domain expertise to do authors' work. Tools can help, and many have been built already. However, most of these tools are targeted toward users assuming some experience in structuring and classifying resources based on specific representation models.

A key feature and challenge in today's ontology-aware applications, including Topic Map-based applications, are Graphical User Interfaces (GUI) [4]. It is largely

L. Maicher, A. Sigel, and L.M. Garshol (Eds.): TMRA 2006, LNAI 4438, pp. 44–55, 2007.

recognized that visualization in the form of a graph can help the user comprehend and analyze information easier. This is particularly important when representing ontological structures, which can be very complicated. Ontology visualization is an active area of research and there are a number of graphical interfaces already available. For example, the ontology editor Protégé [16] alone employs three visualization tools: TGVizTab [1], Jamballaya [20], and OntoViz [26]. In the area of Topic Maps, the available visualization tools include Ontopia's Vizigator [28], TMNav [27], Think-Graph [30], the LIP6' visualization tool [14], etc. Visual interfaces typically provide integrated management of browsing and search in support of users' needs for information exploration. Information visualization normally requires the support of metadata in order to enable intuitive presentation and navigation, as in the case of ontology-based visualization where the interaction is directed by the ontology. Some interfaces provide editing functionality as well, e.g. IsaViz, OntoViz and ThinkGraph.

Topic Maps For e-Learning (TM4L) is an environment for building, maintaining, and using standards-based, ontology-aware e-learning repositories [7]. It targets two groups of users: authors, with a limited or no background of ontologies, and learners, seeking information support in their learning tasks. The goal in its design was to enable users to create, update, browse, and query topic-centered learning repositories without having prior experience with topic maps. The original embodiment of this idea was the TM4L Editor. Later on TM4L was extended with a new functionality aimed at supporting graphical navigation through the learning collection and offering a visual alternative to the available tree structure browsing. The main reason for extending the Editor to allow the use of graphs for interacting with users was the appealing features of graphical notations, especially as an informal graphical front end. They have been found particularly functional in educational settings [3, 5]. Similarly, they have been found intuitive to the ontology engineers, see for example [10, 23].

In this context, the next goal was to exploit the visualization feature in terms of editing Topic Maps-based learning content. The motivation for this was driven by our opinion that automatic topic map construction is not yet an alternative to the manual educational topic map design. Automatic TM acquisition is an expensive operation and more importantly – one with limited reliability. Even if initially accurate and complete, topic maps may need modifications and adaptations at later stages reflecting ontology evolution. This suggests the use of a balanced cooperative modeling and construction approach. Therefore, our goal was focused on employing visualization to provide intuitive editing functionality facilitating TM authoring as much as possible. At present TM4L is an environment for building Topic Map-based e-learning repositories that supports three interactive tasks: editing, browsing and querying. With this multifunctional environment we want to test our insights about how to enable instructors, with limited knowledge of information technology, to populate and maintain ontology-based e-learning repositories relatively easily.

In this paper, we describe TM4L's visualization and editing functionality. This functionality is separated architecturally into two distinct interfaces. The first one is oriented towards hierarchical structures and exploits the semantics carried by *super-class-subclass*, *whole-part*, and *instance-of* relations to make the representation of the domain more intuitive. This aspect is covered in Sections 3 and 4. The second interface addresses more general structures and is intended to provide a combined picture that is particularly useful when dealing with domains that include both hierarchical and non-hierarchical structures. This aspect is covered in Section 5.

2 Interface: Design Goals and Strategies

Information seeking in an e-learning context is a complex activity that originates from a learner's task-related information needs and involves interaction strategies such as searching and browsing information sources. Our approaches to address the challenges inherent in the interaction with and visualization of TM-based e-learning repositories are in line with the techniques used for visualizing semantic net-based information [12].

Exploit syntactic and semantic knowledge to improve the visualization. Two main sources of information can be used to generate effective visualizations for TMs:
- Syntactic knowledge based on the topological properties of the TM.
- Semantic knowledge based on the meaning of the topics and relationships between them captured by the TM.

Provide methods for abstracting and filtering the information space. Reducing the size of the information space is the key to dealing with scaling problems in visualization and can also make the structure of the learning collection more apparent. This reduction can be achieved by developing multi-level filtering and abstraction techniques to hide nodes and relations. Our approach to filtering is based on abstraction criteria that exploit the task context combined with information semantics.

Provide flexible scoping methods. All user interactions defined on TM structures (e.g., editing, searching, navigating) require a specified region (scope) of operation. A region consists of a subset of topics and links drawn from the overall topic map. For example, we can use the notion of a region to identify a set of related topics constituting a "neighborhood". The user's ability to define a region (scope) that is natural and efficient for the task at hand is essential to effective interaction.

Provide a notion of "semantic distance". The concept of "semantic distance" between two topics is critical to developing user-centered navigation and abstraction techniques.

The TM4L interface was designed with the above considerations in mind and according to two basic principles. The first one was that users' interaction with learning content should be easy and intuitive. The second was that both browsing and searching should be supported. These principles were embedded in the following goals:

1. Offer an insightful overview of the learning collection structure.
2. Provide primary information at the earliest point.
3. Support rapid decision making about information relevancy based on multiple views.
4. Support exploratory browsing to develop intuition.
5. Offer contextual support during searching and querying to allow users to correctly express their information needs.
6. Support multiple perspectives and allow their comparison or the retrieval of additional information at a glance.

7. Offer possibilities for constraining the amount of displayed information (e.g. to selected topics of interest).

From a Semantic Web perspective, ontology-based information seeking is a promising approach for enhancing existing interfaces with features that enable learners to improve exploratory search styles and better express their information needs. This involves interacting with concepts and relations embodied in the ontologies that describe the subjects in the area of interest.

3 Two Perspectives on the Interactions

The functionality and visualization strategy of TM4L is defined to support two groups of users: authors and learners. The users from these two groups have different levels of subject knowledge and skills. While the learners have often only a vague understanding of their information needs, the authors, who know the subject domain, are typically aware of what topics they need. Thus authors and learners differentiate in:

- *Navigation and Query formulation:* Which path is more relevant to current information needs? How should one modify the query to find more relevant information?
- *Vocabulary:* Which terms should be used? (While the learners frequently are not familiar with the terminology, authors typically know the jargon of the field.)

The different ways of tackling these questions reflect the gap in terms of knowledge and perception between the authors and the learners. In general, learners need to alternate phases of browsing the TM content with phases of querying it. In the latter they often need to refine their selection criteria according to the obtained results.

In contrast, the authors need efficient support for structuring, organizing, entering, and updating the learning content. These presume functionality of supporting topic maps evolution, which will enable the authors to modify the underlying ontology, instances and resources.

As it is impossible to fulfill all requirements, we adopted a compromised approach to the interface design:

- Allow users who know what they are looking for to quickly and efficiently find it.
- Allow learners who don't know what they are looking for to do *exploratory searching*.

Searching and browsing in TM4L is integrated so that users can move easily between the two options so they can focus their search.

4 Editing and Browsing Support

Visualizing and navigating ontology-based content is a challenging problem faced in many knowledge domains and applications. In particular, visualization is used in tools that support the development of ontologies, such as ontology editors (i.e. Protégé [30], IsaViz [18], WebOnto [9]). The intended users of these tools are ontology engineers that need to get an insight in the complexity of the ontology. Therefore, these tools employ schema visualization techniques that primarily focus on the structure of the ontology, i.e. its concepts and their relationships.

The ontologies currently used for structuring e-learning content are typically light-weight. Light-weight ontologies are typified by the fact that they are predominantly taxonomies, with very few cross-taxonomical links, and with very few logical relations between the classes. Light-weight ontologies are a valid choice in many cases because they are easier to understand, easier to build, and easier to get consensus upon. Topic maps are seen as lightweight ontologies because they are able to model knowledge in terms of topics, their classes, occurrences, and associations. In contrast to other domains in e-learning, instance information along with the resources is often as important (if not more important) as the structure of the ontology that is used to describe them. Therefore, in contrast to the general ontology editors, the TM4L editing facilities enable users to capture the ontology schema, as well as visualize instances, their properties, such as the resources associated with them, and their related topics.

Interfaces that provide multiple views are able to offer users different perspectives on a selected entity. Following this model, the TM4L Editor provides Topic centered, Relation centered and Themes guided views (see Fig. 1).

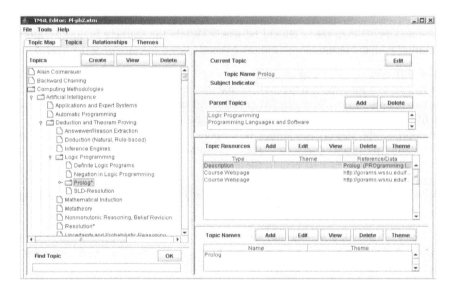

Fig. 1. TM4L Editor: a topic-centered view

In Topic Maps, associations define relations among an arbitrary number of topics. As a primary relation for classifying learning content we have selected the *whole-part* relationship known also as *partonomy*. Like a taxonomy, a partonomy is a hierarchy, but based on the *part-of* relation rather than on a *class-subclass* relation. The reason for picking out partonomy is its important explanatory role in an e-learning context [6]. Explaining what a learning unit is about, often involves describing its parts and how are they composed. For example, we may choose to structure learning material on Programming Languages in terms of its components, i.e. Syntax, Semantics and Pragmatics. However, the learning units describing the syntax, semantics and pragmatics are part of the Programming Languages unit and not subclasses of it. By emphasizing the compositional structure, the partonomy is closer to the approach normally used for representing learning content. Recent research in education also indicates that one technique shown to reduce cognitive load and improve learning is a *whole-part* presentation method [22]. For example, Mayer and Chandler's study [15] suggests that studying initially a part (piece by piece) rather than a whole presentation allows the learner to progressively build a coherent mental model of the material without experiencing cognitive overload.

In many application areas the natural model of the domain requires the ability to express knowledge about the *class-subclass* relation. The *class-subclass*, also known as *is-a* relation, allows organizing objects in the domain with similar properties into classes. The *class-subclass* relation has received a lot of attention and is well-understood. However, the interaction between *whole-part* and *class-subclass* relations has not been studied in detail.

Despite their different purposes, knowledge base, database, object-oriented and e-learning communities heavily rely on conceptual models which have a lot in common. Inter-relationships such as *is-a*, *part-of*, *similar-to*, etc. are used to define and constrain the interactions of concepts within these models. Therefore, in addition to the primary *whole-part* relationship, TM4L contains four other predefined relationship types, including the classic *class-subclass* and *class-instance* extended with *similar-to* and *related-to* relations [6]. By offering this minimal set of five predefined relation types we support TM4L authors that experience difficulties in articulating and naming relationships.

The TM4L Editor interface is a typical tree rendering, with the left pane showing the tree and the right pane showing the properties (facets) of each selected node. The nodes of the tree are topics and the edges denote either the default binary *part-of* relation or a relation chosen by the user (*superclass-subclass* or *class-instance*). The hierarchical tree allows browsing the topic partonomy at different levels of detail. The topic attributes, resources, topic parents and relations are displayed in separate panels.

Because of the tree-centered representation, a multiple inheritance is approximated with the help of "cloned" subtrees, appearing in the list of descendants of every parent. Nodes with more than one parent in the *whole-part* hierarchy are indicated. The learning units organized by the *whole-part* relation not always form trees in the formal sense. TM4L handles the case where these relationships are discontinuous, which implies that it is able to visualize forests as well as trees.

For facilitating the access and selection of topics during the editing, expand-and-contract style selection for the topic class hierarchy is provided. To provide a context of the interactions whenever an element of the visualization is selected, it is highlighted. Besides adding new topic types and relation types to the ontology schema, it is possible to add new instances to topics, new relations, and new resources, as well as to modify or delete their attributes at any time, without instances becoming invalid.

5 Graphical Editing and Exploration

The original TM4L Editor enables authors to create TM-based learning content and repositories, by adding topics, relations, resources and scopes (themes). In a typical scenario, after the collection is created, the author can realize (during a browsing session) that certain modifications are necessary. Then the author updates the learning repository structure by using the general editing functionality of the Editor.

One of the recommendations of the TM4L users was for a global view of the repository structure along with "visual editing" functionality. This prompted us to combine the TM4L graphical viewer with an editor so as to offer the author a graphical view of the collection with the possibility of performing some basic editing operations (such as adding, moving, and deleting) on it. As the typical TM4L users are instructors or students, who typically do not have experience with constructing topic maps, we extended the original environment with a graphical editor (called TM4L-GEV), based on a graph representation. It was supposed to complement both the TM4L Viewer and the original TM4L Editor with editing functionality.

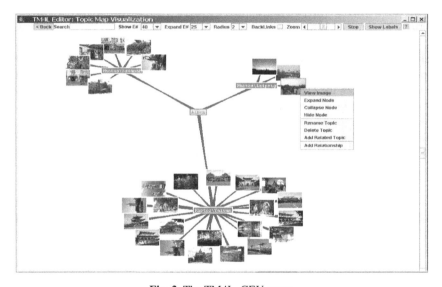

Fig. 2. The TM4L–GEV menu

Currently, the Graphical Editor allows modifications of the TM structure and related properties, such as topic and relationship type names, but not of the resource content. In this section we describe our approach concerning the graphical extension of the TM4L environment.

TM4L-GEV is a GUI for creating and modifying (educational) topic maps. It is a visualizing and editing tool for topic maps, which aims to reconcile topic maps with the semantic network philosophy by providing a set of graphic idioms that cover TM constructs. The graph visualization interface is based on the "TouchGraph" technology [31], an open source graph layout system, which we connected to TM4L and extended to meet its GUI requirements. We studied different tools for visualizing conceptual structures and chose TouchGraph because of its expressive, clear, and intuitive visualization. In addition, it offers a number of advantageous features for visualizing networks, such as high level of interactivity, fast rendering, locality control, pan and zoom capability, etc. These characteristics have been shown to be vital for visualizing large information networks. TouchGraph applies a spring-layout technique, where nodes repel each other while edges attract them, which results in placing semantically similar nodes closer to each other.

GEV provides a graph representation for TM constructs (topics are represented as nodes and relations as edges) and offers capabilities for navigating and editing topic maps. It is a browsing and editing "in-one-view" tool. The simplest editing feature consists of direct editing of the topic name of a selected node. In a similar fashion the author can edit a relation type name. The more complex editing functionality of TM4L-GEV includes:

Create New Topic. This operation consists of creating a new topic in the topic map. This does not link the new topic/node to any other nodes of the displayed graph.

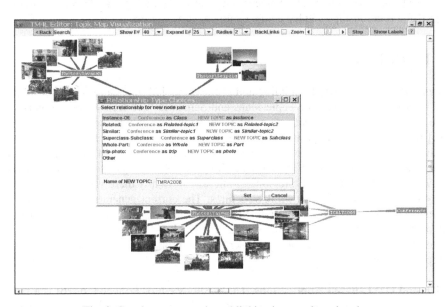

Fig. 3. Creating a new topic and linking it to a selected topic

Add Related Topic. This operation consists of creating a new topic and linking it to the currently selected topic. The user is prompted to select a relation by which to link the two topics.

Delete Topic. This operation consists of deleting an existing topic along with all its resources and associations (linking the deleted topic to some other topics) in the current topic map.

Add relationship of an existing type. The system first asks the user to select a type for the new binary relationship from a list of predefined and user-defined relationship types. Considering the currently selected topic as the player of the first role of the newly created relationship of the selected type, it asks then the user to select a topic to play the second role in the relationship.

Add relationship of a new type. This operation consists of creating a new relationship type in the topic map, followed by performing the "Add relationship of an existing type" operation.

Delete Relationship. This operation consists of disconnecting related topics.

These operations can be selected from a menu, which is activated by right-clicking on a certain graph element. If a user right-clicks on a topic (a node), s/he will see a menu of the options: Rename Topic, Delete Topic, Add Related Topic, and Add Relationship. If a user right-clicks on an edge, s/he will see a menu with the following option: Delete Relationship, and if a user right-clicks on an empty space, s/he will see the following option: Create New Unlinked Topic. Additionally, to enable the display of different perspectives on learning resources matching the learners' level and interests, TM4L-GEV implements theme *filters* that can simplify the display by hiding topics and relationships that have no meaning to certain users.

6 Related Work

The availability of tools for building and prototyping TM applications can considerably improve the reception of Topic Maps and Semantic Web technologies in general. The early examples of visualizations of Web resources include the Hyperbolic Tree [13] for navigation of large trees and The Brain (http://www.thebrain.com) for navigating graphs. A more recent example is Hypergraph [25], a Java application that provides a hyperbolic layout in 2D that allows interactive repositioning of nodes to provide more magnification to regions of interest. Normally these visualizations focus on syntactic structures such as link structures. The current generation of tools represents a new step in this direction in that the emphasis is on interfaces for manipulating information. For example, systems such as Haystack [11] are emerging that concentrate on the concepts important to the users of the information: documents, messages, properties, annotations, etc.

RDF and OWL-based Applications. The ontology editor Protégé [16, 26] is a Java-based knowledge modeling tool. It incorporates hierarchical visualization plug-ins to aid the construction, editing and visualization of ontologies. These include OntoViz [26], which is based on the AT&T GraphViz visualization libraries for graphical representations of hierarchical data, and TGVizTab [1], which also uses Touchgraph, and provides functionality for searching and saving graphs as image files. SHriMP [19] is a modular component that is combined with Protege to form Jambalaya [20], a tool that provides fish-eye views that make use of a continuous zoom for overviews of large data sets. Encoding of data nodes using color and depth cueing in 3D helps to distinguish more important data.

Tools for editing and visualizing graphs of RDF data are available on most platforms. The most common graphical visualization for RDF is IsaViz [18]. It is a visual environment for browsing and authoring RDF models represented as graphs, using

Jena (http://jena.sourceforge.net/). It features a 2.5D user interface allowing zooming and navigation in the graph. It also supports the creation and editing of graphs by drawing ellipses, boxes and arcs. Triple20 [21] is another ontology manipulation and visualization tool for languages built on top of the Semantic-Web RDF triple model. Growl [24] is a visualizing and editing tool for OWL and DL ontologies and provides graphic representation for all OWL constructs and all common Description Logic expressions as well as advanced methods of navigation within large ontologies.

Topic Map-based Applications. In the field of Topic Map-based applications, one of the first interactive Topic Map visualization tools has been implemented by Le Grand and Sotto [14]. The proposed tool supports sophisticated visual and navigational forms, however the presentation is not easily comprehensible and intuitive. TMNav [27] is a combined text and graphical topic map browser that allows users to easily navigate through the topic maps of interest. It is based on the TM4J topic map library and uses Java Swing, TouchGraph, and HyperGraph.

The Omnigator [29] is Ontopia's generic topic map browser. One of its recent additions is the Vizigator [28], which provides a graphical alternative to the text browsing environment. The Vizigator includes two components: the VizDesktop, used by application designers to control colors, shapes, fonts, and icons, and the VizLet, a Java applet that can be embedded in OKS applications.

ThinkGraph [30] is a 2D drawing application specialized for Concept Maps authoring. It uses only standard XML: SVG (Scalable Vector Graphics, a XML language specialized for 2D drawing) is used for the presentation part (shape and graphical attributes) while XTM is used for the data part.

ENWiC [8] is a framework for visualization of Wikis that offers an alternative to the standard text interface. It represents the structure of the Wiki as a topic map, which is visualized using Touchgraph. The graphical representation helps users to see an overview 'map' of the Wiki, which enables efficient navigation. However the visualization is primarily concerned with navigating Wiki's type of websites rather than general educational topic maps.

TM4L. Where Protege is primarily designed as a general ontology editor, TM4L is primarily a Topic Map-based editor and browser with e-learning orientation. What is central to our work is the provided help to authors for logically grouping the repository items by providing a set of predefined relations equipped with adequate visualization interface. Other tools also similar to our work in that they are based on using TouchGraph are the Ontopia's Vizigator and TGVizTab. However these tools provide only visual navigation of the presented conceptual structure, while TM4L-GEV also supports visual editing. Perhaps the closest in spirit to TM4L-GEV is IsaViz, which is also aimed at combining editing and visualization but based on the RDF technology. The distinguishing feature of TM4L is that it supports synchronization between the two editing interfaces thus allowing the author to switch at any time between them.

7   Conclusion

We continue to see the man-machine collaboration as the most powerful ontology producer. Tools have been built and continue to be built to automate some tasks of ontology extraction. However, manual editing in addition to the automated acquisition process will remain as a fundamental method of knowledge capture in the near future. In this relation, to foster development of Topic Maps-based e-learning applications, authors need adequate editing systems and development environments.

In this article, we presented our work on extending the editing and visualization features of TM4L towards a browsing and editing "in-one-view" authoring environment. The focus is on integrating the visualization and editing support. The intuitive, visual interface is discussed in the context of TM4L evolution.

Acknowledgments

This material is based upon work supported by the National Science Foundation under Grant No. DUE-0442702 "CCLI-EMD: Topic Maps-based courseware to Support Undergraduate Computer Science Courses."

References

1. Alani, H.: TGVizTab: An ontology visualisation extension for Protégé. In: Knowledge Capture 03 - Workshop on Visualizing Information in Knowledge Engineering. ACM, Sanibel Island, FL (2003) 2–7
2. Biezunski, M., Bryan, M., Newcomb, S.: ISO/IEC 13250:2000 Topic Maps: Information Technology, Available at: www.y12.doe.gov/sgml/sc34/document/0129.pdf
3. Gaines, B. R. and Shaw M. L. G.: Webmap: Concept mapping on the web. The World Wide Web Journal, 1(1) (1996)
4. Bouquet, P., Serafini, L., Zanobini, S.: Peer-to-Peer Semantic Coordination. J. of Web Semantics, 2(1) (2005)
5. Canas A. J., Ford K., Novak J. D., Hayes P., Reichherzer T., Suri N.: Using concept maps with technology to enhance cooperative learning in Latin America. Science Teacher, 2001
6. Dichev C., Dicheva D.: Contexts as Abstraction of Grouping, Workshop on Contexts and Ontologies, 12th Natl Conf on Artificial Intelligence, AAAI 2005, Pittsburgh (2005) 49-56
7. Dicheva, D., Dichev, C.: TM4L: Creating and Browsing Educational Topic Maps, British J. of Educational Technology - BJET, 37(3) (2006) 391-404
8. Espiritu C, Stroulia E., Tirapa T. ENWIC: Visualizing Wiki semantics as Topic Maps. In: Proc. of 8th Int. Conf. on Enterprise Information Systems. Paphos, Cyprus (2006)
9. Fluit, C., Sabou, M, van Harmelen, F.: Ontology-based Information Visualisation. In: Geroimenko, V., Chen, C. (eds.): Visualising the Semantic Web, Springer-Verlag, London (2002) 36-48
10. Gaines B. R.. An interactive visual language for term subsumption languages. In IJCAI'91, (1991)
11. Karger, D., Bakshi, K., Huynh, D., Quan, D., Sinha, V.: Haystack: A Customizable General-Purpose Information Management Tool for End Users of Semistructured Data. Proc. of the 2nd Biennial Conf. on Innovative Data Systems Research, Asilomar, CA, USA (2005)
12. Keller, R.M., Hall, D.R.: Developing Visualization Techniques for Semantics-based Information Networks, In Proc. Workshop on Information Visualization in Knowledge Capture Technologies, 2nd Int. Conf. on Knowledge Capture, Sanibel Island, FL (2003)

13. Lamping J, Rao R, Pirolli P.: A focus+context technique based on hyperbolic geometry for visualising large hierarchies. In: ACM Conf. on Human Factors in Software (1995) 401–408

14. Le Grand B, Soto M.: Topic Maps Visualization, In Geroimenko, V. and Chen, C. (eds.): Visualizing the Semantic Web: XML-based Internet and Information Visualization, Springer-Verlag, London (2003) 49-62

15. Mayer, R. E., Chandler, P.: When learning is just a click away: Does simple user interaction foster deeper understanding of multimedia messages? J. of Educational Psychology, 93 (2) (2001) 390-397

16. Musen, M.A., Fergerson, R.W., Grosso, W.E., Noy, N.F., Grubezy, M.Y., Gennari, J.H.: Component-based support for building knowledge-acquisition systems. Proc. Intelligent Information Processing (IIP 2000) Conf. Int. Federation for Processing (IFIP), World Computer Congress (WCC'2000), Beijing, China (2000) 18-22

17. Pepper S., Rath H. H.: Topic Maps: Introduction and Allegro, Markup Technologies 99, Philadelphia, USA (1999)

18. Pietriga, E.: Isaviz: A visual authoring tool for RDF. WorldWideWeb Consortium. (2003) Available http://www.w3.org/2001/11/IsaViz/

19. Storey, M.A., Wong, K., Fracchia, F.D., Muller, H.A.: On Integrating visualization Techniques for Effective Software Exploration. Proc. IEEE Symp. on Information Visualization (InfoVis'97), Phoenix, Arizona, USA (1997) 38-45

20. Storey, M.A., Musen, M., Silva, J., Best, C., Ernst, N., Fergerson, R., Noy, N.: Jambalaya: Interactive visualisation to enhance ontology authoring and knowledge acquisition in Protégé. Workshop on Interactive Tools for Knowledge Capture, K-CAP-2001, Canada (2001)

21. Wielemaker J., Schreiber G., Wielinga B.: Using triples for implementation: The Triple20 ontology-manipulation tool, in Y. Gil et al. (Eds.): International Semantic Web Conference - ISWC 2005, LNCS 3729, Springer-Verlag Berlin Heidelberg (2005) 773-785

22. Price J.L., Catrambone R.: Part-Whole Statistics Training: Effects on Learning and Cognitive Load, CogSci, Chicago (2004)

23. Sowa , J. F.: Conceptual structures: Information processing in mind and machine. Addison-Wesley (1984)

24. URL: http://ecoinformatics.uvm.edu/technologies/growl-knowledge-modeler.html

25. URL: http://hypergraph.sourceforge.net/

26. URL: http://smi-protege.stanford.edu/svn/ontoviz-tab/

27. URL: http://tm4j.org/tmnav.html

28. URL: http://www.idealliance.org/proceedings/xml04/papers/311/311.html

29. URL: http://www.ontopia.net/omnigator/

30. URL: http://www.thinkgraph.com/english/index.htm

31. URL: http://www.touchgraph.com/

Documentation for Aircraft Maintenance Based on Topic Maps*

Kay Kadner[1] and David Roussel[2]

[1] SAP AG, SAP Research, Chemnitzer Str. 48, 01187 Dresden, Germany
kay.kadner@sap.com
[2] EADS CRC, 4 av. Didier Daurat, 31700 Blagnac, France
david.roussel@eads.net

Abstract. Fast and easy processing of documentation for maintenance and overhaul is of high importance for many companies, especially in the aircraft domain. The documentation of a certain aircraft often comprises thousands of pages, which today mostly exist as paper-based documents. To use the benefits of electronic technical manuals, we define a description language for storing Aircraft Maintenance Manuals (AMM) based on Topic Maps, which is called XTM-P (XML Topic Map for Procedures). Besides syntactic information, this language is used to capture semantic information for supporting smart adaptation to multiple output devices and modalities. Several concepts of this language are described.

1 Introduction

Aircraft maintenance, repair, and overhaul (MRO) is a critical process with strict requirements to safety, security, and quality. Hence, its execution is standardised by international bodies like the Air Transport Association). Since a substantial portion of costs for operating an aircraft can be attributed to MRO, efficiency is crucial. Efficiency includes the maintenance itself as well as the processing of maintenance documentation. The thousands of documentation pages for a particular aircraft are used by maintenance workers for execution and authors for continuous improvement. A study at EADS in 2004 revealed that 50% of time is spent on information search because most documents exist only on paper.

XTM-P was developed within the SNOW project [1] as content description language for maintenance procedures. Its main purpose is to provide a content format for documentation, which can be enhanced by semantic information for supporting the adaptation to user interface description languages like HTML and VoiceXML. XTM-P specifies how to use XTM 1.0 and benefits from many results provided by the Topic Maps community to build the needed resources (e.g., published set of types and generic tools). The paper is structured as follows. Section 2 contains a discussion about related work. In section 3, we describe the application scenario of typical maintenance work. Concepts of XTM-P are described in Section 4 followed by a brief introduction of the XTM-P authoring environment. The paper closes with a conclusion and an outlook to future work.

---

* Work on this paper has been partially funded by the EU in FP6 IST SO 2.3.2.6, [1].

L. Maicher, A. Sigel, and L.M. Garshol (Eds.): TMRA 2006, LNAI 4438, pp. 56–61, 2007.
© Springer-Verlag Berlin Heidelberg 2007

2   Related Work

In the area of technical documentation, XTM-P is related to specifications such as S1000D and DITA. S1000D [10] proposes a specification for technical publications that covers creation, management, compilation and publishing of information. It allows to define metadata, data modules, datasets and rules while leaving some specification aspects opened for tailoring for a specific use. Like other OASIS/OPEN standards, Topic Maps are eligible for extending the S1000D specification with components addressing electronic publication indexes in data module headers or relationships between notes and other content units (S1000D chapter 3.9.3) or more specifically the merging of a given airline dictionary with simplified Technical English dictionary (S1000D chapter 3.9.1) in order to ensure both consistent vocabulary and adapted technical names.

DITA [5] is an architecture for creating topic-oriented content that can be reused in a variety of ways while reusing common output transformations and design rules. DITA aims at maintaining a piece of content in a specific context that physically resides in one topic, but is reused in other topics [7]. The coupling of XTM-P and D3ML (Device-independent MultiModal Markup Language [6]) extends the DITA topics formalisation and contextualised interpretation for multimodal and device independent information adaptation.

According to [8], we claim that low-level syntactical transposing of existing structured information does not provide a general solution for information adaptation especially for multimodality and device independence. Therefore, we propose a semantic redesign, which is based on standards like Topic Maps because this allows defining alternate forms of structured content that are easy to retrieve and interactively guide the user through the relevant information. The semantic enrichment of structured content is the main advantage of XTM-P over the related approaches mentioned before.

3   Application Scenario and System Architecture

In SNOW's main use case, the maintenance worker is at the aircraft and performs several maintenance procedures. He can use a mobile device to retrieve necessary documents directly on-site. The same device can be used to contact remote experts, if the worker needs additional expertise as well as to record annotations, which are used for giving feedback to authors for improving the procedures. Besides normal interaction modalitities like keyboard and display, the worker can select voice or gestures for acquiring information.

Although maintenance is SNOW's main motivation, the architecture was developed as domain-independent as possible [9]. The processing flow of XTM-P is shown in Figure 1 and further explained in [4]. After the maintenance procedure is created using the Authoring Environment, it is stored in the Procedure Database. The Documentation Application fills D3ML templates with content from XTM-P and forwards it to the Dialog and Adaptation Manager. As XTM-P contains only the content of procedures, D3ML is used for styling and layouting procedures, which can afterwards be adapted to multiple output formats.

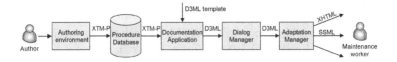

Fig. 1. Processing flow of XTM-P within the SNOW architecture

4   XTM-P Concepts

The structure of XTM-P is strongly aligned to AMM procedures (Aircraft Maintenance Manuals). Each *procedure* consists of several *phases*. The first phase ("General warnings") informs the worker about potential dangers when executing the procedure. The second phase ("Reason for the Job") gives a rationale for this procedure while the third phase ("Job Set-up Information") contains a set of necessary resources (tools, consumables, explanatory documents...), which are relevant for execution. The three remaining phases ("Job Set-up", "Procedure", and "Job Close-up") tell the worker what he has to do for preparing the workplace, executing the procedure and cleaning up the workplace. Each phase contains a list of *steps*, which shortly describe the intended task. For detailed information about a particular step, the worker can rely on *instructions* for further explanation. Each structural element optionally contains additional information like notes and warnings as well as references to explaining images or sub-procedures, among others. All structural elements (procedure, phase, step, instruction) are realised as topic types in XTM-P. Particular elements of a procedure are instances of those types and therefore topics as well. This typing mechanism is used to generate separate Topic Maps for types as well as instances of topics, which are merged according to unambiguous subject indicators.

The semantic enrichment of this syntactic structure is described below in subsection 4.1. In subsection 4.2, we describe concepts that do not create semantic relations between XTM-P elements but rather support the output generation. However, a clear distinction between these two categories is hard to define.

4.1   Semantic Enrichment of Content

Compared to the SGML structure of existing maintenance procedures after conversion from paper, semantic enrichment is mainly realised by associations. Procedures and phases as well as phases and steps are associated by a *composition* association, which is a simple association between the compound and a constituent. In addition to that, we defined the association type *Rhetorical relation*. For instance, the *background* association and the *elaboration* association respectively as instances of *Rhetorical relation* are employed for modelling that some notes are used to increase the understanding of an element (e.g., subtask, place, action) or to elaborate the description of a step.

Furthermore, we defined the association type *Pragmatic relation*, which has also various subtypes. *Pragmatic relations* are used for explicitly linking pieces of texts to other kinds of information, such as graphics or references. This association might be used to add additional icons in the visual output according to their type. Phases as well as steps are interconnected by associations of type *order*. This logical order can be used to create additional navigation links when rendering the procedure. Additionally, a desired order between instructions can be realised by using *variantNames* associated to specific scopes.

Scopes of topic basenames play an important role in XTM-P. They can be used to capture alternative representations of that topic for enabling multiple languages and detail levels of the topic's content. For example, languages are introduced by scopes to *en* or *fr*. An accurate definition is given by *designation*, whereas a *denomination* is used to provide an easy to understand representation.

4.2 Rendering Hints

Another type of content enrichment is the augmentation with rendering hints, which directly affect the user interface generation. For example, the types *warning*, *note* and *caution* denote information with different semantics resulting in different rendering styles, e.g., warnings may be printed in red color and bold face. This can be amplified by a scope such as *important* or *very_important*.

Additional rendering hints are introduced because XTM-P provides content for multimodal user interfaces. To ensure a high-quality user interface for modalities besides display, the content description must provide information for assisting the adaptation to those modalities as well as the adaptation in general. For supporting audio output, the author can augment every topic with a basename scoped to *tts-synthesis-adaptation*, which contains speech synthesis markup.

By scoping associations to *non-breakable* or images (realised as occurrences) to *non-scalable*, XTM-P directly influences the output generation by preventing the adaptation manager from paginating the document at this point [11] or scaling the image. Pagination can occur if the document does not fit to certain rendering capabilities (e.g., a display). Image scaling might be prevented because the image contains information, that will be lost when the image is scaled down to a lower resolution (e.g., a detailed exploded view).

Additionally, XTM-P can describe the nature of actions by typing the topic of a certain information piece with a communication act. As suggested by [3], the communication acts currently used are extendable to enable the system to refine the interactions with the user (e.g., confirmation, check for comprehension).

Listing 1 contains a simple example of XTM-P. It describes the association of a step with an image. The association is *non-breakable* preventing the two items to appear on different output pages. The image is *non-scalable* for ensuring that the user can read its content. Showing examples of the other concepts would exceed the page limit due to their complexity.

5   Authoring Environment

A considerable part of the SNOW project is the development of authoring environments for the respective languages. Figure 2 shows a screenshot of the

Listing 1. XTM-P example

```
<association>
  <instanceOf> <topicRef xlink:href="#Info_unit-graphic" /> </instanceOf>
    <scope> <topicRef xlink:href="#non-breakable" /> </scope>
  <member>
    <roleSpec> <topicRef xlink:href="#compound" /> </roleSpec>
    <topicRef xlink:href="#step_5"/>
  </member>
  <member>
    <roleSpec> <topicRef xlink:href="#constituent" /> </roleSpec>
    <topicRef xlink:href="#step_5_description_image" />
  </member>
</association>

<topic id="step_5_description_image">
  <instanceOf> <subjectIndicatorRef xlink:href="#graphic" /> </instanceOf>
  <occurrence>
    <instanceOf> <topicRef xlink:href="#non-scalable"/> </instanceOf>
    <resourceRef xlink:href="Bonding_details.tif" />
  </occurrence>
</topic>
```

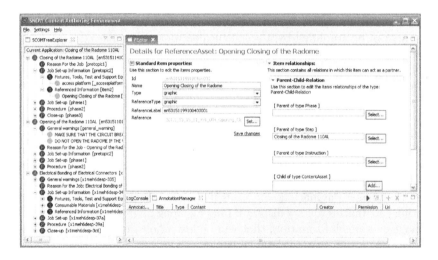

Fig. 2. Screenshot of the XTM-P authoring environment

XTM-P authoring environment, which is realised as an Eclipse Rich Client Platform (RCP) application. The tree-view on the left side shows the structure of opened procedures: procedure, phase, step, instruction, additional information and references. On the right side, the author can modify the details of each selected item. Since the authoring environment is currently in a beta stage, not all features of XTM-P are supported. On the lower right, the author can access the annotations, which were created by maintenance workers during procedure execution. The author can use them for improving the procedure's accuracy and completeness, delete them after consideration or even discuss them with the worker. Like the overall SNOW system, the annotations can leverage the full modality range of SNOW like text, images, videos or audio.

6 Conclusion and Outlook

Topic Maps are an active research domain that meets several industrial requirements. We presented our approach of realising technical documentation for aircraft maintenance manuals based on Topic Maps. This primarily rather structural description was augmented with semantic information and rendering hints for influencing and assisting the adaptation process to multimodal and device-independent user interface descriptions.

Future efforts will increase the semantic expressiveness of XTM-P. It is planned to include additional rendering hints with a stronger impact on the adaptation, for instance information about additional modalities like gesture input. The current language only supports presentation of information. Upcoming versions might also support filling input forms and even navigation branching based on these inputs. Additionally, a schema for validation needs to be specified, e.g., based on TMCL (Topic Map Constraint Language, [2]).

References

1. Services for NOmadic Workers (SNOW) project. http://www.snow-project.org.
2. The Topic Maps Constraint Language. http://www.isotopicmaps.org/tmcl/.
3. H. C. Bunt. Information dialogues as communicative action in relation to partner modelling and information processing. In M. M. Taylor, F. Neel, and D. G. Bouwhuis, editors, *The Structure of Multimodal Dialogue*, pages 47–73. North-Holland, Amsterdam, 1989.
4. Rodger Burmeister, Christoph Pohl, Siegfried Bublitz, and Pascale Hugues. SNOW - A multimodal approach for mobile maintenance applications. In *Proceedings of the 4th International Workshop on Distributed and Mobile Collaboration*, 2006.
5. Darwin Information Typing Architecture. www.oasis-open.org/committees/dita/.
6. Steffen Göbel, Falk Hartmann, Kay Kadner, and Christoph Pohl. A Device-Independent Multimodal Mark-up Language. In *INFORMATIK 2006: Informatik für Menschen, Band 2*, pages 170–177, 2006.
7. The Rockley Group Inc. Preparing for DITA: What you need to know, August 2005. http://www.rockley.com.
8. Giulio Mori and Fabio Paternò. Automatic semantic platform-dependent redesign. In *sOc-EUSAI '05: Proceedings of the 2005 joint conference on Smart objects and ambient intelligence*, pages 177–182, New York, NY, USA, 2005. ACM Press.
9. Alessandro Costa Pereira, Falk Hartmann, and Kay Kadner. A Distributed Staged Architecture for Multimodal Applications. In *Software Engineering 2007*, 2007. To appear.
10. S1000D^{TM}- International specification for technical publications utilizing a common source database. http://www.s1000d.org/.
11. Axel Spriestersbach, Thomas Ziegert, Guido Grassel, Michael Wasmund, and Gabriel Dermler. Flexible pagination and layouting for device independent authoring. In *Proceedings of the WWW2003 - Emerging Applications for Wireless and Mobile Access Workshop*, 2003.

From Biological Data to Biological Knowledge

Volker Stümpflen, Richard Gregory, and Karamfilka Nenova

Institute for Bioinformatics (MIPS), GSF - National Research Center for Environment and Health, Ingolstädter Landstrasse 1, D-85764 Neuherberg, Germany
{v.stuempflen,richard.gregory,karamfilka.nenova}@gsf.de

Abstract. Large scale biological knowledge still organization remains a challenge in life sciences. Not only because related information is spread across several distributed information resources, but also because context dependent information retrieval suffers from an absence of semantic capabilities in biological databases. This prevents intelligent interpretation of data beyond simple key word searches as well as the inference of implicit biological knowledge. We will discuss in this paper the urgent need for semantic technologies for knowledge organization in life sciences and a prototype based on Topic Maps and distributed technologies.

1 Introduction

Since knowledge is a prime prerequisite for successful research in life sciences, powerful techniques for knowledge organization and management are a necessity to cope with the flood of information. However, biological knowledge management deals with all kinds of information related to a subject, like pieces of a puzzle, mostly incomplete and sometimes contradictory. This information has to be collected from numerous highly distributed data resources.

At the conceptual level, biological information is highly interconnected and often context dependent. In practice, genomic data and its associated information generated by experimental or computational methods is stored in hundreds of independent, overlapping, and heterogeneous data resources that continue to emerge. Up to now still major weaknesses can be observed in the process of transforming primary information into biological knowledge as well as in selecting and integrating information relevant to answer a specific scientific question.

Considering the following almost trivial question of a biologist: (show me) "yeast proteins involved in signal transduction". By intuition, the biologist would search all databases containing related information and compile the results in many cases manually from the output of the resulting web pages. At the moment there is no option to ask a computational system for the right answer. Even internet search engines (assuming every related resource is indexed) fail. Google returns 1.45 million hits but the majority of the results are only poorly related to the original question. Obviously, the manual evaluation of the results is inadequate and unsystematic. There are several reasons for the difficulties to find a generic solution for the problem. One reason is the diversity of the provided data access techniques. Some databases provide direct access to the data, while other databases offer access via Web Services. Some

L. Maicher, A. Sigel, and L.M. Garshol (Eds.): TMRA 2006, LNAI 4438, pp. 62–66, 2007.

database providers offer just large flat files or even only via the web-based portals. To overcome the obvious limitations, uniform access mechanisms are required, delivering structured information independent of the underlying resource. In addition, there are even more complex conceptual obstacles for interoperability between the highly heterogeneous formats of biological data resources. Search mechanisms based on relational queries fail if they have to interpret the meaning of the question. Even the interpretation of individual words is problematic and a well-known barrier to data integration. Serious problems with ambiguity of terms persist [1]. These range from ambiguous gene identifiers (synonyms/homonyms) to ambiguities due to different meanings of the same term, for example "allele", in varying communities.

2 Large Scale Biological Knowledge Organization

Since not only the volume but also the complexity of the biological data sets is continuously growing, novel knowledge organizational methods are urgently needed to support the process of knowledge identification. As an implementation to demonstrate how biological knowledge can be organized on a semantic level, we integrated the two largest systems provided by the MIPS group: PEDANT and SIMAP. Both systems contain together more than 1.2 TB biological data organized in approx. 450 databases. The semantic linkage of these distributed database systems will provide access to huge amounts of protein sequences and associated data for more efficient exploration enabling biological discovery. Foundation for general aspects of information integration is on GenRE the Genome Research Environment developed at MIPS [2]. GenRE is a component oriented n-Tier architecture based on the J2EE middleware. The basic idea behind the multi tier approach is the segregation of the system in weakly connected layers performing distinct tasks. The architecture allows any of the tiers to be modified or replaced independently as requirements or technology change. Within GenRE [see Fig. 1] we deliver by default XML objects as output from the implemented components. This transformation is an important step to level differences between the underlying data sources.

In the context of component-based software architectures, an independent module as part of the middleware has been developed with the main purpose of structuring and organizing distributed data on a semantic level. This component, called Dynamic Topic Map Generation Engine [see Fig. 2] adds semantics to the syntactically integrated data by applying the Topic Maps concepts and methods. One of the main goals of semantic web technologies is to allow machines to interpret web-based information in the right context by appending computer "readable" meanings to the information. Web Services provide mechanisms to support interoperable machine-to-machine interaction over a network. Here we briefly present an implementation of a rational, concept-driven integration of two systems containing large-scale distributed biological data by combining these technologies.

The PEDANT genome database contains pre-computed bioinformatics analyses of publicly available genomes. The main purpose of this system is to close the gap

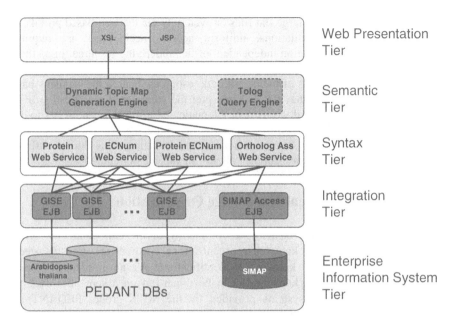

Fig. 1. The GenRE multi-Tier architecture. The system is extended with a semantic layer capable to access the underlying integration tier without the requirement for systems modification.

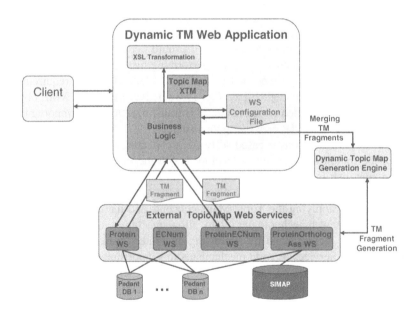

Fig. 2. An overview of the dynamic Topic Map engine. Topic Map fragments are generated on demand during runtime avoiding the need to store complete maps of biological information which may easily grow up to several tera bytes.

between the high-quality protein sequence databases and the enormous amounts of other protein sequences produced by independent genome sequencing projects. The entire PEDANT genome system actually consists of, at the time of writing, 441 single genome databases, which hamper a simultaneous cross comparison among multiple genome databases and so a more efficient protein analysis. Additionally, the SIMAP (Similarity Matrix of Proteins) database contains pre-computed homologies of over than 5.4 million protein sequences. The integration on semantic level of these two distributed database systems will provide access to huge amounts of data for better and faster exploration of protein data.

The integration of the 441 PEDANT genome databases is realized on the fly via Web Services which use particular components provided by the middleware layer to access the individual databases. The semantic linking of PEDANT databases with SIMAP is also achieved by applying Web Services.

When the integrative system receives a request, the required data will be collected from the selected databases at runtime and then further processed and converted into semantically relevant data by the Topic Map component. The resulting data has the standard XML-based topic map data format (XTM). The generated XML documents can be then processed and displayed to the user by the presentation tier. The advantage of this approach is that no new database is created and no redundant data is produced. Information is interconnected within a huge knowledge network navigable in any direction.

3 Discussion

For large scale knowledge organization based on distributed resources within life sciences we feel it is also important to discuss some experiences we made with Topic Maps compared to the considerable alternative RDF technology. RDF follows the idea of a semantic annotation of each resource available at the web. However, beside a few use cases [3] [http://expasy3.isb-sib.ch/~ejain//rdf/] resources on the web are not generally RDF annotated and it is questionable regarding the funding situation of biological databases [4] if such a solution can be realized in the foreseeable future. Topic Maps are an open standard providing a reference model for the semantic structuring and organization of any knowledge domain. Topic Maps represent a top-down approach and hence provide the possibility to model a specific knowledge domain explicitly without having a complete semantic annotation.

Combination of Topic Maps with J2EE middleware and Web Service technologies are a straight forward way to organize even distributed biological knowledge in a way capable to reflect the demands of the real users, the life scientists. We achieved this by simple extension of the GenRE multi-Tier architecture, hence reusing existing and mature components for biological information integration. The development of our Dynamic Topic Map Generation Engine provides a seamless and dynamic way to organize biological knowledge without the need for reengineering established information systems.

References

[1] Stein,L.D. (2003) Integrating biological databases. Nat. Rev. Genet. 4, 337-345.
[2] Mewes,H.W., Frishman,D., Mayer,K.F., Münsterkotter,M., Noubibou,O., Pagel,P., Rattei,T., Oesterheld,M., Ruepp,A., & Stümpflen,V. (2006) MIPS: analysis and annotation of proteins from whole genomes in 2005. *Nucleic Acids Res.* 34, D169-D172.
[3] Cheung,K.H., Yip,K.Y., Smith,A., Deknikker,R., Masiar,A., & Gerstein,M. (2005) YeastHub: a semantic web use case for integrating data in the life sciences domain. Bioinformatics. 21 Suppl 1, i85-i96.
[4] Merali,Z. & Giles,J. (2005) Databases in peril. Nature 435, 1010-1011.

Remote Topic Maps in Learning

Stian Lavik, Tommy W. Nordeng, Jarle R. Meløy, and Tore Hoel

Cerpus AS, N-8432 Alsvåg, Norway
{stian,tommy,jarle}@cerpus.com
Oslo University College
P.O. Box 4, St. Olavspl., 0130 Oslo
tore.hoel@hio.no

Abstract. Topic Maps is becoming a recognized way of structuring and navigating knowledge. Since the digital world is moving towards a more and more service oriented reality, it is appropriate to focus on solutions for using topicmaps remotely as services. Two current cases for how this can be done is displayed here, both carried out by Cerpus AS, a small Norwegian company that works with topicmaps in the e-Learning domain. This is discussed in the light of topicmaps in a service-oriented architecture and along the axis of virtual learning environments (VLEs) and personal learning environments (PLEs). We conclude that using remote topicmaps is a viable road to travel in the learning domain, as well as in other domains.

1 Introduction

Topic Maps (ISO 13250) is on its way to consolidate its position as a powerful way to manage, structure and navigate knowledge [1]. The general idea behind topicmaps is to organize information by subjects and relation between subjects, and to use a knowledge layer to organize the information layer. This subject centricity is useful, it gives a proper focus: on the subject one are examining, not on files, formats, headlines or other meta information.

From a learning perspective the support for associative structures is interesting and useful. According to some knowledge theory, there are two basic building blocks in learning; concepts and propositions (the relation of two or more concepts into a meaningful unit, typically a semantic expression) [2]. Topics from Topic Maps correspond to concepts and associations correspond to propositions. Hence, according to the theory of knowledge consisting of concepts and propositions, Topic Maps inherently supports the basics of learning. And to quote Dubai:

"Bodies of knowledge in general are associative systems. Associations are not only aids to understanding, they are also proven mnemonic devices: The richer the associative network, the higher the probability that the item will be stored and retrieved" [3].

One of the fascinating aspects of Topic Maps is the idea of using the domain knowledge itself to index domain information. If this is capitalized upon, we can experience a very rewarding way of modeling knowledge (and its relation to

L. Maicher, A. Sigel, and L.M. Garshol (Eds.): TMRA 2006, LNAI 4438, pp. 67–73, 2007.

information); (most of) the metadata of the domain model can be built inside the domain model. This is especially interesting from the angle of learning. When it comes to learning it is crucial to relate new knowledge to existing knowledge. Ausubel claims that "the single most important factor influencing the learning process is what the learner already knows" [4]. And he expresses further in-depth theory that stresses the importance of this building of understanding by relating new knowledge to prior knowledge, not just merely memorizing information. So, it's a good idea to build metadata or context inside the domain model. To use Topic Maps in learning effectively, it is also necessary to have a Topic Maps based repository that lasts a long time, so that the learner can graft new knowledge into the knowledge base.

2 Virtual Communities

In light of the ongoing globalization and the "Internet wave", the rise of virtual communities seems natural and almost inevitable. An increasing number of communities are available, they be commercially, culturally, ideally motivated, or motivated based on beliefs or interest in a special domain. Some examples are Yahoo groups, flickr.com, youtube.com and lots of others.

Within the domain of learning, the virtual communities have been around for some time. In Norway there are currently two major vendors (Fronter and it's learning) of *Virtual Learning Environments* (VLE) (sometimes called *Learning Management Systems* (LMS)). There are also some open source solutions around, such as Sakai and Moodle.

Common for all the VLEs are that they mean to offer a complete environment that facilitates a range of pedagogical activities, and (not least) administration features to administrate the environments. They all have some way to model the everyday schooling, including users, subjects, classes, access control, etc. This is a top down perspective, and rather system centric. Still, it matches what most teachers probably expect of a learning environment, since it more or less reflects the working environments they are used to.

The *Personal Learning Environments* (PLE) have a different starting point than the VLEs; the main focus here is on the individual learner and his context. The learner himself configures his virtual learning environment (controls access levels, etc.). There is little or no course management here. Instead, one will typically find services the learner subscribes to (learning activity tools, RSS feeds, etc.), links to other important resources, etc. Elgg is a good example of a PLE that has received much positive publicity lately [5].

As the learner is the center in the PLEs, there data will also live independently of what education institution the learner is enrolled at. The educational institutions are in general more toned down than in the VLEs. Metadata from the educational institutions (such as groups, classes, courses, terms, etc.) may serve as a mean or supportive structure in the PLE, but not as a framework that that dictates or limits the learners' own preferences in terms of structuring his learning and knowledge.

When it is the learner that decides what courses, methods and activities (maybe together with a supervisor) he will use to learn what he is supposed to learn, it is natural that he himself also decides what tools and services he will use to reach his goals. The digital learning environments are driven towards a more service-oriented architecture. Instead of the system (the digital learning environment) giving a set of predefined activities and resources, the learner himself can subscribe to services that support his own style of learning.

In Norway, the government has already established the first version of "Citizen portal" ("Min side"). This is meant as personal web page for each citizen of Norway where they can find personal information about and interact in relation to health services, taxation, etc. And we have launched the idea of "My learning portal" ("Min læringsside") as a web page to be a kind of "personal portal" for learning. If this site is to be anything like the described ideas, it will be more or less a hundred percent service-oriented. Each citizen would subscribe and unsubscribe to whatever services they want to in relation to their learning, and thereby create their own learning environment.

3 Service Oriented Architecture (SOA)

Within the XML community service oriented architecture (SOA) has been discussed and nourished for quite some time, and more and more websites/organizations offer web services to other websites/organizations and virtual communities. And along the lines of Web 2.0, web services and distribution of content is essential [6].

The growth of virtual communities displays an inherent need of thinking in terms of exchanging services and the growth of web services fuels virtual communities so they become more viable to attract users and to last.

SOA has a very simple basic philosophy. We acknowledge the fact that we cannot be experts in every field ourselves, so we ask the some experts to do the job for us [7]. We simply make the desired output available to our users.

As already mentioned, there exist a vast number of virtual communities and websites on the Internet and more and more of them offer services from other sites through web services (e.g. Amazon, eBay, Google, etc.). Many of them also offer web services themselves, to be used in other communities and applications.

3.1 Remote Topic Maps

Many learning applications and systems don't use Topic Maps, and they may not implement it in any near future. Still, we want to bring the power of Topic Maps into their domain, because we think building topicmaps is a good way of documenting acquired knowledge and building a deeper understanding of the knowledge domain.

The SOA way of building software has reached the Topic Map community. Ontopia has recently released the Topic Maps Remote Access Protocol (TMRAP) as "a web service interface for remotely accessing topicmaps" [8]. The reasoning behind TMRAP is exactly what it sounds like; to be able to interact with a topicmap remotely. The interface consists of a number of methods that can be applied to the topicmap remotely, and the output can then be used to one's liking.

4 Topicmap Server

In response to the demand for service-oriented architecture and on the basis on the belief in the Topic Maps technology, Cerpus built the Topicmap Server. Our goal was to develop technology for offering Topic Maps in external systems without having to implement topicmap engines in those systems. The Topicmap Server is a server to host topicmaps for various applications and systems that can be accessed and used via web services. Our customers will be organizations that want the power of topicmaps in their applications without implementing topicmap support themselves. The idea is that such organizations buy an account on the Topicmap Server and host their topicmap there, and then use the topicmap in their own application over web services (with TMRAP).

The Topicmap Server will have some editing applications for users to edit the topicmaps directly. And to regulate access between users, applications and topicmaps, the Topicmap Server has a managing application called TMBuilder Application (Topic Map Builder Application). The TMBuilder Application also handles web service requests from external systems.

The Topicmap Server can be used to serve external VLEs or PLEs, and it can empower those systems with support for Topic Maps. For example, a VLE could use a topicmap to index all the resources belonging to a given user and display the relation between his resources (associations in the topicmap) by fetching the necessary fragment of the topicmap from the Topicmap Server. Or, as we will see in a moment, topicmaps could be used to display the knowledge domain itself, organized by subjects and associations.

5 BrainBank Learning, Integration with Moodle

5.1 Background

One of our current tasks is the integration of BrainBank Learning and VLEs, represented by Moodle (Modular Object-Oriented Dynamic Learning Environment). From a BrainBank Learning perspective, Moodle is an interesting VLE to use as a case for this kind of integration. Firstly, Moodle has roots in the same learning philosophy as BrainBank Learning, namely constructivism [9, 10]. Secondly, Moodle is open source (and hence easy to deal with, business-wise).

BrainBank Learning and Moodle complement each other well. Moodle is a richly featured VLE, including features to support a typical school everyday (e.g. course management). BrainBank Learning is more focused on the individual learner and his learning process, with a clear emphasis on the bottom up perspective.

In addition to a genuine interest in integrating BrainBank Learning with VLEs, we are currently in working together with the County of Nordland (Nordland Fylkeskommune) in a project that is concerned with computer aided learning in schools. This project is a catalyzer for the integration work.

5.2 The Integration

BrainBank Learning was designed to be a tool for meaningful learning [2] within a constructivist learning environment [11, 12, 13]. It is a web application for learning of concepts (their meaning) and context (how concepts relate). The core of the suite is BrainBank, the ontology of a topic map for acquired knowledge in a lifelong perspective. As the Topic Maps standard defines an effective way of representing information (through topics and associations etc.) [1], BBL uses Topic Maps technology to represent the data in the application. The application is installed on a central server, making users connect to the very same repository of data. This makes it easy for a learner to change schools (or even use BrainBank Learning after finished education) without loosing any data.

BrainBank Learning is mainly focused on aiding each user to build his own knowledge map (in the form of a topicmap), from a bottom up perspective. The focus is on the learner, and he can decide how to build his knowledge base himself. In this sense, BBL has more in common with PLEs than with VLEs.

Moodle calls itself "A Free, Open Source Course Management System for Online Learning". Furthermore, Moodle is presented as a course management system (CMS) on the official website [14].

The architecture of Moodle strongly suggests that there is one installation per educational institution, even though you probably could combine several schools in one installation. (That would in any case be a bit limiting in terms of customization for each school.) This also implies that the expected time for data to live in Moodle is significantly shorter than for BrainBank. A given users data will live at the Moodle installation as long as the user is a student at that school. If he wants to carry it further, it needs to be exported as a package, to be imported in another system later. This way of handling data is the general way of going about it in the VLE world, Moodle does not stand out from other VLEs in this matter.

Moodle's dictionary module and the BrainBank topicmap are natural connection points between BrainBank Learning and Moodle. By using the Moodles dictionary module learners can build their own dictionaries. The module also facilitates to use words from the dictionary as "hot words" in the rest of Moodle, which means that whenever a word that exists in the dictionary is used in another text in Moodle, Moodle automatically creates a link to the entry for that word in the dictionary.

We have created an updated version of the Moodle dictionary that contains functionality to connect every word in the dictionary to topics in BrainBank. If the topic does not exist in the users BrainBank, it will automatically be created. When a word is connected, there is a link that can take the user directly to the corresponding topic in BrainBank Learning. On the BrainBank Learning side, there will be created a resource to the given topic that represents the entry in the Moodle dictionary.

We have built a component in BrainBank Learning that will accept request from other applications over web services and use parameters from the request to perform operations within BBL. This is of such nature that it also opens up possibilities for easily integrating with other VLEs and PLEs in the future.

Obviously, there are limitations to the integration. For the integration to work, users must be users in BrainBank Learning as well as in Moodle.

It makes sense to apply topicmaps in such a context and to do it via BrainBank Learning, since BrainBank Learning is a learning application allowing learners to build their own topicmaps. Words can be linked to topics in BrainBank as resources and the knowledge map is enriched with associations etc. The integration amplifies the effect of the Moodle dictionary on one hand, and on the other it improves BrainBank Learnings connection to resources located externally and makes it more useful to the VLE as well as PLE community in general.

From a pedagogical point of view it makes perfect sense to tie the produced resources (in this case essays, WIKI pages, forum discussions, multiple choice tests, etc. in Moodle) stronger to the knowledge map (the learners' BrainBanks). As mentioned above, it is important to relate all new knowledge to prior knowledge. In this way, the learners' knowledge maps can play a key role in the production of learning resources in Moodle.

There are many other potential areas for integration, and there is also a great potential for improvement in today's model. For example, it would probably be useful if there were some kind synchronization between the topics in BrainBank and the Moodle dictionary, so that changes in one place automatically changed the data in the other repository.

Likewise, we see possibilities for extending the integration, such as using fragments of the learners' knowledge maps from BrainBank for navigation inside Moodle, etc. Still, the integration has begun, and the chosen approach seems like a useful place to start.

6 Conclusions

We see a clear potential for remote topicmaps in learning. The cases of the Topicmap Server and the integration of BrainBank Learning and Moodle display two ways of doing it. And most likely, there will emerge more and new ways of using topicmaps remotely in the near future.

In the case of BrainBank Learning and Moodle we use remote topicmaps to reach a specific goal, namely integrating the VLE Moodle with BrainBank Learning. In the case of Topicmap Server, the use of remote topicmaps is on a more general level, and we hope to see this generating new possibilities to use Topic Maps in learning.

To use topicmaps over web services seems to be a viable solution in the learning domain, and it fits with the development that is going towards PLEs, where the learner himself configures what services he wants and what suits his learning style.

References

1. Garshol L. M. & Moore G. (2005) *ISO/IEC 13250 Topic Maps: Topic Maps — Data Model*. http://www.isotopicmaps.org/sam/sam-model/. Accessed 30.05.2006.
2. D. P. Ausubel, Novak, J.D. & Haneisan, H. (1978) *Educational Psychology: A Cognitive View*. 2 edn, Holt, Rinehart and Winston.
3. Dubai, Y. (2002) *Memory from A to Z*. Oxford University Press.
4. Ausubel , D., (1968) *Educational psychology: A cognitive view (context)*. New York: Holt, Rinehart & Winston.

5. O'Hear, S. (2006, March 7th) *A space on the web that we control.* Article in The Guardian. http://education.guardian.co.uk/elearning/story/0,,1724614,00.html. Accessed 07.06.2006.

6. O'Reiily, T. (2005) *What Is Web 2.0 - Design Patterns and Business Models for the Next Generation of Software.* http://www.oreillynet.com/pub/a/oreilly/tim/news/2005/09/30/what-is-web-20.html Accessed 09.06.2006.

7. He, H. (2003) *What Is Service-Oriented Architecture?* http://www.xml.com/pub/a/ws/2003/09/30/soa.html . Accessed 07.06.2006.

8. Garshol, L. M. (2005) *TMRAP – Topic Maps Remote Access Protocol.* In: *Charting the Topic Maps Research and Applications Landscape: First International Workshop on Topic Map Research and Applications, TMRA 2005.* pp. 53 - 68. Ed. Maicher L. & Park J. Springer Berlin / Heidelberg. ISBN: 3-540-32527-1.
http://dx.doi.org/10.1007/11676904_5. Accessed 07.06.2006.

9. Moodle Documentation. http://docs.moodle.org/en/Philosophy. Accessed 30.05.2006.

10. Wikipedia: *Constructivism (learning theory)* http://en.wikipedia.org/wiki/Constructivism_%28learning_theory%29. Accessed 30.05.2006.

11. Lavik, S., Meløy, J. R. & Nordeng, T. W. (2004) *BrainBank Learning - building personal topic maps as a strategy for learning.* In: Proceedings of XML 2004 Washington, DC, http://www.idealliance.org/proceedings/xml04/papers/21/brainbank.pdf Accessed 30.05.2006.

12. B Wilson. (1996) *Constructivist learning environments: Case studies in instructional design.* New Jersey: Educational Technology Publications.

13. Jonassen, D.H & Rohrer-Murphy, L. (1999) *Activity theory as a framework for designing constructivist learning environments*, Educational Technology Research and Development. 47, 61-79.

14. Moodle - *A Free, Open Source Course Management System for Online Learning.* http://moodle.org. Accessed 30.05.2006.

Design and Users' Evaluation of
a Topic Maps-Based Korean
Folk Music Retrieval System

Sam Gyun Oh[1] and Ok nam Park[2]

[1] Department of Library and Information Science, Sungkyunkwan University,
Myongryun-Dong 3-53, Jongro-Gu, Seoul, Republic of Korea
samoh@skku.edu
[2] The Information School, University of Washington, Box 352840, Suite 370,
Mary Gates Hall, Seattle, WA 98195-2840
parko@u.washington.edu

Abstract. The purpose of the study is to compare the performance between a
Topic Maps-Based Korean Folk Music (Pansori) Retrieval System (TMPRS)
and a representative Current Pansori Retrieval System (CPRS). The study is an
experimental effort using representative general users. Participants are asked to
carry out several predefined tasks and their own queries. The study measures
objective and subjective performance of the two systems. The methods of data
analysis are described and suggestions for improving current retrieval systems
using Topic Maps are presented.

Keywords: User evaluation, Information retrieval, Topic Maps-Based System,
Korean Folk Music, Pansori.

1 Introduction

Ontology, as "an explicit specification of a conceptualization" [2] has received much
attention recently in many disciplines and research communities such as artificial
intelligence, knowledge representation, and the semantic web community. Many
researchers have claimed the potential for ontologies, the needs of ontology use, and
appropriateness of ontology use in their disciplines as an emerging area [2]. There are
two standard ontology languages: W3C RDF and Web Ontology Language (OWL)
and ISO/IEC SC34 Topic Maps(TM). Both languages are complimentary because
RDF/OWL is strong in supporting inferences from existing concepts, but Topic Maps
has its strengths in implementing semantic data modeling, expressing rich
relationships among topics and collocating related items. Comparatively speaking,
there have been more RDF/OWL-based ontologies than TM-based ones. The research
domain for this study, Korean Folk Music(Pansori), seems to be well-suited for TM
because users of a Pansori retrieval system are likely to benefit richer expression of
relationships and collating related items rather than inferences from topics. This is
why the TM ontology language was selected for this study over RDF/OWL.

Despite considerable expectation, there have not been many studies which
demonstrate how much and in what ways ontology is valuable to satisfying users'

L. Maicher, A. Sigel, and L.M. Garshol (Eds.): TMRA 2006, LNAI 4438, pp. 74–89, 2007.
© Springer-Verlag Berlin Heidelberg 2007

needs. Previous studies have been conducted in somewhat limited ways in that no study has conducted evaluations based on categories of task types in spite of the close relationship between user evaluations and tasks. Most studies have been concerned with objective measurements such as search time, mistakes made, etc. There have been no users' evaluations of Topic Maps-based retrieval systems. Since Topic Maps has the potential to improve the limitation of current retrieval systems, conducting in-depth user-centered evaluation of Topic Maps-based information retrieval (IR) systems seemed necessary. Comparing the performance of the Topic Maps-based system with existing information (IR) system also seemed useful.

Motivated by this, the purpose of this paper is to implement a TM-based Korean Folk Music (Pansori) Retrieval System (TMPRS) and to conduct user evaluations of TMPRS and a representative Current Pansori Retrieval System (CPRS). This study attempts to tease out different aspects of system performance, both objective and subjective in nature. Evaluation is based on multiple tasks in the order of increasing complexity. Search steps taken, search time spent for given tasks, search completeness, ease of system usage, system efficiency, appropriateness of search support, and users' satisfaction are also measured. Through the study, the research aims to find strengths and weaknesses of a TM-based retrieval systems compared to a current retrieval systems. We also hope to suggest ways for improving current retrieval systems by utilizing the power of Topic Maps technology.

The topics to be discussed in this paper include research questions, related works, basic concepts of Topic Maps, description of TMPRS and CPRS, research design, analysis methods, and future research directions and conclusion.

1.1 Research Questions

There are papers that deal with usability and strengths of Topic Maps (TM) in terms of information organization and retrieval. However, there has been no study discussing strengths and weaknesses of TM-based IR systems from the users' perspective.

The purpose of this article is to experimentally evaluate two IR systems: TMPRS and CPRS. Various dimensions from users' perspectives are considered and users will be asked to evaluate both retrieval systems by conducting multiple pre-defined tasks as well as a query of their own. The following general research questions will be addressed in this study:

- Are there objective performance differences between TMPRS and CPRS?
- Are there subjective performance differences between TMPRS and CPRS?

2   Related Works

Guo et al. [3] evaluated four knowledge base systems based on OWL semantic web application with respect to 14 benchmark queries. For evaluating system performance, they employed three criteria - query response time, search completeness, and soundness as the percentage of the answers located for each query. The study identified what knowledge base system is good in terms of scalability. In addition, the study suggested some directions for future research with regard to what system is effective given queries employed.

Kim [5] showed the evaluation of an ontology-based retrieval system by comparing it to a free text searching system. She recruited 10 domain expert searchers, and conducted an evaluation study using 20 questions with respect to search time and relevance. The study revealed that the ontology-based system showed better performance in precision and was efficient in reducing search time for questions assigned. However, the study did not describe the evaluation part in detail with regard to the search engine employed, questions they asked, and relevance judgment criteria.

Sure and Iosif [11] also conducted an evaluation of an ontology based system. The research compared two ontology based systems to a free–text searching system. The study demonstrated that users of the ontology-based system made fewer mistakes and took less time to complete tasks. The study did not investigate the participants' more qualitative assessments of system usefulness or satisfaction and did not specifically explain the procedure used for task assignments.

Other current studies have some limitations. First, while many IR and information behavior studies have shown close relationships between user evaluation and search tasks [6], [7], [9], few studies have conducted the evaluation according to task categories. Second, most studies have employed objective measurements such as search time, mistakes made, search completeness, etc. The studies have not measured user criteria such as satisfaction, appropriateness, and ease to use. Also, these studies have evaluated ontology-based systems against free-text searching systems. Many researchers in library and information science (LIS) compared controlled vocabularies and free-text searching for a long time [10]. Rowley's work [10] extensively surveyed related research discussing issues of controlled vocabulary versus free-text search. Throughout these studies, researchers have reached consensus that controlled vocabularies and free text searching do not compete, rather they have their own advantages, benefiting from each other's strengths, and counterbalance each other's weaknesses. Ontology and controlled vocabularies are somewhat different in that ontology allows representing more flexible associations than controlled vocabularies. Therefore, studies to compare an ontology-based system with a free text based system could naturally be expected to show similar results and were not of interest as a consequence. What was of value for this investigation was any improvement an ontology-based system could bring compared to a thesaurus-based system. Finally, we could not discover studies employing user evaluations of Topic Maps-based systems. The main strength of Topic Maps is their capability to support flexible representation of diverse associations among topics and to categorize search results into meaningful groups. It was considered valuable to investigate how Topic Maps-based systems might work for users from the users' perspective.

3   Korean Folk Music-Pansori

Pansori (판소리) is a domain which Koreans are familiar. Koreans have many opportunities to hear Korean folk music and it is studied by students during the early years of their schooling. Before we can implement a topic map, it is necessary to model the domain of Pansori. The relationships in Fig1 provide an informal way of domain modeling employing polygons to express classes of Korean Folk Music. There is an ISO new work item (NWI) which suggests a design for a graphical notation to express Topic Maps ontologies. What is being proposed here can be a part of the new proposal for Topic Map graphical notation.

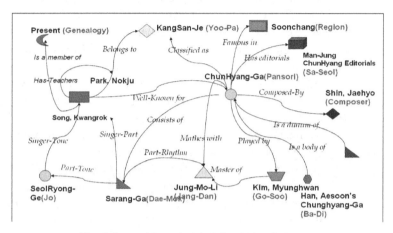

Fig. 1. Pansori Domain Modeling Using Polygons

Since there is no rigorous modeling tool for Topic Maps as of today, UML was employed to model an ontology for the Korean Folk Music domain considering that readers are familiar with this notation. Pansori UML modeling is displayed in the Fig. 2 below. The definition of Pansori terms is provided in Appendix.

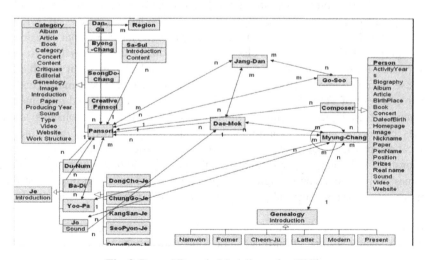

Fig. 2. Pansori Domain Modeling using UML

The *Pansori(판소리)* is being used for two major reasons. One reason is to represent a knowledge domain for this study, the domain of Korean Folk Music, and the other reason is because it represents a specific and narrow well-structured knowledge base which has a clear meaning as a particular branch of Korean Folk Music. The *Pansori(판소리)* domain can be divided into several sub-groups. The first group offers relationships among *Myoung-Chang(명창)* of Pansori. *Myoung-Chang(명창)* is associated with *genealogy(계보)*, *Yoo-Pa(유파)*, *Jo(조)*, *Dae-Mok(대목)*, and *pansori(판소리)*. For example, *Sanghyun Cho(조상현)* as a *Myoung-Chang(명창)* belongs to the 'present-period' *Myoung-Chang(명창)* genealogy, to *KangSan-Je(강산제)* sect, is famous for singing well a particular song called, *ChunHyang-Ga(춘향가)*, and his teacher is *Nokju Park(박녹주)*. A famous *Myoung-Chang(명창)* of *JinYang-Jo(진양조)* as a tone *is KwangRok Song(송광록)* and *Mansoon Park(박만순)* is well known for singing the *Love-Song(사랑가)*. The second group forms relationships with Pansori. Pansori has relationships with *Myoung-Chang(명창)*, *Dae-Mok (대목)*, *Yoo-Pa (유파)*, *Region(유명지역)*, *Sa-Seol(사설집)*, *composer(작곡가)*, *dunum(더늠)*, *Ba-Di(바디)*, *Go-Soo(고수)*, and *Jang-Dan(장단)*. There are complicated relationships among many groups in the Pansori knowledge structures. That is, *a Myoung-Chang(명창)* with *a Pansori, a Dae-Mok(대목)* of Pansori with *a Myoung-Chang(명창)* and *a Pansori, a Jo(조)* with *a Myoung-Chang(명창)* and *a Dae-Mok(대목)*, *a Go-Soo(고수)* with *a Jang-Dan(장단)* and *a Pansori*, and *a Yoo-Pa(유파)* has relationships with *a Myoung-Chang(명창)* and *a pansori*. Therefore, it is important to represent related information among groups of the domain effectively and efficiently to users.

From the perspective of data modeling, Topic Maps provides an effective way to change a data schema flexibly. While current database technology has no way to escape from losing some of the meaningful relationships captured by UML and ER modeling between concepts since it only provides for relationships that are 1:1, 1:M, or M:N. But Topic Maps enables us to implement a system without any loss of meaningful relationships between classes. It seems likely that it may lead to better performance for navigation and retrieval of information. It also makes it possible for a database designer to spend less time and effort in changing schemas. This is a valuable benefit of Topic Maps with respect to database modeling and implementing systems. For example, the current implementation of these relationships among classes cannot be kept structurally. All the relationships must be maintained by application program level, which becomes very difficult to maintain as those relationships may increase or change and therefore to perform future data mining becomes problematic. The strength of Topic Maps is the ability to implement these complex relationships structurally and provide them to a retrieval system without any loss.

Based on this modeling and domain study, we grounded concepts by TAO – Topics, Associations, and Occurrences - in Topic maps as shown in the table 1 below. Types represent a schema of each TAO.

Table 1. Pansori Domain TM Structure

Topic Types	Association Types	Occurrence Types
◦ Je		◦ Contents
◦ Yoo-Pa		◦ Concert
◦ KangSan-Je	◦ Belongs to	◦ Article
◦ DongPyon-Je	◦ Classified as	◦ Paper
◦ DongCho-Je	◦ Composed by	◦ Work Structure
◦ SeoPyon-Je	◦ Consists of	◦ Nick Name
◦ ChungGo-Je	◦ Famous in	◦ Real Name
◦ People	◦ Has Editorials	◦ Image
◦ Go-Soo	◦ Hierarchical relationship	◦ Sound
◦ Composer	◦ Is a body of	◦ Introduction
◦ Myung-Chang	◦ Is a dunum of	◦ Genealogy
◦ Genealogy	◦ Is a member of	◦ Producing Year
◦ Pansori Type	◦ Master Of	◦ Book
◦ Creative Pansori	◦ Matches with	◦ Type
◦ Pansori	◦ Part-Rhythm	◦ Position
◦ Dan-Ga		◦ Editorial
◦ Byon-Chang		◦ Video
◦ SeungDo-Chang	◦ Part-Tone	◦ Critique
◦ Chang-Guk	◦ Played by	◦ Prize
◦ Dae-Mok	◦ Singer-Part	◦ Albums
◦ Ba-Di	◦ Singer-Tone	◦ Web site
◦ Jang-Dan	◦ Tambour-Rhythm	◦ Homepage
◦ Jo	◦ Teacher-Student	◦ Date Of Birth
◦ Region	◦ Well-Known for	◦ Activities Year
◦ Sa-Sul		◦ Birth Place
◦ Pansori Elements		◦ Pen Name

4 TM Pansori Retrieval System Using Topic Maps (TMPRS) vs. Current Pansori Retrieval System (CPRS)

4.1 Topic Maps-Based Pansori Retrieval System (TMPRS)

TMPRS was implemented based on TM structures extracted from the domain modeling. LTM (Linear Topic Map Notation), which is a simple textual format for Topic Maps, was employed to represent Topic Maps, and Ontopia Knowledge Suite (OKS) as a general application tool was used to build topic maps. We built an interface to demonstrate the Topic Maps based Pansori retrieval system. Topic types are placed in the top as shown in Fig 3 below. If a user clicks a topic type in the top menu, the interface shows its hierarchical relationships, scoped names, instances, and occurrences as shown in Fig 3. If the user clicks any topics, the system displays associations in the left section, occurrences in the middle section, and its hierarchical relationship in the right section. Therefore, the user can identify all kinds of associations, and occurrences related to that topic in one display window. For example, if a user finds Chun-Hyang Ga (춘향가), which is an instance of Pansori as

Fig. 3. TMPRS Topic Types Example

Fig. 4. TMPRS Topic Search Example

a topic type, s/he can see all the associations and information resources in a one page display shown in Fig 4.

4.2 A Current Pansori Retrieval System (CPRS)

The reasons why the study selected the 'Pansori.com' as a comparison site among several Pansori systems are as follows. 'Pansori.com' contains exhaustive contents, well comprised categorization, and various types of data such as sounds, pictures, and text that are related to Pansori. In addition, it has been kept updated since 1996 and the system statistics reveal high traffic by users.

CPRS (Pansori.com) is based on the hierarchical browsing system by classification of categories. The main page of CRPS consists of 19 top categories, each top category usually has several sub categories, and most top categories have one-level sub categories except for some categories which have two-levels of sub categories. The main access method of CPRS is by browsing. The system does not provide any keyword retrieval function. Therefore, a user can retrieve items only by browsing. As shown in the Fig 5, if a user desires to find *dong-Pyon Je(동편제)*, which is one type of a *Yoo-Pa(유파)*, a user needs to keep track of categories by browsing and by clicking consequently in the order *of Je(제)*, *Yoo-Pa (유파)*, and *Dong-Pyon(동편제)*.

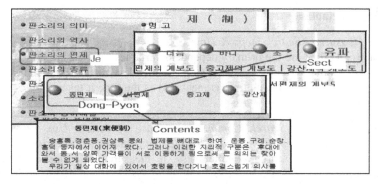

Fig. 5. Search Examples of CRPS

5 Research Design

5.1 Experiment Participants

Twenty LIS students in Korea were randomly selected for the study. While these students due constitute a convenience sample to some degree, they are as representative of a general Pansori-aware audience.

5.2 Variables

Conceptualization of research variables are shown in the Fig 6 below.

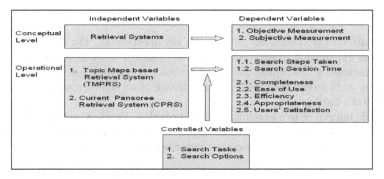

Fig. 6. Conceptualization of Research Variables

Independent Variables

Retrieval Systems
The systems included in this study are Topic Maps-based Pansori Retrieval System based on Topic Maps (TMPRS) and a Current Pansori Retrieval System (CRPS). We employed UML for modeling and developed a new interface using JSP and the Ontopia Topic Maps Engine OKS to demonstrate the power of TMPRS. For CRPS, the Pansori retrieval system available from Pansori.com (http://www.pansori.com) was selected.

Dependent Variables

Objective Measures – Search Steps & Time
Search steps and time are the primary dependent variables for measuring the objective performance of both systems. A search step is defined as a participant's click to find what s/he is looking for. Search time is measured as the time it takes for a participant to finish a search.

Subjective Measures – Search Completeness, Ease of System Use, Efficiency of Retrieval Systems, Appropriateness, and Subject' Satisfaction with Retrieval
A dependent variable, search completeness, is measured in terms of how well participants are able to complete tasks using each system. Ease of use is defined as the degree to which participants felt that the system was easy to use. Efficiency is also used as a variable. It is defined as the degree to which participants felt that they were able to quickly find the information that they needed. Appropriateness is defined as the degree to participants felt that the system was appropriate for search. Satisfaction is measured as a degree to which a subject is satisfied with service provided by each retrieval system. 7-point Likert scale is employed to measure subjective dependent variables from 1 point as highly disagree to 7 point as highly agree.

Control Variables – Task Types and Search Option
Task types and search options, in this study, are employed as control variables since they may have an effect on search performance. Six different pre-defined search tasks are assigned to each participant. And they are also asked to perform their own query. Only a browsing search option is employed since CPRS does not provide keyword search function.

5.3 Procedure

All test sessions were conducted in the same lab environment. The lab session started with a brief explanation of test procedures and requirements. During this explanation session, participants' informed consent was obtained allowing for those who choose to continue an observation of their search behavior along with a continuous recording of their screen displays.

A simple tutorial of two systems was also provided. Two test queries were given to allow participants to explore the two systems and become familiar with systems use before the real session begins. Two exploration queries are as follows:

- Query 1: Find the "Je (제)" of Pansori and examples of "Je (제)" of Pansori
- Query 2: Find types of genealogy of Myung-Chang (명창) in Pansori

When participants felt that they were ready to proceed, the experimental sessions started, and a researcher began screen recording and observation. To reduce the order effect, half of the participants were asked to use TMPRS first followed by CPRS. This order was reversed for the other 10 subjects. Tasks were also randomly assigned. When a participant completed each task for the two systems, s/he was required to complete a specific questionnaire pertaining to the task. After a subject completed all the steps required in the experiment, s/he also completed a general questionnaire pertaining to the overall experiences of using the two systems.

5.4 Research Methods

Three different methodologies were used in this study to collect data for user performance evaluation. Questionnaires, Screen Recordings, and Observation/Note-Taking were employed for quantitative and qualitative data collection and analysis. Each method is described in detail in the following:

Questionnaire
Questionnaire was employed for a quantitative subjective variable data collection method. A questionnaire was employed to study the various subjective performance measures such as completeness, ease of use, efficiency, and satisfaction after each task, and to study subjective performance measures in general after all tasks were completed.

Screen Recording
Screen Recording was used to determine various quantitative and qualitative data such as search session time per task and search steps per task as well as users' interaction with systems, if any.

Observation & Note-Taking
Observation by a researcher was also employed as a qualitative data collection method for additional participants' interaction and experience with each system.

5.5 Search Tasks

Assigned tasks were categorized based on the query complexity. The complexity was based on the numbers of concepts, hierarchies, and the degree of relationships between concepts [1]. [12]. Lia and Palvia's notion of task complexity [8] was applied here. Task categories and task examples assigned are as follows:

Table 2. Query Types

Task Group 1: Simple Task	Search for information about Jang-Dan (장단)
Task Group 2: Complex Task 1	Search for famous Myoung-Chang and works of Dong-Pyon-Je (동편제)
Task Group 3: Complex Task 2	Search for the birth year for SoHee Kim (김소희)
Task Group 4: Hierarchical Relationship Task	Search for hierarchical category information for Seo-Pyon-Je (서편제). That is, Look for lower or higher level of Seo-Pyon-Je (서편제)
Task Group 5: Association and Cross Reference related Task 1	Search for generation which NokJu Park (박녹주) belongs to, and find three Myoung-Chang(명창) in the same generation
Task Group 6: Association and Cross Reference related Task 2	Search for a famous Myoung-Chang for a Je-Bi (제비후리러 나가는 대목) part and find the birth place for that Myoung-Chang.
Task Group 7: User Own Query	Search for information in your interest.

After participants finished the assigned tasks, they were asked to describe what query they would like to search for their own interest. To conserve participants' time, each one was told to do only one personal interest query. The same query was searched again using the other system.

6   Results and Analyses

For objective measurement of normally distributed data, paired t-tests were employed to see whether there were significant differences in the means between the two systems following [4]; Wilcoxon's signed ranked tests were also used to analyze non parametric data. For subjective measures, since the differences between participants' measures were not normally distributed, Wilcoxon's signed rank test was used to investigate the magnitude of differences.

As seen in Table 3, in tasks 1 and 7, the differences between the two systems were not significant across five subjective criteria. For tasks 2 through 6, the five subjective criteria (completeness, ease of use, efficiency, appropriateness, and satisfaction) were found to be statistically significant. However, in task 7 (users' own query) the difference between the two systems was insignificant.

Task 1 involved an uncomplicated query such as "Search for information about Rhythm" that could be resolved by finding information on the main page as shown in Fig 7. In task 7, which allowed self-formulated queries, most participants opted for simple interests such as "Search for information about Tambour" or "Search for Seo-Pyon-Je (서편제)." As TMPRS outperformed CPRS when the nature of the given task was either complex, hierarchical, or associative & cross- referential, one may conclude that users' domain knowledge is a crucial factor that determines the overall performance TMPRS.

Measures on time spent repeated the pattern of subjective data: In tasks 2 through 6, use of TMPRS was shown to have demanded less time than that of CPRS, while in tasks 1 and 7, differences between the two systems were insignificant. For the steps taken, TMPRS outperformed CPRS in tasks 3, 5, and 6, while the result was clearly reversed in task 1; no significant differences were found in tasks 2, 4 and 7. It is suggested that the use of CPRS took fewer steps than that of TMPRS in task1 due to the methods of content display: In one page CPRS showed contents and categories together where TMPRS showed only categories, making it necessary for its users to click on a category (i.e., an extra step) to see its content.

Table 3. Results on Subjective Measures - |S| value

	T1	T2	T3	T4	T5	T6	T7	Overall
Completeness	0.75	0.0215	0.0039	0.0014	0.6475	0.0032	0.0523	0.0039
Ease of Use	0.4275	0.0032	<.0001	0.0034	0.0239	<.0001	0.9938	<.0001
Efficiency	0.7032	0.0017	<.0001	0.0009	0.0334	<.0001	0.6062	0.0001
Appropriateness	0.8516	0.0012	<.0001	0.0002	0.0426	<.0001	0.7021	0.0019
Satisfaction	0.2479	0.0004	<.0001	0.0002	0.0318	<.0001	0.8395	0.001

Table 4. Results on Subjective Measures – Means of differences between two systems & their standard deviations

Measure \Task		T1	T2	T3	T4	T5	T6	T7	Overall
Complet eness	Mean	-0.15	0.85	1.1	1.55	0.1578947	1.9	-1.55	1.25
	SD	1.42441	1.42441	1.37267	1.82021	1.6754156	2.3597502	3.0860467	1.681947
Ease of Use	Mean	0.4	1.4	2.5	1.35	1.3157895	3.15	0	2.45
	SD	1.98415	1.72901	1.5728	1.8432	2.2659442	1.6944181	3.4182175	1.538112
Efficie Ncy	Mean	0.15	1.45	2.85	1.35	1.3684211	3.6	-0.55	2.2
	SD	1.81442	1.73129	2.03328	1.42441	2.2659442	1.8180383	3.7763112	1.852452
Appro priat eness	Mean	-0.05	1.5	2.7	1.7	1.2631579	3.5	-0.35	1.75
	SD	2.11449	1.60591	1.65752	1.49032	2.3532981	1.8209309	3.7735227	2.022895
Satis faction	Mean	0.6	1.8	2.8	1.85	1.3157895	3.4	-0.05	1.85
	SD	2.32605	1.70448	1.76516	1.63111	2.3582628	2.1126187	3.3635038	1.954078

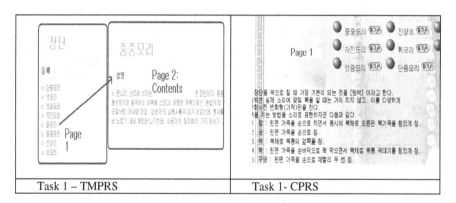

Task 1 – TMPRS	Task 1- CPRS

Fig. 7. Task 1 Search

Overall, objective measures mirrored subjective measures: In simple task, there were no big differences between TMPRS and CPRS while in complex tasks such as 3, 5 and 6 in particular, TMPRS was shown to have performed better than CPRS.

The study also noted that tasks 3 and 6 yielded bigger means of differences between TMPRS and CPRS (See Tables 4 and 5). In other words, TMPRS seemed more suitable for task 3 and task 6. However, in terms of types of tasks, tasks 2 and 3 form a group, while tasks 5 and 6 belong to another. It is hard to explain why tasks 3 and 6 were better than tasks 2 and 5 for TMPRS. However, it seems that task 3 and task 5 require occurrence information while task 2 and task 6 include association information. Because CRPS embedded occurrence information in the text, participants needed more time to read it to find occurrence information for the tasks.

Participants were asked to evaluate their overall feelings and experience of the two systems on five subjective criteria.

On completeness, participants reported that they did better with TMPRS since its structure was more specific, detailed and categorical, which meant less clicks for information search. With CPRS, participants found it hard to complete some tasks as they needed to explore hierarchical relationships between categories of information first, which meant more time and energy.

On ease of use, participants noted that TMPRS was superior to CPRS: TMPRS made movement from categories to categories easy and flexible and allowed them to find information on one page. On the other hand, with "fragmented" and "unrelated" information structures, CPRS forced them to explore and repeat categories and to identify the structures on their own.

On efficiency, participants responded that TMRPS triggered lots of information in one click, allowing them to retrieve information with fewer clicks and less browsing. CPRS made it hard to find information efficiently from hierarchical structures; participants needed more time since they had to combine fragments of information from different structures; some also noted that they had to read a long text to find information.

On appropriateness, participants also thought TMPRS was better than CPRS. With TMPRS they could finish their tasks, but with CPRS they experienced difficult guessing work and unfinished tasks. They thought CPRS was particularly inappropriate for tasks that involved linked and complex information.

On satisfaction, TMPRS was found to give more information with greater ease that gave them conceptual pictures of knowledge of a domain. On the other hand, CPRS gave very limited information. It did not link to other theme of information and how a category is related to others, and it required reading of texts for information retrieval. Most of them mentioned that they are not satisfied with the structure of category and it took more time and more browsing.

Table 5. Objective Measures Results – Measn of difference between two systems & its standard deviation

Measures /Task		T1	T2	T3	T4	T5	T6	T7
Time	Mean	-5.157895	24.47368	58.78947	31.15789	21.16667	135.10526	11.631579
	SD	12.659047	42.31281	62.14104	48.9935	57.01522	140.8679	50.450427
·Step	Mean	-3.947368	1.421053	3.789474	0.789474	2.888889	7.5263158	0.1578947
	SD	3.51937	4.658514	3.408795	2.615742	4.587565	8.7519421	3.6706517

Table 6. Objective Measures Results - |S| or |t|

Measures /Task	T1	T2	T3	T4	T5	T6	T7
Time	|t|= 0.0926	|S|=0.0044	|S|<.0001	|t|=0.0126	|S|=0.0313	|S|<.0001	|S|=0.3549
Step	|S|=<.0001	|S|=0.4307	|S|=0.0001	|S|=0.3029	|S|=0.0191	|S|=0.0002	|S|=0.9119

CPRS was mostly frequently characterized as "fragmented" , "unrelated" or "not systematically structured" , while "more information", "flexible", "well structured", "fewer browsing and less time", "related information" and "help with understanding of a domain at the conceptual level" were most dominant descriptors of TMPRS.

Overall the data from the experiment suggest that TMPRS performed better than CPRS in objective and subjective measurements, especially in tasks 2 through 6. However, no significant differences were found in measurements involving users' own queries and task 1. It seems that simplicity is a factor at work. It may therefore be valuable to see whether or not domain expert users employ more complex queries and show different evaluation.

7   Conclusion and Future Work

ISO/IEC SC34 Topic Maps is an ontology language with strong implications for implementations of semantic data modeling. It can express rich relationships among topics and collate related items. Despite its potentials and ensuing expectations, however, studies that demonstrate how much and in what ways Topic Map based systems can satisfy users' needs have been scarce, if not non-existent. Previous studies were somewhat limited in that none evaluated categories of task types even though user evaluations and tasks are closely related. Most studies have only employed objective measurements such as search time, mistakes made, etc.

We attempted two things in the current study: First we implemented a Topic Map based system named Korean Folk Music (Pansori) Retrieval System (TMPRS) and then conducted a comparative study on user evaluation between this system and a representative Current Pansori Retrieval System (CPRS). Twenty LIS students were randomly selected and assigned to multiple pre-defined tasks as well as a query of their own. At completion of each task, they were asked to fill out a questionnaire for that task comparing the performance of the two systems. A general evaluation questionnaire about the overall experience of the two systems was also given at the end of each experiment session. It was believed that Pansori, a genre in traditional Korean music, was well-suited for Topic Maps. Users of a Pansori retrieval system may benefit from enriched expressions of relationships and collated items rather than from simple inferences from topics.

The study sought to tease out different aspects of system performance, both objective and subjective in nature. Evaluation was based on multiple tasks in the order of increasing complexity. Search steps taken, search time spent for given tasks, search completeness, ease of system usage, system efficiency, appropriateness of search support, and users' satisfaction were measured.

Based on the results from the experiments, we found that TMPRS generally outperformed CPRS in objective and subjective measurements. TMPRS was much better than CPRS for tasks 2 through 6. However, there were no significant differences in objective and subjective measurements for users' own query and task 1. It was suggested that this statistical insignificance was accounted by the simplicity of the tasks. TMPRS was superior to CRPS for complex task, hierarchical task, and association & cross reference task.

In addition, TMPRS performed better than CPRS especially in tasks 3 and 6, when compared to the data from tasks 2 and 5. Commonality in types (nature) of task could not explain the differences. It was therefore suggested that occurrence information of tasks 3 and 6 may have caused the unexpected results. However, it is premature to generalize this finding at the current stage.

Overall reaction towards the two systems was somewhat different as well and seems to have affected responses of completeness, ease of use, efficiency, appropriateness, and satisfaction of the participants.

To conclude, TMPRS performed well in complex tasks rather than in simple tasks. TMPRS' methods of modeling and structuring information allowed users to locate information with more information, and seemed to promise fewer browsing and less time. It also provided a conceptual understanding of a domain.

The current study has a number of implications for future research. First, an extension of the study involving users with a domain expertise would certainly add to the evaluation of TMPRS. The current study employed college students with limited subject knowledge of Pansori. As a result their self-formulated queries had no depth. It would be valuable to see the effect, if any, of domain expertise on the level of complexity in self-formulated queries and on evaluation results. Second, an extension of the study to users outside a LIS domain would be valuable to validate the study. The current study employed only LIS students and it assumed that LIS students have no impact on the results. To verify no impact of the sampling in the study and to generalize the result, it is necessary to investigate how users in different population evaluate two systems. Third, this study controlled task types and search options as control variables since it was assumed that they may have an effect on search performance. However, it did not control interface design or the information available, which might have an effect on search performance. Therefore, it would be good to control these factors as well to compare two systems in the future study. Fourth, the relevance between types of tasks and TMPRS need more specification and consistency. The current study, for instance, identified that TMPRS performed better in tasks 3 and 6 than in tasks 2 and 5. Such results, however, were not expected by the researchers because tasks 2 and 3 shared a type and tasks 5 and 6 shared another. Finally, as the study was limited to one domain, which makes it difficult to generalize its findings, expansion of the current research into different domains seems also necessary.

References

1. Bystrom, K. Jarvelin, K. : Task complexity affects information seeking and use. Information Processing and Management 31.2 (1995) 191-213.
2. Gruber, T.R What is an ontology? (1994) <http://www.ksl.stanford.edu/kst/what-is-an-ontology.html>
3. Guo, Y, Pan, Z., Heflin, J. : An Evaluation of Knowledge Base Systems for Large OWL Datasets. Third International Semantic Web Conference, Hiroshima, Japan, LNCS 3298, Spinger, (2004) 274-288
4. Janes, J. : Comparing the means of two groups – the t-test, Library Hi Tech 20.4 (2002) 469-471

5. Kim, H.H. : Ontoweb: Implementing an ontology-based web retrieval system. Journal of the American Society for Information Science and Technology 56.11 (2005) 1167-1176.
6. Kim, K-S, Allen, B.: Cognitive and task influences on web searching behavior. Journal of the American Society for Information Science and Technology 53(2) (2002) 109-119
7. Kim, S., Soergel, D. : Selecting and Measuring Task Characteristics as Independent Variables. In.: Procs of the 68th Annual ASIST meeting (2005)
8. Liao, C., Palvia, P.C.: The impact of data models and task complexity on end-user performance: an experimental investigation. International Journal of Human-Computer Studies 52.5 (2000) 831-45
9. Nielsen, M L.: Task-based evaluation of associative thesaurus in real-life environment. In.: Procs of the ASIST 2004 Annual Meeting (2004)
10. Rowley, J. : The Controlled Versus Natural Indexing Languages Debate Revisited: a Perspective on Information Retrieval Practice and Research. Journal of Information Science 20.2 (1994) 108-119
11. Sure, Y., Iosif, V. : First results of a semantic web technologies evaluation. In.: Procs of the Common Industry Program (2002) 69-78
12. Vakkari, P. : Task complexity, problem structure and information actions integrating studies on information seeking and retrieval. Information Processing and Management. 35 (1999) 819-837

Appendix: Pansori Terms Explained

- Pansori: A type of Korean Folk Music
- Dae-Mok: A special part of a pansori ("A long song" is a part of the pansori "ChunHyanGa")
- Yoo-Pa/Je: Four types of Pansori (Dong-Pyon, Seo-Pyon, Chung-Go, Kang-San)
- Myung-Chang: A person who sings a Pansori
- Go-Soo: A person who plays a korean drum
- Dunum: Famous Myung-Chang + "Je" + A special part of Pansori (E.g,Kwon, Sam Duk-Je-A love song)
- Ba-Di: Famous Myung-Chang + "Je" + Pansori (E.g, E.g,Kwon, Sam Duk-Je-ChunHyanGa)
- Jo: Melody of a Pansori
- Jang-Dan: A special kind of rhythm of Pansori
- Sa-Seol: A form of lyric written for Pansori

Towards a Formal TMQL Semantics

Robert Barta

Bond University
School of Information Technology
rho@bond.edu.au

Abstract. TMQL, the upcoming standardized Topic Maps query language, may become the main work horse for semantic web applications based on the Topic Maps paradigm. While the current specification uses prose to declare the intended meaning of various language constructs, this work is an approach to a complete formal semantics. It details the *static semantics* as a translation from TMQL expressions into TMRM path expressions and presents for these low-level expressions a structural definition and the *dynamic semantics*.

1 Introduction

TMQL [3] [1] (Topic Maps query language) is designed to be a data access and query language for content being organized along the Topic Maps paradigm [6]. The draft specification at the time of writing describes a *functional language*: given a valid TMQL expression, a set of variable bindings and a minimal ontological framework (predefined types, functions and predicates), the expression can be evaluated without any further global context.

This design choice has several consequences, one of the most eminent ones being that any evaluation model does not need a concept of *state*. This makes any mapping into other functional programming languages simpler and therefore more efficient; the missing state context also opens a pathway for optimizers which can effectively be expression-to-expression transformers. And finally at evaluation time, expressions can be more easily farmed out onto grids and cluster architectures.

Apart from providing a precise evaluation definition, the main motivation for a *formal* semantics for TMQL is to have a strict foundation for these optimization techniques. Only with a rigorous mathematical approach rules for minimizing the computational complexity can be formulated and—more importantly—proven to maintain the intended meaning of a TMQL expression. This is even more relevant when contextual knowledge, such as ontological information about the maps being queried or various usage patterns are to be exploited for optimization.

Given a set of variables which are assigned to Topic Map item and other values (variable bindings), a formal semantics for TMQL has to describe the result of evaluting a query expression on this binding set. As primitive values we use those which are predefined by TMQL (integer, float, etc.), for topic maps we commit to those items following TMDM [4] (Topic Maps data model). As

L. Maicher, A. Sigel, and L.M. Garshol (Eds.): TMRA 2006, LNAI 4438, pp. 90–106, 2007.

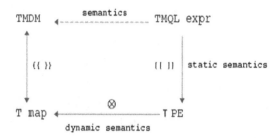

Fig. 1. Overall Semantics

TMDM is not directly amenable to a concise formalization we choose a slightly different route (Fig. 1). In that we postulate that there is a structural mapping between a TMDM instance and a *subject map* according to TMRM [5], the TM reference model. Several such attempts (e.g. [2]) for such a mapping exist; here we symbolize this mapping with {{ }} brackets. When applied to a TMDM item, the mapping will construct an equivalent subject map. That mapping also has to include map navigation inside a TMDM instance.

The *static semantics* [[ ]] is then defined as a mapping of TMQL expressions into TMRM path expressions: every valid syntactic form in the TMQL grammar is translated into these low level path expressions. The *dynamic semantics* is then directly given by the definitions of TMRM path expressions which detail the results when a path expression is applied to a subject map.

To keep the paper more self-contained, first relevant parts of TMQL itself are presented. Then follows a rather minimalistic presentation of the T model (section 3) which—in its latest form—underlies TMRM subject maps, together with primitive map traversal facilities. To model query results we then define tuple sequences in section 4 and various operators to combine them. Equipped with these, we then move on to T path expressions and define how they are evaluated on a subject map (section 5).

Based on this low-level machinery we then turn to TMQL path expressions and declaratively define the static semantics [[ ]] (section 8), first for TMQL path expressions. While this is relatively straighforward, the mapping of TMQL FLWR and TMQL SELECT expressions needs first a mechanism to eliminate variables (section 9). We close with yet untackled issues.

2   TMQL Overview

TMQL offers 3 different *surface syntaxes*, mainly to appeal to different developer communities and to adapt to differing development scenarios. The SELECT style mimics the functionality known from SQL statements, but is actually an expression, rather than a statement:

```
select-expression -> 'select'    tuple-expression
                  [  'from'    value-expression ]
```

```
[ 'where'  boolean-expression ]
[ 'order' 'by' tuple-expression ]
[ 'unique'  ]
[ 'offset' value-expression ]
[ 'limit'  value-expression ]
```

The FROM clause is used to determine (or compute) the map a query expression is effectively applied to, and the WHERE clause specifies the constellation of values one is interested in by providing a boolean constraint over a set of variables. For each constellation so characterized, the SELECT clause with its tuple expression is evaluated. That renders each a tuple sequence, all so computed sequences are then concatenated together to form an overall result. It is worth noting, that the evaluation of the tuple expression in the SELECT clause may result in zero, one or more tuples. This feature implicitly provides *grouping* functionality, so that no other special language constructs have to be provided.

To extract, for example, the name and the age of all persons from a map, one could write:

```
select $p / name, $p / age
where
   $p isa person
```

Since the variable $p is not explicitly quantified inside the boolean expression, it will be regarded there as *free*, i.e. it will be freely assigned to all items of the queried map. Each of such an assignment is then tested whether the value is an instance of **person**.

The boolean expressions in TMQL are quite conventional. They can be combined with the propositional operators (*and*, *or* and *not*), but TMQL also provides *exists* and *forall* quantification as in

```
exists $n in $p / name
   satisfies fn:contains ($n, "Dr.") or $n * = academic-title
```

The whole clause is then **True** when there exists one (or more) **name** characteristics of the value currently bound to $p where the name—automatically converted into a string—contains "Dr." as a substring. The prefix **fn** is predefined and indicates the namespace for the TMQL-intrinsic functions. The clause is also satisfied if the type of the name is actually a subclass of **academic-title**: The postfix * uses the name characteristics as starting point and computes all types and their supertypes. Each of them will be compared to **academic-title**. Here the *exists semantics* is implicit.

The second syntax style is more adequate with line-oriented interfaces or where the syntactic sugar should be kept at a minimum. The processing pattern is quite simple: First content—which can be constants of any of the available data types or topic map content—is generated. Then postfixes are applied one by one to transform or filter the content:

```
path-expression -> content [ postfix-chain ]
postfix-chain   -> postfix [ postfix-chain ]
postfix         -> filter | projection
```

Postfixes are either filters or projections. Filters are characterized via a boolean expression which is used as predicate:

```
filter -> [ boolean-expression ]
```

When applied to a tuple sequence, for every tuple in the sequence this boolean expression is evaluated. If the result is `True`, then that very tuple will be part of the result tuple sequence. Otherwise it will be ignored.

Projections also work on the basis that each tuple of the incoming tuple sequence is considered. For each tuple, a tuple expression which characterizes the projection is evaluated. Again the partial results—each a tuple sequence—are concatenated. The following path expression may serve as example:

```
%_ [ . * = person ] ( . / name, . / age )
```

It first references all items in the queried map (indicated by the special variable `%_`), then it filters out those items which are direct or indirect instances of the concept **person**. After that filter it then computes pairs of values for each of the **person** instances. The first component of every pair is the value of the name of a person, the second component is the data value for the **age** occurrence.

The third syntax flavour, FLWR, allows a much more fine-grained control on the use of variables and also provides syntax to generate not only tuple sequences as result structure, but also XML and Topic Map content. As we ignore XML and TM content in this context, FLWR expressions specialize to

```
flwr-expression -> { 'for' < variable-association > }
                     'where' boolean-expression
                     'return' tuple-expression
```

whereby any number of variables can be introduced and can be associated with values (in the grammar we use the brackets <> to group phrases which must occur at least once and are separated by commas and to group phrases which may occur any number of times). As the variables so introduced range over the values provided by the variable associations, every so generated constellation is tested with the boolean expression inside the WHERE clause. Only those combinations of values which satisfy this constraint are considered and only with such combinations the content in the RETURN clause is generated.

Following the example stream, an equivalent FLWR expression could look like this:

```
for $p in %_ [ . * = person ]
return
   ( $p / name, $p / age )
```

Accordingly, the variable $p *iterates* over all instances of **person** and with each such iteration the tuple expression in the RETURN clause is evaluated.

All three TMQL styles can be freely mixed, as the developer might find appropriate. To reduce further syntactic noise, the language also offers a number of shortcuts for rather frequent programming patterns. As examples we list **// person** which actually stands for the more canonical form **%_ [. * = person]**. The dot itself stands for **@_[0]** where the variable **@_** represents the current context tuple. And the ***** is only a short form to navigate to all types of an item, so it stands for the navigation along the *classes* axis: **classes :>:**.

There are several such navigational axes in TMQL, most of these are mandated by the TMDM data model itself. Examples are *find all occurrence items of a given item of a type* **age** (written as **characteristic :>: age**) or *find all names of a given item* (written as **name :>:**). All these axes can be moved along in *forward* or *backward* direction. To find all instances of a concept, say **person**, the path expression would use the navigation **person classes :<:**.

3   TMRM Model

The low-level model defined in TMRM assumes that subjects in the universe are represented by *subject proxies*. Each proxy is characterized by a finite number of properties (see Fig.2). Each proxy is thought to be uniquely linked with a label, so that if the label is known, the proxy can be looked up and if a proxy is known, its label can be somehow computed. Apart from that, labels have no relevance.

The properties of a proxy are simply pairs, a *key* together with a *value*. Keys are always proxy labels, values can be proxy labels too, but can also be literals from a set of predefined types, such as **Integer**, **String** and so forth. A *subject map* is then simply a collection of proxies.

In the following we will first formalize the above and will then extend this model by primitive navigation. For this, we postulate two sets: the (finite) set of *labels* $\mathcal{L}$ and a set of values $\mathcal{V}$ in which all literals (**Integers**, **String**) together with their type are collected. Also this set is supposedly finite, and it includes also all values from $\mathcal{L}$.

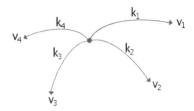

Fig. 2. Proxy Structure

3.1   Properties, Proxies and Maps

A *property* is a pair $\langle k, v \rangle \in (\mathcal{L} \times \mathcal{V})$. The first component in such tuples is called the *key* and the second the *value* of the property. We denote all such properties with $\mathcal{P}$. A *subject proxy* (or short *proxy*) is then simply a finite set of properties, $\{p_1, \ldots, p_n\}$, with $p_i \in \mathcal{P}$. For the set of all such proxies we use $\mathcal{X}$ and with it we define a *subject map* (short *map*) to be any finite subset of $\mathcal{X}$.

3.2 Subclassing

TMRM does not make any ontological commitment, the only exceptions are two widely used concepts, that of *subclassing* and the *type-instance* relationship. Mathematically, both are binary relations whereby TMRM only mandates some minimal properties:

- Two proxies c, c' can be in a *subclass-superclass* relationship, whereby we equivalently say that either *c is a subclass of c'* or *c' is a superclass of c*: $\mathrm{sub} \subseteq \mathcal{X} \times \mathcal{X}$. sub is supposed to be reflexive and transitive. *Reflexive* implies that any proxy is technically a subclass of itself, regardless whether the proxy is used as a class in the map or not. *Transitive* implies that if a proxy c is a subclass of another c' and that in turn subclasses c'', then c is also regarded to be a subclass of c''.
- Two proxies a, c can be in an *isa* relationship, whereby we equivalently say that either *a is an instance of c* or *c is the type of a*: $\mathrm{isa} \subseteq \mathcal{X} \times \mathcal{X}$. For isa we only expect it to be non-reflexive, so that no proxy can be an instance of itself. Additionally, whenever a proxy a is an instance of another c, it is also implicitly true that a is an instance of any superclass of c.

How these relationships are modelled within a TMRM map is left unconstrained. In the following we will interpret the relationships always in the context of a given map m and write for this sub_m.

3.3 Navigation

Given a map m and particular proxies $x, y \in m$, the following *navigation operators* are defined:

- A postfix operator $\downarrow$ to return the multiset of *all local keys* of a given proxy:

$$x \downarrow = \{k \mid \exists v \colon \langle k, v \rangle \in x\} \tag{1}$$

- A postfix operator $\uparrow_m$ to retrieve the *remote keys* of a proxy inside a given map m. These are those where the given proxy *is* the value in another proxy:

$$x \uparrow_m = \{k \mid \exists y \in m \colon \langle k, x \rangle \in y\} \tag{2}$$

- The postfix operator $\rightarrow k$ retrieves the *local values* for a particular label $k \in \mathcal{L}$:

$$x \rightarrow k = \{v \mid \exists \langle k, v \rangle \in x\} \tag{3}$$

The generalization $\rightarrow_m k^*$ also honors transitive subclassing on the specified key:

$$x \rightarrow_m k^* = \{v \mid \exists \langle k', v \rangle \in x \wedge k' \ \mathrm{sub}_m \ k\} \tag{4}$$

Again, this operator depends on a given map, this time because the subclassing is interpreted only relative to a map.

- The postfix operator $\leftarrow_m k$ navigates to all proxies in the given map which use a given value v together with a certain label $k \in \mathcal{L}$:

$$v \leftarrow_m k = \{x \in m \mid \exists \langle k, v \rangle \in x\} \tag{5}$$

If subclassing concerning the provided key should be respected relative to a given map m, then the operator $\leftarrow_m k^*$ does this:

$$v \leftarrow_m k^* = \{x \in m \mid \exists \langle k', v \rangle \in x \wedge k' \text{ sub}_m k\} \tag{6}$$

It is straightforward to generalize all these navigation operators from individual proxies (and values) to multisets of proxies (and values). The benefit of this is that operators can now be *chained*, i.e. applied consecutively to a proxy (or a multiset of proxies). This effectively provides a simple postfix language.

4 Tuple Sequences

Tuples of values are a convenient way to capture the result of one pattern match. All these partial results can then be organized into a tuple sequence.

We denote a single tuple with values from a value set $\mathcal{V}$ as $\langle v_1, v_2, \ldots, v_n \rangle$. Obviously tuples are identical if all their values in the corresponding positions are. Tuples can be concatenated, simply by collating their values: $\langle u_1, \ldots, u_m \rangle \cdot \langle v_1, \ldots, v_n \rangle = \langle u_1, \ldots, u_m, v_1, \ldots, v_n \rangle$. This allows us to represent tuples as products of singleton tuples:

$$t = \prod_{i=1}^{n} \langle v_i \rangle = \langle v_1 \rangle \langle v_2 \rangle \ldots \langle v_n \rangle \tag{7}$$

When we organize tuples into sequences we write for a single sequence

$$s = \sum_{i=1}^{m} t_i = [t_1, \ldots, t_m] \tag{8}$$

Such sequences can be ordered or unordered; for our purposes here, though, we will treat them as multisets (bags), together with union, subtraction and intersection.

Sets of values can be interpreted as tuple sequences in such a way that every value builds exactly one singleton tuple: For a given set $\{v_1, \ldots, v_n\}$ we can so build the tuple sequence $\sum_{i=1}^{n} \langle v_i \rangle$. We denote this conversion simply as $\langle \{v_1, \ldots, v_n\} \rangle$. Under this interpretation, a map $m = \{x_1, \ldots, x_n\}$ can be represented as the tuple sequence $[\langle x_1 \rangle, \ldots, \langle x_n \rangle]$. Conversely, we can also interpret a tuple sequence as map when the tuples it contains are single proxies.

Tuple sequences can be concatenated

$$\sum s_i + \sum t_j = [s_1, \ldots, s_m, t_1, \ldots, t_n] \tag{9}$$

simply by interleaving freely the tuples of the second operand with those in the first. This corresponds to multiset union (as long as ordering is ignored). Tuple sequences can also subtracted from each other; we use the binary infix operator $-$ for that. Its meaning corresponds to multiset subtraction. Finally tuple sequences can be compared, in the sense that the resulting tuple sequence only contains tuples common to both (multiset intersection). We use the symbol $=$ for this.

Tuple sequences can also be combined by *multiplying* (joining) them. Informally, every tuple of the left operand sequence is concatenated with every other of the right-hand one. The way this is defined below is to cut off the first value of each tuple of the second operand and to combine that with every tuple of the first operand. This is then repeated until the second operand does not have tuples with any values left. Formally, the product between two tuple sequences is defined recursively via

$$(s)\left(\sum_{j=1}^{m}\langle v_{1j}, v_{2j}, \ldots, v_{lj}\rangle\right) = \left(s\sum_{j=1}^{m}\langle v_{1j}\rangle\right)\sum_{j=1}^{m}\langle v_{2j}, \ldots, v_{lj}\rangle \tag{10}$$

$$\sum_{i=1}^{n} t_i \sum_{j=1}^{m}\langle v_j\rangle = \sum_{i,j=1}^{nm} (t_i\langle v_j\rangle) \tag{11}$$

Tuples and proxies are also otherwise related. Obviously, we can take all values out a proxy and arrange them into a value tuple. If a certain order matters, then we postulate an order on keys and sort the values according to that. Conversely, a value tuple can be converted into a proxy, given that we have a tuple of keys available

$$\langle v_1, \ldots, v_n\rangle \yen \langle k_1, \ldots, k_n\rangle = \{\langle k_1, v_1\rangle, \ldots, \langle k_n, v_n\rangle\} \tag{12}$$

This *zipping* operation can be easily generalized to tuple sequences by repeating the process with every tuple of the sequence. In that, it allows to interpret every tuple sequence as a sequence of proxies whereby we arbitrarily can choose some keys. Once we have a sequence of proxies, that can then be interpreted as map.

5 $\mathcal{T}$/TMRM Path Expressions

A particular path expression can be interpreted as an *expression of interest*, i.e. as a pattern to be identified in a map. Given a tuple sequence s, we can apply a path expression p to it, expecting to get another tuple sequence in return. We symbolize this application as $s \otimes_m p$ and note that this operation is to be understood in the context of a map m. If that is implicit, we drop the index.

The set of path expressions $\mathcal{T}$ we characterize as the smallest satisfying the following conditions:

1. The *empty* postfix ε is in $\mathcal{T}$. When it is applied to a sequence, the same sequence is returned.
2. Every value from $\mathcal{V}$ (and consequently every proxy label) is in $\mathcal{T}$. If such a value is applied to a sequence, then the sequence itself is discarded. Instead a new sequence with a singleton tuple is created in which the value is used.
3. The navigation operators $\uparrow$, $\downarrow$, $\leftarrow k$ and $\rightarrow k$ are in $\mathcal{T}$. When applied to a tuple sequence these operators are applied to every tuple:

$$\left(\sum_{i=1}^{n} \langle v_{1i}, v_{2i}, \ldots, v_{li} \rangle \right) \otimes \leftarrow k = \sum_{i=1}^{n} \prod_{j=1}^{l} \langle v_{ji} \leftarrow_m k^* \rangle \tag{13}$$

$$\left(\sum_{i=1}^{n} \langle v_{1i}, v_{2i}, \ldots, v_{li} \rangle \right) \otimes \rightarrow k = \sum_{i=1}^{n} \prod_{j=1}^{l} \langle v_{ji} \rightarrow_m k^* \rangle \tag{14}$$

Above we simply iterate over each tuple and compute an intermediate result for this one tuple. This intermediate result is achieved by applying the navigation to each value in the current tuple. As one such application results in a multiset of values, that is converted into a singleton tuple sequence. All these singleton tuple sequences are multiplied and all these intermediate results are then concatenated into the overall result.

An analogous approach is used for finding keys:

$$\left(\sum_{i=1}^{n} \langle v_{1i}, v_{2i}, \ldots, v_{li} \rangle \right) \otimes \downarrow = \sum_{i=1}^{n} \prod_{j=1}^{l} \langle v_{ji} \downarrow \rangle \tag{15}$$

$$\left(\sum_{i=1}^{n} \langle v_{1i}, v_{2i}, \ldots, v_{li} \rangle \right) \otimes \uparrow = \sum_{i=1}^{n} \prod_{j=1}^{l} \langle v_{ji} \uparrow_m \rangle \tag{16}$$

4. Given path expressions $p_1, \ldots, p_n$ and a function $f : \mathcal{V}^n \mapsto \mathcal{V}$ then also $f(p_1, \ldots, p_n)$ is in $\mathcal{T}$. When an n-ary function $f : \mathcal{V}^n \mapsto \mathcal{V}$ is applied to a tuple sequence, we can interpret it as one which takes a value tuple of length n and renders one value from $\mathcal{V}$. To apply it to a tuple sequence, we apply it to every individual tuple and organize the singleton results back into a sequence:

$$f\left(\sum t_i \right) = \sum \langle f(t_i) \rangle \tag{17}$$

5. The *projection* postfix π_i is in $\mathcal{T}$ for any positive integer i. It can be used to extract a certain column from a given tuple sequence:

$$\sum_{i=1}^{n} \langle v_{1i}, v_{2i}, \ldots, v_{li} \rangle \otimes \pi_j = \sum_{i=1}^{n} \langle v_{ji} \rangle \tag{18}$$

Projection here plays a similar role like in query languages like SQL, except that we here use an index for selection instead of names.

To organize values freely into a new tuple sequence, we can use the *tuple projection* $\langle p_1, \ldots, p_n \rangle$ with p_i being path expressions. For a single tuple it evaluates all the path expressions and builds the product of all partial result sequences:

$$t \otimes \langle p_1, \ldots, p_n \rangle = \prod_{i=1}^{n} t \otimes p_i \qquad (19)$$

When applied to a tuple sequence, all applications to its tuples are concatenated. As a special case, the *empty projection* $\langle\rangle$ always returns an empty tuple sequence.

6. The *conditional* $p?q : r$ is in $\mathcal{T}$ for path expressions p, q and r. When it is applied to a tuple sequence, every tuple is tested whether it produces a result when p is applied to it. If that is the case, the *then* branch is used, i.e. the tuple will be subjected to q and these results will be added to the overall result. Otherwise, the tuple will get r applied:

$$\left(\sum_{i=1}^{n} t_i \right) \otimes (p?q : r) = \sum_{i=1}^{n} ([t_i \otimes q \mid t_i \otimes p \neq \emptyset] + [t_i \otimes r \mid t_i \otimes p = \emptyset]) \quad (20)$$

7. For two path expressions p and q the *alternation* $p + q$, the *reduction* $p - q$, and the *comparison* $p = q$ are in $\mathcal{T}$:

$$s \otimes (p + q) = (s \otimes p) + (s \otimes q) \qquad (21)$$

$$s \otimes (p - q) = (s \otimes p) - (s \otimes q) \qquad (22)$$

$$s \otimes (p = q) = (s \otimes p) = (s \otimes q) \qquad (23)$$

8. For two path expressions p and q also the *concatenation* $p \circ q$ is in $\mathcal{T}$. Here we simply define that

$$s \otimes (p \circ q) = (s \otimes p) \otimes q \qquad (24)$$

If—from the context—it is clear that two path expressions are to be concatenated, we omit the infix.

6   TMQL Environment

The TMQL specification defines a minimum runtime environment. In that any implementation is supposed to provide a set of predefined functions and predicates. All these are organized into topic maps which all combined form the static ontological environment.

When the application initiates a query evaluation, then it may also pass in parameters into the query process. This is done in form of variables which are bound to values, be they primitive ones, lists or complete maps. For the evaluation of the query expression all these variables effectively behave as constants, i.e. their values will be directly inserted into the query expression, so that these variables are eliminated.

Again, the following assumes a mapping {{ }} of all Topic Map related information into TMRM.

7 Content Generation

When content has to be generated, then it can either be of a simple nature or not:

```
simple-content -> ( atom | item-reference ) [ navigation ]
```

(No variables have to be considered here as they must have already been eliminated. Any remaining variable occurrences here would lead to an error.) In its simplest form this may result in a constant of predefined data types (numbers, strings, etc.). Content also can refer to items in the queried map in which case this has to be translated into a proxy label. Any simple content is organized into a singleton tuple sequence. If an optional navigation chain exists, the navigation operators as translated according to {{}}:

```
[[ atom ]]           = < atom >
[[ item-reference ]] = {{ item-reference }}
[[ navigation ]]     = {{ navigation }}
```

If otherwise content is produced via a nested query expression or via a tuple expression, these will have their own static semantics.

7.1 Tuple Expressions

For composite tuple expressions the used binary operators are mapped in a straightforward way into their $\mathcal{T}$ equivalents:

```
[[ tuple-expr-1 '++' tuple-expr-2 ]] = [[ tuple-expr-1 ]] + [[ tuple-expr-2 ]]
[[ tuple-expr-1 '--' tuple-expr-2 ]] = [[ tuple-expr-1 ]] - [[ tuple-expr-2 ]]
[[ tuple-expr-1 '='  tuple-expr-2 ]] = [[ tuple-expr-1 ]] = [[ tuple-expr-2 ]]
```

Any if-then-else construct is mapped onto $\mathcal{T}$ conditionals, whereby a missing else branch defaults to the empty projection:

```
[[ 'if' tuple-expr-1
   'then' tuple-expr-2
   'else' tuple-expr-3 ]] = [[ tuple-expr-1 ]] ? [[ tuple-expr-2 ]]
                                                : [[ tuple-expr-3 ]]
[[ 'if' tuple-expr-1
   'then' tuple-expr-2 ]] = [[ tuple-expr-1 ]] ? [[ tuple-expr-2 ]] : <>
```

Should the tuple expression be of the form of a comma-separated list of value expressions (v1, v2, ..., vn), then these expressions have to be translated separately and have to be organized into a $\mathcal{T}$ projection:

```
[[ tuple-expression ]] = [[ v1, v2, ..., vn ]]
                       = < [[ v1 ]] , [[ v2 ]] , ... , [[ vn ]] >
```

7.2   Value Expressions

The value expressions themselves are only used in the language grammar to organize values into algebraic expressions, be these formed with the predefined infix and prefix operators (such as + and *), or be it via explicitly named functions. As all operators will be mapped eventually into one of the predefined functions, we only have to deal with value expressions of the form f (v1, v2, ..., vn):

```
[[ f '(' v1, v2, ..., vn ')' ]] = {{ f }} ( < [[ v1 ]], [[ v2 ]] , ... , [[ vn ]] > )
```

As each of the value expressions above might result in one or more (or even zero) values, any evaluation will end up in arbitrary many parameter sets. This is directly modelled in with $\mathcal{T}$ function semantics.

8   TMQL Path Expression Semantics

The evaluation model of TMQL PEs is quite simple: At first *content* is produced, then a chain of postfixes is applied, one postfix at a time. If the chain is empty then [[content]] represents the complete static semantics. Otherwise, we define the application of postfixes to be left associative and use the $\mathcal{T}$ path expression concatenation:

```
[[ content postfix-chain ]] = [[ content ]] [[ postfix-chain ]]
[[ postfix postfix-chain ]] = [[ postfix ]] [[ postfix-chain ]]
```

8.1   Projections

Projections in TMQL PEs directly correspond to $\mathcal{T}$ projections:

```
[[ '(' tuple-expression ')' ]] = [[ tuple-expression ]]
```

8.2   Filters

Filters are supposed to suppress all tuples of the incoming tuple sequence which do not satisfy a certain predicate. This can be based on the $\mathcal{T}$ conditional:

```
[[ '[' boolean-expression ']'  ]] = [[ boolean-expression ]] ? epsilon : <>
```

Hereby the boolean expression is down-translated into a $\mathcal{T}$ path expression in such a way that it will render a non-empty result when it is supposed to be satisfied. Is this the case for a particular tuple then the application of ε (epsilon) will return that very tuple. Otherwise the empty projection will not forward any tuple, effectively suppressing the incoming tuple under consideration.

8.3   Association Predicates

Association predicates are effectively shorthand forms for TMQL PEs. For example, the predicate

```
is-composed-by (opera: $opera, composer: puccini, ...)
```

is equivalent with

```
// is-composed-by [ . -> opera = $opera ] [ . -> composer = puccini ]
```

Both state that all instances of associations of the type `is-composed-by` are to be selected and then tested whether each of these associations has one role `opera` with a value which is identical to what the variable `$opera` currently is bound to. Also the association under consideration is tested whether another role `composer` exists which happens to have as value the topic `puccini`. Given further that the pseudo postfix `//` `is-composed-by` is actually only a shorthand notation for `(%_)` `[ . * = is-composed-by ]`, the overall static semantics of association predicates is fully covered by that of TMQL PEs.

But this is only true for association predicates which contain a trailing ellipsis (...). That indicates that any matching association is allowed to have further roles apart from those mentioned, `opera` or `puccini` in the case above. This *non-strict* interpretation contrasts a *strict* interpretation if there is no ellipsis:

```
is-composed-by (opera: $opera, composer: puccini)
```

where any association must have exactly these two roles, and no others.

To model a strict interpretation of association predicates we first remove the ellipsis from the association template as if it were non-strict, but then append a further filter postfix which ensures that no other role may appear. This is best demonstrated along the example:

```
[[ is-composed-by (opera: $opera, composer: puccini) ]] =
    [[
        is-composed-by (opera: $opera, composer: puccini, ...)
        [ not . roles :>: - ( opera ) - ( composer ) ]
    ]]
```

In that, the `roles` axis finds all roles of the currently examined association. This tuple sequence is then reduced by first a single `opera`, and then by a single `composer` tuple. Note that this seemingly straightforward interpretation hides a subtlety. Should one association in the queried map have two roles with type `opera`, then such an association whould *not* match that very predicate. Something which most likely is intended.

9   Variables

While TMQL path expressions have no capabilities to declare new, locally scoped variables, this is possible with the other surface syntaxes. In each of these cases the variables are *quantified*, i.e. they are supposed to range over a defined multiset of values. In the FLWR syntax this is made explicit, as in:

```
for $opera in // opera
return
    ( $opera / name )
```

with SELECT-style expressions this is only implicit:

```
select $opera / name
where
   $opera isa opera
```

As $opera is the only free variable inside the WHERE clause, it implicitly is supposed to range over all items in the context map, at least conceptually.

In any case, the structure of the language guarantees that the list of values over which variables should iterate are computable by a TMQL path expression. This, and the obvious fact that with $\mathcal{T}$ projection once computed values can be forwarded on to postfixes later in the chain allows to completely eliminate all such variables. The only variables which remain after this process are regarded as placeholders for constant values. The application has to provide values when it initiates a query evaluation.

This elimination process of one variable $v associated to an expression p is denoted as | $v => p and such a transformation is applied to another expression. As the formal definition exceeds the scope of this presentation, this is only shown in a rather simple example. To eliminate, for instance, the variable $opera from the tuple expression in the above RETURN clause, we let it range over all opera items:

```
[[ for $opera in // opera
   return
      ( $opera / name ) ]] = [[ ( $opera / name ) ]] | $opera => // opera
                           = [[ // opera ]] [[ . / name ]]
```

Should—within the same syntactic scope—two (or more) variables only differ in the number of primes, such as $a and $a', then this *variable semantics* has to be made explicit by simply appending a filter postfix such as [not $a = $a'] appropriately before down-translating to $\mathcal{T}$.

10   Boolean Expressions

Boolean expressions in their simplest form are either the constant **True** or **False**. We map these into tuple sequences, the first being a tuple sequence representing the whole context map (using the special variable %_), the other being the empty sequence:

```
[[ True ]]  = [[( %_) ]] ? epsilon : <>
[[ False ]] = <>          ? epsilon : <>
```

If boolean expressions are combined with the boolean operators | (*or*) and & (*and*), then their meaning can be expressed with the alternation and the concatenation operators + and $\otimes$ (we omit this in the following):

```
[[ boolean-expr-1 & boolean-expr-2 ]] = ( [[ boolean-expr-1 ]]   [[ boolean-expr-2 ]] )
                                      ? epsilon : <>
[[ boolean-expr-1 | boolean-expr-2 ]] = ( [[ boolean-expr-1 ]] + [[ boolean-expr-2 ]] )
                                      ? epsilon : <>
```

If a boolean expression is to be negated (not), then the unnegated expression is translated first. The translation process guarantees that the result is a $\mathcal{T}$ condition. To manifest the negation, the *then* and the *else* branches are swapped.

10.1 Exists and Forall Clauses

An EXISTS clause such as

```
some $o in // opera
    satisfies $o / premiere-date < "1900"^^xsd:date
```

has to be translated into a conditional $\mathcal{T}$ path expression so that that generates non-empty content if *there exists at least one item in the context map which is an instance of **opera** and which has at least one occurrence of type **premiere-date** which has a literal value less than 1900, interpreted as date.*

First the boolean expression inside the EXISTs clause has to be transformed. This results in expression e_1:

```
{{ op:date-less }} ($o {{ characteristics :>: premiere-date }}, {{ 1900-0-0:00:00:00 }})
    ? epsilon
    : <>
```

The prefix op is also predefined and indicates all TMQL operators. Also the path expression to which the variable $o is associated is translated (e_2):

```
[[ (%_) ]] ( ( pi_0 {{ classes :>: }} = {{ opera }} ) ? epsilon : <> )
```

whereby the whole map is traversed in the first term and in the second a $\mathcal{T}$ conditional tests whether any of these map proxies is an instance of what opera corresponds to. This is done by projecting the first (and only column) with π_0 and computing its types.

To eliminate $o in e_1 we have to use the variable elimination operator on it, so that the overall result becomes e1 | $o => e2.

In the general case the EXISTs clause might introduce not a single, but several variables v1, v2, ..., vn, each with their respective path expressions e1, e2, ..., en:

```
[[ 'some' < variable-association > 'satisfies' boolean-expression ]]
  = [[ boolean-expression ]] | v1 => e1 | v2 => e2 | ... | vn => en ? epsilon : <>
```

As EXISTS and FORALL quantifiers are complementary, the static semantics for FORALL boolean expressions indirectly follows from that of EXISTs clauses:

```
[[ 'every' < variable-association > 'satisfies' boolean-expression ]]
  = [[ 'not' 'some' < variable-association > 'satisfies' 'not' boolean-expression ]]
```

11 TMQL FLWR Semantics

The static semantics for FLWR expressions is quite straightforward, given that their structure strongly insinuates the intended meaning. The objective is to produce content (in our simplified presentation here only via a tuple expression), so we will do this last in a path expression interpretation. Before that, variable bindings are to be generated, wich the boolean expression is used to filter, so that will have to go right the translated tuple expression. We are always guaranteed a WHERE clause (it defaults to WHERE True if it missing).

All variables introduced in variable associations are explicit together with a path expression to specify the range of values the variable is supposed to iterate over. All these variables v1, v2, ..., vn (in lexical order of appearance) and their respective path expressions e1, e2, ..., en are then used for variable elimination. The overall semantics of a FLWR expression is then

```
[[ flwr-expression ]] = [[   { 'for' < variable-association > }
                             'where' boolean-expression
                             'return' tuple-expression ]]
                = ([[ boolean-expression ]] [[ tuple-expression ]]) | v1 => e1
                                                                       ...
                                                                     | vn => en
```

12   TMQL Select Semantics

While a complete SELECT expression consists of several clauses, we concentrate only on the mechanics concerning the SELECT and the WHERE clause. Intuitively, the WHERE clause is used to *generate* variable binding sets in such a way that these bindings are constrained by the boolean expression in the WHERE clause, so that an evaluation returns True. Once such a binding set has passed this test, it is used in the value expressions in the tuple expression inside SELECT clause. The resulting tuple sequences combined are then the overall result.

The *generation of binding sets* is semantically captured by first identifying the variables in the WHERE clause which are yet unbound and are *free*, in that they are not introduced with a variable association inside the boolean expression. These free variables v1, v2, ..., vn will then range over all items in the map, at least conceptually, generating all possible combinations thereof. Each combination builds a binding set and all these binding sets are organized into a sequence. From this sequence then all those binding sets are removed which do not satisfy the boolean condition. The overall semantics of SELECT expression is then

```
[[ select-expression ]] = [[ 'select'   tuple-expression
                             'where'    boolean-expression ]]
                = ( [[ boolean-expression ]] [[ tuple-expression ]] ) | v1 => e1
                                                                         ...
                                                                       | vn -> en
```

whereby here the order of variable elimination is irrelevant, in contrast to FOR clauses where the nesting implies a visibility scope.

Worth noting is, that only the free variables inside the WHERE clause are considered, not any variable which appears in the SELECT clause. All additional variables there are treated as constants, i.e. as those which the environment has to pass in before evaluation begins. If such a variable is then not bound at this evaluation time, that will result in an error.

13   Remaining Issues

This work at hand mainly concentrated on the main mechanical aspects of TMQL, so that by implementing this machinery an important subset of TMQL expressions can be evaluated. For practical work, though, additional management features have to be covered:

Adding ordering will involve that tuple expression themselves will have to get another quality, namely that they can be ordered or unordered. It also means that all operators concerning tuple sequences have to be redefined for the cases that ordering matters or should be maintained (stable operators). Finally, two new operators have to be introduced into $\mathcal{T}$, one which makes an unordered sequence ordered and vice-versa. Once this is provided the formal semantics is almost complete as ordering *only* applies tuple expressions within TMQL. There is, though, a difference how sorting will be interpreted in SELECT expressions compared to those following the FLWR flavour. Another list-oriented operation we have ignored here is slicing. It is trivial to define on sequences and that semantics can be directly carried over into TMQL.

Nothing has been said here about *atomification*, i.e. the process under which a data value is extracted from an occurrence or name topic map item. A discplined approach is necessary here as this might be a potentially expensive operation, triggering implicit data type conversion (*coercing*). No coverage is given for XML and TM content generation.

References

1. R. Barta. TMQL preview, 2006. Bond University, Technical Report, http:// topicmap.bond.edu.au/docs/41/toc.
2. R. Barta and L. Heuer. A TMDM Disclosure using Tau, 2005. TMRA'05 - International Workshop on Topic Map Research and Applications, http:// www.informatik.uni-leipzig.de/ tmra05/PRES/BH.pdf.
3. L. M. Garshol and R. Barta. Iso 18048: Topic maps query language (tmql) - draft, 2006. JTC1/SC34 SC34/WG3, http://topicmap.bond.edu.au/junk/tmql.pdf.
4. L. M. Garshol and G. Moore. ISO 13250-2: Topic Maps - data model, 2003-11-02. http://www.isotopicmaps.org/sam/.
5. S. R. Newcomb, P. Durusau, and R. Barta. ISO/IEC JTC1/SC34, Topic Maps - reference model, editor's draft, 2006. http://www.isotopicmaps.org/tmrm/.
6. S. Pepper. The TAO of Topic Maps. 2000. XML Europe 2000, http://www.gca.org/ papers/xmleurope2000/papers/s11-01.html.

Toma -
TMQL, TMCL, TMML

Rani Pinchuk, Richard Aked, Juan-Jose de Orus, Els Dessin,
David De Weerdt, Georges Focant, and Bernard Fontaine

Space Applications Services, Leuvensesteenweg 325, B-1932 Zaventem, Belgium
{rani.pinchuk, richard.aked, juan.jose.de.orus,
els.dessin, david.de.weerdt, georges.focant,
bernard.fontaine}@spaceapplications.com
http://www.topiwriter.com/

Abstract. Toma is a Topic Map Query Language, Topic Map Manipulation Language and Topic Map Constraint Language. Although its syntax is similar to that of SQL, it has a powerful path expression syntax which allows to access elements of the topic map. Toma offers the SELECT, INSERT, UPDATE and DELETE statements, used to query and manipulate the topic map. The MERGE statement is used to merge topic maps, and the EXPORT statement is used to export the topic map to XTM. Set of statements are provided for defining and managing constraints. Finally, Toma provides functions which allow to modify, convert and aggregate the data coming from the topic map.

1   Introduction

Toma, as presented in this paper, is based on the early version of the Toma language used in the AIOBCT project - a question answering system over Topic Maps created for the European Space Agency. The goal for that early version was to have a Topic Map Query Language (TMQL) which can be useful in the implementation of question answering systems. The name Toma was chosen because, originally, Toma was based on ideas taken from **To**log[1] and AsTMa[2].

That early Toma version has been submitted as a candidate for the TMQL ISO standard. Since then, many changes and additions have been introduced in Toma. Today, Toma is a TMQL (Topic Map Query Language), meaning that it allows the user to formulate queries over topic maps. It is a TMCL (Topic Map Constraints Language), meaning that it provides ways to define constraints over the topic map. It is also a TMML (Topic Map Manipulation Language), meaning that it lets the user manipulate (insert, update, delete) the topic map.

Toma is designed to be simple to learn and to use, and is quite similar to the well known SQL[3]. An implementation of the language does exist, as a Topic Maps engine called TopiEngine. The language is also used as the interface language of the TopiWriter product. This paper presents Toma and explains the different choices in the language design.

L. Maicher, A. Sigel, and L.M. Garshol (Eds.): TMRA 2006, LNAI 4438, pp. 107–129, 2007.

2   General Features

The syntax of Toma is quite straightforward. Apart from the inclusion of XTM[4] (and in the future, possibly, other Topic Maps representation languages), Toma can be implemented using a LALR(1) grammar - thus it can be implemented using YACC[5].

Each Toma statement ends with a semicolon. White spaces are used in order to identify tokens. Apart from that, white space characters and new-lines have no meaning, and they can be used to indent statements. The language is case sensitive, although the reserved words of the language are case insensitive (like in SQL).

Toma strings are defined by single quotes (like in SQL). A backslash before a quote escapes that quote.

Comments are written by using the hash sign (#). Any text following the hash sign and till the end of the line, is ignored.

Topic Literals. A topic literal is an expression that is resolved to a topic. Table 1 details the available topic literals.

Table 1. Topic Literals

Expression	Resolved to	Example
id(<*quoted-string*>)	a topic with that id	id('host-location')
bn(<*quoted-string*>)	topics with that basename	bn('Processor')
var(<*quoted-string*>)	topics with that variant	var('CPU')
al(<*quoted-string*>)	topics with that alias[1]	al('CPU')
si(<*quoted-string*>)	a topic with that subjectIndicator	si('http://www.topicmaps.org/ xtm/1.0/core.xtm#scope')

A *naked identifier* (that is, a string without quotes around it) is another way to write the *id* topic literal.[2] It can be located within *typing brackets*, following the scope operator (the at sign - @) or as a role (after or before the arrow in the association expression). For example, oc(id('location')) and oc(location) are both resolved to the occurrences whose type has the id "location". In the same way the following can be written:

```
$topic.bn@en # equivalent to $topic.bn@id('en')
```

---

[1] An *alias* is both base name and variant. In natural language, base names as well as variants may be used in order to refer to topics. While designing a question answering system over Topic Maps for the European Space Agency, it was found that referring to base names and variants together simplifies the automatic generation of queries from questions formed in natural language.

[2] Note that this paragraph refers to Toma syntax that is explained later on. Typing brackets are explained in section 3.6, scopes are explained in section 3.7 and associations syntax is explained in section 3.4.

Hence, by default, Toma uses topic ids to refer to topics. However, other topic literals provide a way to refer to topics using other reference than the topic id (which is often automatically generated).

Variables. Toma allows to define variables. Each variable has a type. The types of the variables can be:[3]

- topic
- subjectIdentity
- baseName
- variant
- occurrence
- association

The type of the variable is determined by the syntax or the semantics of the statement. The default type of a variable is *topic*.

A variable is written as a dollar sign followed by any letter (upper or lower case) or a underscore and optionally followed by any alphanumeric or underscore characters. For example: `$var1`

Often, a variable is used only once. In that case, we do not care about its value, nor about its name. The only thing we care about is that it is different from any other variable in the statement. In those cases we can use the *anonymous variable* `$$`. The anonymous variable is a variable like any other variable, but without a name. If there are several anonymous variables in a statement, they are all interpreted as *different* variables.

Nulls. NULL indicates 'unavailable'. For example, when selecting a base name together with its scope, if the base name is available but has no scope, NULL will be returned for the scope.

3 Toma Path Expression

In order to address different elements in the topic map, Toma provides path expressions. The path expressions are chained using a dot. All the path expressions of Toma might have an input, an output and a result value.

Input: The input is what comes to the left of the path expression. For example, in the path expression `$topic.bn.var`, `$topic` is the input of `.bn` and `$topic.bn` is the input of `.var`.

Output: The output is the result of the expression itself. For example, in the path expression `$topic.bn.var`, the output of `$topic.bn` is the baseName branch and therefore it is possible to ask about its variant.

---

[3] No special type is defined for scopes, types or member roles as the engine which implements Toma always reifies the scopes, types and the member roles - and therefore they are always topics.

Result: The result value is the textual representation of the output. For example, the result value of a baseName, is the baseNameString. The result value is taken into account only if this expression is the last (right-most) expression in the path. For example, the result value of the expression $topic.bn.var is the actual variant (resourceRef or resourceData) of the base name of the topic $topic.

Path expressions can work with sequences. For example, a topic might have more than one base name. In that case, the path expression $topic.bn is resolved to a sequence of base names.

3.1 Elementary Path Expressions

Elementary path expressions are accessors which refer to specific element in the topic map. Table 2 details the available elementary path expressions.

Table 2. Elementary path expressions

Expr.	Input	Output	Result
.id	topic / baseName / variant / occurrence / association	id of the input	The same as the output
.bn	topic	baseName of the input	baseNameString as a string
.si	topic	subjectIdentity of the input	topicRef, resourceIndicatorRef or resourceRef of the subjectIdentity as a string
.tr	subjectIdentity	topicRef of the input as a string	The same as the output
.sir	subjectIdentity	subjectIndicatorRef of the input	The same as the output
.var	baseName	variant of the input	The resouceData or resourceRef of the variant as strings
.sc	baseName, variant, occurrence, association	A topic which is the scope of the input	The topic id of the output
.rr	subjectIdentity / occurrence / variant	resourceRef of the input	The same as the output
.oc	topic	occurrence of that topic	resourceRef or resourceData of the occurrence as a string
.rd	occurrence / variant	resourceData of the input	The same as the output
.player	association	A topic which is a player of the input	The topic id of the output
.role	association	A topic which is a role of the input.	The topic id of the output

3.2   .al and .reify

Unlike the elementary path expressions, these two path expression do not refer to any single Topic Maps element. They are presented in table 3:

Table 3. .al and .reify

Expr.	Input	Output	Result
.al	topic	None	baseNameString or resourceRef or resourceData of a variant
.reify	baseName / variant / occurrence / association	The topic that reifies the input	The topic id of the output

As explained before, alias is both baseNames and variants. It is provided in order to be able to find a topic by its base name or its variant. It should be noted that alias is not an element type in Topic Maps, and therefore, .al returns a string (or a sequence of strings) which cannot be used as an input for another path expression.

3.3   Instantiation and Inheritance

There are four path expressions that refer to the instantiation hierarchy and the inheritance hierarchy defined in Topic Maps. Those path expressions are listed in table 4.

The LEVEL parameter can be any non-negative number, an asterisk or a range. Level zero means the actual topic, level one means the type / instance / super / sub of the topic, level two indicates the type / instance / super / sub of the type / instance / super / sub of the topic and so on. An asterisk is used to refer to any level (including zero). A range, for example 1..*, is defined by a non-negative number, two dots and a greater number or an asterisk.

Table 4. Instantiation and inheritance path expressions

Expr.	Input	Output	Result
.type(LEVEL)	topic	The topic that is the type of the input at the chosen levels	The topic id of the output
.instance(LEVEL)	topic	The topic that is the instance of the input at the chosen levels	The topic id of the output
.super(LEVEL)	topic	The topic that is the super-class of the input at the chosen levels	The topic id of the output
.sub(LEVEL)	topic	The topic that is the sub-class of the input at the chosen levels	The topic id of the output

Example:

```
$topic.type(1).super(*) # any direct type of the topic, or any
                        # parent (through superclass-subclass
                        # association) of that direct type.
```

3.4   Associations

An association path expression is written as follows:

```
association_id(association_type)->role
```

The whole path expression is resolved to a topic playing the given role in an association of the given type. The association id, the association type and the role can all be expressions that are resolved to topics.

If the *association_id* is not needed, it can be omitted. However, in case it is omitted, two different expressions can refer to two different associations. For example:

```
    (host-location)->host = $h
and (host-location)->location = $l
```

In the two expressions above, $h and $l can be players of *different* associations of type *host-location*. If we want to refer to two players of the same association, we have to use the same association variable in both expressions:

```
    $a(host-location)->host = $h
and $a(host-location)->location = $l
```

Note that a much better approach is to chain the two players as described later. Note also that in the following example, $a and $b can but do not have to refer to the same association:[4]

```
    $a(host-location)->host = $h
and $b(host-location)->location = $l
```

The main feature of the association path expression is that it has no input, thus it starts the path expression (much like a topic literal or a variable). Although this feature by itself is sometimes very useful, it can be a major disadvantage when trying to refer to a chain of associated topics as demonstrated in the following example. In this example, we refer to all the topics that are connected to a topic which is connected to the topic *finger*:

```
    $a(connect_to)->$r1 = id('finger')
and $a(connect_to)->$r2 = $middle
and $b(connect_to)->$r3 = $middle
and $b(connect_to)->$r4 = $topic
and $a != $b
```

---

[4] It is possible of course to add a condition to the statement which states that $a should (or should not) be equal to $b.

Another disadvantage is the awkward way in which one must control the expressions using the association variables in such a chain (here we have to state that $a should not be equal to $b).

Those disadvantages have been solved by introducing the left arrow as described below.

Chaining players. In order to chain players, the association path expression above is extended to include also the role of the input player in the same association:

```
.role1<-association_id(association_type)->role2
```

This path expression is resolved to a player that plays the *role2* in the association of type *association_type* where the input player (the one coming to the left of the association path expression) plays the role *role1* in the very same association. If more than one such association path expression is chained, the associations of two consecutive players are never the same.

For example, we can refer to all the topics which are connected to a topic that is connected to the topic *finger*:

```
id('finger').$r1<-(connect_to)->$r2
            .$r3<-(connect_to)->$r4 = $topic
```

3.5   Square Brackets - Range

The output of a path expression (its right side) can be either empty, one element or a sequence. In the following example, the number of base names that are returned by $topic.bn is determined by the number of base names that are defined in the topic map for the topic *mouse*:

```
select $topic.bn where $topic.id = 'mouse';
```

A quoted string containing the value of the chosen item within square brackets specifies one item out of a sequence and can come after any path expression. For example:

```
$topic.bn['central processing unit'] # the base name 'central
                                     # processing unit' of
                                     # the topic $topic.
```

Another way to specify the items within a sequence is to use a variable in square brackets:

```
$topic.bn[$bn] # $bn will get the values of the sequence.
               # we can use $bn in another place to limit
               # the sequence.
```

This lets us control the sequences in a better way. For example we can select only basenames of topic *foo* starting with 'a':

```
select $topic.bn[$bn] where $topic.id = 'foo' and $bn ~ '^a';
```

This also provides a way to access intermediate players in a long chain of associations. For example, the following statement gets all the possible paths between the topic *stomach* and the topic *insulin* through three associations, wherein the first is of type *connect_to*.

```
select 'stomach', 'connect_to', $p1, $at1, $p2, $at2, 'insulin'
where id('stomach').$$<-(connect_to)->$$[$p1]
                  .$$<-($at1)->$$[$p2]
                  .$$<-($at2)->$$ = 'insulin';

'stomach'|'connect|$p1     | $at1  | $p2     | $at2  |'insulin'
         |_to'    |        |       |         |       |
---------+--------+--------+-------+--------+-------+---------
  stomach |connect_|duodenum|connect|pancreas|produce| insulin
          |to      |        |_to    |        |       |
(1 row)
```

Note the use of the anonymous variable as the roles (because we do not need the roles in any other place).

3.6 Brackets in Path Expressions

Apart from using brackets to indicate the level of the inheritance and instantiation path expressions as explained in section 3.3 above, brackets are also used to indicate a type. Brackets can follow several path expressions or precede the association arrow in the association expression (see table 5). In such cases they allow to specify the types of the elements.[5]

Table 5. Usage of bracket in path expressions

baseName	.bn(type)
occurrence	.oc(type)
association	association_id(type)->role

The type itself can be specified as an expression that is resolved to a topic, that is, a topic literal (including a naked identifier), a variable containing a topic or a path expression that is resolved to a topic.

Examples:

```
$topic.oc(description) # the occurrence of type "description"
                       # of the topic $topic.
$a(part-whole)->part # the player playing the "part" role in
                     # the association $a that is of type
                     # "part-whole".
```

---

[5] Variants have no types according to the XTM standard, but have types according to the TMDM. We have decided not to include the types of variants in this version of Toma as their use was not clear.

In addition, brackets can be used within a path expression in order to group expressions and to control precedence. For example:

```
($association_class.instance(1))->($role_class.instance(1)).bn
```

The above returns the baseNames of a player in the association. The type of the associations is any instance of `$association_class`. The role of the player is any instance of `$role_class`.

3.7   Scope - @

The scope sign allows to specify the scope of a baseName, an occurrence or an association. It also allows to specify the parameters of a variant (which are described as scopes in the coming XTM 2.0[6]) and therefore also allows to specify the scope of an alias.

The scope sign should be followed by an expression that is resolved to a topic and is written as shown in table 6:

Table 6. Scope path expression

baseName	`.bn@scope`
	`.bn(type)@scope`
variant	`.var@scope`
alias	`.al@scope`
occurrence	`.oc@scope`
	`.oc(type)@scope`
association	`association_id(association_type)@scope->role`

Note that the @ sign comes always right *after* the brackets that indicate type. For Example:

```
$topic.bn@en # the base name of the topic in the English scope
$topic.oc(size)@metric # the occurrence of type 'size' in the
                       # metric scope
```

3.8   Precedence

Toma path expressions are evaluated from left to right. For example in the expression `$topic.oc(description)@en.rd`, `$topic` is evaluated first. Then its occurrence of type *description* in the scope *en* is evaluated. Finally the resource-Data of this occurrence is evaluated.

Expressions in brackets (including those in *typing brackets*) have higher precedence. For example, in the expression `$topic.oc($a.type)@en.rd`, the type of the occurrence is evaluated as a whole (the type of the variable `$a`) before the occurrence is evaluated.

4   The USE Statement

The USE statement lets the user declare which topic map is to be queried or manipulated.

```
USE topic_map_path;
```

topic_map_path is a quoted string or a URI[7][6] that indicates the path to the location where the topic map is kept. For Example:

```
use './db/computers.db';
use file:///usr/local/topiengine/db/computers.db;
```

The declaration that is done by the USE statement is applicable until another definition is done by another USE statement.

5   SELECT Statement

The SELECT statement is used in order to define queries over topic maps. The SELECT statement syntax is as follows:[7]

```
SELECT [ ALL | DISTINCT ] navigation_list
  [ WHERE formula ]
  [ { UNION | INTERSECT | EXCEPT } [ ALL ] other_select ]
  [ ORDER BY expr1 [ ASC | DESC ] [, expr2 [ ASC | DESC ] ...] ]
  [ LIMIT integer ]
  [ OFFSET integer ];
```

In general, variables can be introduced in the WHERE clause but also in the SELECT clause.

5.1   SELECT Clause

The SELECT clause of a query is used to define *projections* over the values of the variables found in the WHERE clause. The SELECT clause defines how rows[8] in the result look like in a similar manner to the SELECT clause in SQL. The *navigation_list* controls which values will be presented in the result set. It is possible to introduce new variables in the *navigation_list* and to use any path expression.

The DISTINCT keyword will cause that no duplicated rows are returned. The ALL keyword is the opposite and is the default behavior.

---

[6] It is impossible to refer to relative paths using URI. This is the reason that the path can also be define using quoted string.

[7] In the notation presenting the syntax of the different statements, any clause surrounded by square brackets is optional. In addition, curly brackets are used to group possible options and a vertical bar symbol ("|") is used as disjunction between those options.

[8] Rows are referred to in the SQL sense.

The result is arranged as rows in a similar manner to the results that are returned from relational databases. Any returned variable will be represented by the id of its value:

```
select $topic, $topic.id where $topic.al = 'CPU';

 $topic    | $topic.id
-----------+----------
 processor | processor
(1 row)
```

Note that the SELECT clause returns elements of the values that are already chosen in the WHERE clause. For example:

```
select $topic.bn where $topic.bn = 'lung';
 $topic.bn
----------
 lung
 long
(2 rows)
```

In this example, we select *all* the topics that have the base name *lung*. Then we ask to show the base names of the topics we found. We find one topic that has the two base names *lung* and *long*. So the $topic.bn in the SELECT clause means that we want to see all the base names of the topic objects that can be $topic according to the WHERE clause.

This behavior is a useful feature. For example, if we need to "translate" base names between scopes we can write:

```
select $topic.bn@dutch where $topic.bn@english = 'lung';

 $topic.bn@dutch
-----------------
 long
(1 row)
```

The ability to include new variables in the selection part allows to generate one column which is totally dependent on the value of another column. For example, it is possible to retrieve the scope of the base name that is shown in the result set as follows:

```
select $topic.bn@$scope, $scope.id where $topic.bn = 'lung';

 $topic.bn | $scope.id
-----------+----------
 lung      | english
 long      | dutch
(2 rows)
```

In this example, $topic is set in the WHERE clause, and then its base names are listed in the SELECT clause. However, the $scope variable is introduced in the selection clause as any scope of the listed base names of $topic. Therefore, $scope gets a value for each row in the result set.

5.2 WHERE Clause

The WHERE clause may contain the following sub-clauses:

EXISTS: The EXISTS sub-clause consists of a path expression.

```
EXISTS path_expression
```

If the result of evaluating the path expression is not empty, the sub-clause is evaluated to true.

Comparison sub-clauses: A comparison sub-clause consists of two expressions and a comparison operator between them:

```
expression1 = | != | ~ | ~* | !~ | !~* expression2
```

An expression might be any path expression, a variable or a quoted string. When using the regular expression comparison operators, both expressions must be evaluated to a string.

A comparison operator can be one of the following:

= Equality operator. The two expressions around the equal sign should be equal to each other.

!= Inequality operator. Negation is used in Toma as filtering (unlike in SQL). Therefore, the inequality operator is used to filter out any equality between the two expressions.

~ Case sensitive regular expression match operator. The regular expressions that can be used are Perl-like regular expression. See Perl Compatible Regular Expressions (PCRE)[8] for details.

~* Case insensitive regular expression match operator.

!~ Negation of ~.

!~* Negation of ~*.

IS NULL Has the same meaning as NOT EXISTS.

IS NOT NULL Has the same meaning as EXISTS:

NOT sub-clause: The NOT sub-clause consists of one search condition.

```
NOT formula
```

As mentioned above, negation in Toma is used for filtering. Thus the negation adds constraints on the value of the variables in the WHERE clause. Note that in the notation above formula can be any of the WHERE sub-clauses.

AND sub-clause: The AND sub-clause consists of two search conditions.

```
formula1 AND formula2
```

Both formulas should be evaluated to true - that is, the variables in those formulas should get values so that both formulas are true. If there are no such values, the AND sub-clause is evaluated to false.

OR sub-clause: The OR sub-clause consists of two search conditions.

```
formula1 OR formula2
```

At least one of the formulas should be evaluated to be true - that is the variables in the formulas will get all the possible values so that at least one of the formulas is true. If there are no such values, the OR sub-clause is evaluated to false.

IN sub-clause: The IN sub-clause consists of an expression, the IN keyword and a list of comma separated expressions within brackets:

```
expression IN ( expression1, expression2 ... )
```

The IN sub-clause is evaluated as:

```
( expression = expression1
  OR expression = expression2
  OR ... )
```

Another way to write the IN sub-clause is by using a sub select instead of the list of expressions:

```
expression IN (sub-select-statement)
```

The selection part of the sub select should be of exactly one expression. It is forbidden to use variables from the main SELECT statement in the sub select statement. Example:

```
# all the base names of the topics of type
# 'mechanical device' which have an occurrence of type
# 'mass' which is equivalent to one of the occurrences
# of the same type of topics of type 'pc card'
select $topic1.bn
  where $topic1.type.bn = 'mechanical device'
    and $topic1.oc(mass) in (select $topic2.oc(mass)
                               where $topic2.type.bn =
                                 'pc card');
```

5.3   UNION

```
select1 UNION [ ALL ] select2
```

UNION appends the result set of the first SELECT statement to the result set of the second SELECT statement. It also eliminates all duplicates (so it runs DISTINCT on the result) unless the ALL keyword is used. In order for UNION to work, both selects must have similar selection clauses: they have to have the same number of expressions, and each expression in one select has to resolve to the same type (topic, association, base name etc.) of the expression in the other select in the same position.

5.4 INTERSECT

```
select1 INTERSECT select2
```

INTERSECT returns all the results that are in both result sets. Both selection clauses must be similar, as described in section 5.3 above.

5.5 EXCEPT

```
select1 EXCEPT select2
```

EXCEPT returns all the results that are in select1 but not in select2. Both selection clauses must be similar as described in section 5.3 above.

5.6 ORDER BY Clause

The ORDER BY clause controls the way the result is ordered.

```
ORDER BY column_number [ ASC | DESC | NASC | NDESC ]
    [, column_number [ ASC | DESC | NASC | NDESC ] ...]
```

The list of the column numbers which follows the ORDER BY keywords defines ordering constraints over the variables used in the SELECT clause. The first column can be referred to as number one, the second, as number two etc. Each one can be preceded by one of the keywords ASC (ascending), DESC (descending), NASC (numerical ascending) or NDESC (numerical descending). ASC is the default. ASC and DESC are for ordering alphabetically (so 10 comes before 2). NASC and NDESC are for ordering numerically. In that case, any value that is not a number is resolved to 0.

5.7 LIMIT and OFFSET Clauses

The LIMIT and OFFSET clauses provide a way to retrieve only a portion of the result.

```
[ LIMIT integer ]
[ OFFSET integer ]
```

The LIMIT value specifies the total number of rows to be retrieved, and the OFFSET controls the row to start from.

6 INSERT Statement

The INSERT statement is used in order to insert topics, topic elements and associations into the topic map. The INSERT statement syntax is as follows:

```
INSERT value INTO simple_path_expression
    [ , value INTO simple_path_expression2 [ ... ] ];
```

The *simple_path_expression* is indeed simple because of the following reasons:

- No variable is allowed. This means that the path expression usually starts with a topic literal or an association.
- Only literals are allowed to follow the at sign (@) and to be placed in type brackets.
- Only right-arrow association expressions are allowed.

The *simple_path_expression* should be resolved to a not yet existing value,[9] and *value* is inserted as that value. The *simple_path_expression* can refer to other values that do not exist yet (such as not yet existing scopes or types). Those will *spring* into existence.

Pairs of *value* and *simple_path_expression* can be written in one INSERT separated by commas. Those pairs are inserted one after the other. For example, the INSERT:

```
insert 'http://www.the.site.of.cpu.com/'
  into id('cpu').si.rr,
       'CPU'
  into id('cpu').(bn@long)['central processing unit'].var@short,
       'The processor processes all the instructions.'
  into $topic.oc(description)@textual;
```

creates the topic:

```
<topic id='cpu'>
  <instanceOf>
   <topicRef xlink:href="#processing-part"/>
  </instanceOf>
  <subjectIdentity>
   <resourceRef xlink:href="http://www.the.site.of.cpu.com/"/>
  </subjectIdentity>
  <baseName>
   <baseNameString>central processing unit</baseNameString>
   <scope>
    <topicRef xlink:href="#long"/>
   </scope>
   <variant>
    <parameters>
     <topicRef xlink:href="#short"/>
    </parameters>
    <resourceData>CPU</resourceData>
   </variant>
  </baseName>
  <occurrence>
   <resourceData>
```

---

[9] If the value already exists, the INSERT fails.

```
      The processor is the device that processes all instructions.
    </resourceData>
    <instanceOf>
     <topicRef xlink:href="#description"/>
    </instanceOf>
    <scope>
     <topicRef xlink:href="#textual"/>
    </scope>
   </occurrence>
  </topic>
```

In the example above, some elements were not explicitly mentioned to be inserted, although they are. For example, the topic *cpu* itself or its long base name and the scopes *long* and *short*. Those elements implicitly sprong into existence in order to be able to insert of the values that are explicitly inserted in the statement.

If the INSERT statement contains association path expressions, all of them are assumed to belong to the very same association. This allows to insert a new association by listing its players. Thus, the INSERT:

```
insert 'adapter'
  into (provider-provided-receiver)->provider,
       'laptop'
  into (provider-provided-receiver)->receiver,
       'electricity220'
  into (provider-provided-receiver)->provided;
```

creates the association:

```
<association id="_a1">
  <instanceOf>
    <topicRef xlink:href="#provider-provided-receiver"/>
  </instanceOf>
  <member id="_mem1">
    <roleSpec>
      <topicRef xlink:href="#provider"/>
    </roleSpec>
    <topicRef xlink:href="#adapter"/>
  </member>
  <member id="_mem2">
    <roleSpec>
      <topicRef xlink:href="#receiver"/>
    </roleSpec>
    <topicRef xlink:href="#laptop"/>
  </member>
  <member id="_mem3">
    <roleSpec>
```

```
      <topicRef xlink:href="#provided"/>
    </roleSpec>
    <topicRef xlink:href="#electricity220"/>
  </member>
</association>
```

7   UPDATE Statement

The UPDATE statement is used in order to update the values of topic elements or associations in the topic map. The UPDATE statement syntax is as follows:

```
UPDATE expression1 = string [ WHERE formula ];
```

expression1 is a path expression. *string* is a quoted string. In the UPDATE statement only one variable is allowed. For example, in the UPDATE statement below, we change the base name "processor" to the base name "Processor":

```
update id('processor').bn['processor'] = 'Processor';
```

8   DELETE Statement

The DELETE statement is used to delete topics, topic elements or associations.

```
DELETE expression WHERE [ formula ];
```

In the DELETE statement only one variable is allowed. In the following example, we delete all the occurrences of type *mass* in the scope *textual* of all the topics of type *device*:

```
delete $topic.oc(mass).sc['textual']
 where $topic.type.id = 'device';
```

9   MERGE Statement

The MERGE statement provides the ability to merge topic maps:

```
MERGE [XTM] WITH uri
  [ MARK topic_literal1 [ , topic_literal2 ... ]];
```

or:

```
MERGE XTM <<content_separator
content
content_separator
  [ MARK topic_literal1 [ , topic_literal2 ... ]];
```

The currently used topic map (defined by the last USE statement) will be merged with the other topic map. The *uri* is the URI of a file which contains the topic map. This file can be other Topic Map storage,[10] or any supported definition of Topic Maps.[11] If that file is not another Topic Map storage, the XTM keyword should be given.

If no *uri* is given, then a content block must be provided. When a content block is provided, note that a new line must follow the *content_separator*. Note also that a content block cannot represent a Topic Map storage, and therefore the XTM keyword must be present.

If the MARK clause is used, the topics resolved from the *topic_literals* will be added as scopes to all the characteristics of the merged topic map.

Examples:

```
use 't/db/columbus-epds.db';
merge with file::://.db/columbus-msm.db
 mark columbus-msm;

use columbus-epds;
merge XTM <<EOF
    <topicMap id="only-mlu">
      <topic id="mlu">
        <instanceOf>
          <topicRef xlink:href="#device"/>
        </instanceOf>
        <baseName>
          <baseNameString>module lighting unit</baseNameString>
        </baseName>
      </topic>
    </topicMap>
EOF;
```

10   LOCK, UNLOCK and SHOW LOCKS Statements

The LOCK statement provides the ability to lock topics and associations of certain scopes. This feature is provided to be able to merge a topic map but prevent changes to the merged parts that are marked by a given scope:

```
LOCK BY topic_literal;
```

More than one LOCK statement can be issued. Each locking scope will contribute to the set of locked topics and associations.

The UNLOCK statement provides the ability to unlock topics and associations of certain scopes:

---

[10] Topic Map storage is the topic map as kept by the engine which implements Toma. This can be a file, or anything else which can be referred to by a URI.

[11] TopiEngine currently supports only XTM.

```
UNLOCK [ BY topic_literal ];
```

If no BY clause is provided, all the locks are removed.

The SHOW LOCKS statement returns the scopes by which topics and associations are locked.

```
SHOW LOCKS;
```

Each scope is returned in a row - the first column of the row is the id of the scope and the second row is one of its base names.

11   EXPORT Statement

The EXPORT statement allows to export topic maps as a Topic Maps representation (such as XTM).

```
EXPORT [ TO file_path ] [ AS XTM ];
```

The *file_path* can be a quoted path or a URI. It refers to the location of the file to which the topic map is exported. If no *file_path* is given, the EXPORT is written to the standard output. The AS clause is optional and allows to define alternative formats to be written.[12] XTM is the default format.

12   DEFINE CONSTRAINT Statement

The constraint definition syntax is as follows:

```
DEFINE CONSTRAINT identifier
  EACH TOPIC | ASSOCIATION variable
    [ WHERE formula1 ]
    SATISFIES formula2;
```

Each constraint has a unique name - the *identifier*. A constraint cannot be redefined. In order to change a constraint, it has to be deleted first.

The two formula blocks are similar to the formula explained in the SELECT statement. If the WHERE clause is omitted, the value of *variable* is all the topics or associations (according to the variable definition - TOPIC or ASSOCIATION in the beginning of the statement). The constraint is broken when *formula2* is false.

Examples:

```
# each topic must have a base name
define constraint basename_constraint
  each topic $topic
    satisfies exists $topic.bn;
```

---

[12] TopiEngine supports currently only the XTM format.

```
# each topic of type 'device' must have occurrences of
# type 'mass' and 'description' and it must play the
# role 'host' in a 'host-location' association.
define constraint device_constraint
  each topic $topic
    where $topic.type.id = 'device'
    satisfies exists $topic.oc(mass) and
              exists $topic.oc(description) and
              (host-location)->host = $topic;
```

13   Managing Constraints Statements

The DROP CONSTRAINT statement removes a constraint.

```
DROP CONSTRAINT identifier;
```

Constraints can be disabled and re-enabled by using the statements

```
DISABLE CONSTRAINT identifier;
```

```
ENABLE CONSTRAINT identifier;
```

The SHOW CONSTRAINT statement is provided in order to list constraints:

```
SHOW CONSTRAINT [ identifier ];
```

If no *identifier* is defined, all the constraints of the topic map are returned. If *identifier* is defined, only that constraint is shown. Each constraint is returned in a row with three columns: the identifier of the constraint, the Toma definition of that constraint and "enabled" or "disabled" value.

14   CHECK CONSTRAINT Statement

An enabled constraint can be checked by running the following statement:

```
CHECK CONSTRAINT [ identifier ];
```

If identifier is not provided, all the constraints are checked. For each broken constraint, the statement returns one or more rows which contains three columns - the identifier of the broken constraint, 't' or 'a' to indicate that the constraint is broken by a topic or by an association, and the id of the topic or association that breaks the constraint.

15   Toma Functions

15.1   String Functions

The operator and functions in this section can be used only on strings.

| | The double pipe operator concatenates two strings.

LOWERCASE(`string`) Converts all characters in the string to lower case characters.

UPPERCASE(`string`) Converts all characters in the string to upper case characters.

TITLECASE(`string`) Converts all characters to lower case except for the initial characters which are converted to upper case characters.

LENGTH(`string`) Returns the length of a string.

SUBSTR(`string, from, [ length ]`) Retrieves a specific part of the string. It returns a sub-string of *string* starting from the *from* character (the first character is at index 1). If *length* is provided, the returned string will be of that length.

TRIM(`string, [ LEADING | TRAILING | BOTH ], [ chars ]`) Trims the string. It removes occurrences of any character in *chars* from the start and/or end of *string*. If LEADING, TRAILING or BOTH are not provided, BOTH is taken as the default. If *chars* is not provided, space is taken as the default.

15.2 Conversions Functions

TO_NUM(`text`) Converts text to a number if possible. For example, the text "3.4 kg" will be converted to the number 3.4. The text "PDU" will be converted to NULL.

TO_UNIT(`text, target_unit`) Convert between units. The function expects that the *text* contains a number and a unit indicator, for example "200cm" or "3.4 kg", and tries to convert that number to the target unit. The following statement returns the mass of the parcel in kg:

```
select to_unit($topic.oc(mass), 'kg')
  where $topic.bn = 'parcel';
```

15.3 Aggregation Functions

Aggregation functions can be used only in the selection clause of a SELECT statement. If an aggregation function is present in a selection clause, all the expressions of that selection clause must be aggregation functions.[13]

COUNT(`expression`) Counts the number of values in the result denoted by the expression.

SUM(`expression`) Sums the TO_NUM conversions of the result set represented by the expression. If one of the values is converted to NULL, it is valuated as zero by the SUM function.

MAX(`expression`) Returns the maximum value among the TO_NUM conversions of the result set represented by the expression. NULL is valuated as zero by the MAX function.

---

[13] This is due to the fact that currently there is no grouping in Toma. If grouping turns out to be needed, it will be added to Toma in the future.

MIN(`expression`) Returns the minimum value among the TO_NUM conversions of the result set represented by the expression. NULL is valuated as zero by the MIN function.

AVG (`expression`) Calculates the average of values among the TO_NUM conversions of the result set represented by the expression. NULL is valuated as zero by the AVG function.

CONCAT (`expression`, [`string`]) Concatenates the values of the result specified by the expression. If *string* is defined, it is placed as a separator between the values. Example:

```
select concat(id('mlu').al, ', ');
# returns: MLU, module lighting unit
```

16   Conclusion

Toma provides a very powerful path expression syntax which allows to refer to any Topic Maps element. It uses syntax similar to that of SQL, which makes it relatively simple to learn (assuming SQL is well known). It provides statements not only for querying the topic map, but also for manipulating it and for defining constraints on it, and therefore is an "all-in-one" TM*L language: TMQL, TMCL and TMML.

An implementation of Toma exists as a Topic Maps engine called TopiEngine. This implementation delivers the promised power of the language with attractive performance.

Acknowledgment. An early version of Toma has been developed as a TMQL in the AIOBCT project. This project was a question answering system over Topic Maps developed for the European Space Agency (ESA contract number 17612/03/NL/LvH/bj).

Toma has been developed further by Space Applications Services, as part of the TopiWriter project, as a co-funded activity with the European Space Agency (ESA contract number 19077/05/NL/PG).

References

1. Lars Marius Garshol, Ontopia. tolog - A topic map query language
   http://www.ontopia.net/topicmaps/materials/tolog.html
2. Robert Barta, Bond University. AsTMa* Language Family
   http://astma.it.bond.edu.au/astma-family.dbk
3. Donald D. Chamberlin and Raymond F. Boyce, 1974. SEQUEL: A structured English query language. International Conference on Management of Data, Proceedings of the 1974 ACM SIGFIDET (now SIGMOD) workshop on Data description, access and control, Ann Arbor, Michigan, pp. 249-264.
4. Steve Pepper, Graham Moore. XML Topic Maps (XTM) 1.0.
   http://www.topicmaps.org/xtm/

5. S. C. Johnson. YACC: Yet another compiler-compiler. Unix Programmer's Manual Vol 2b, 1979.
6. Lars Marius Garshol, Graham Moore, ISO/IEC JTC1/SC34, Topic Maps - XML Syntax, http://www.isotopicmaps.org/sam/sam-xtm/
7. T. Berners-Lee, R. Fielding, L. Masinter, Uniform Resource Identifier (URI): Generic Syntax. RFC3986, January 2005, http://tools.ietf.org/html/rfc3986
8. Philip Hazel, University of Cambridge, PCRE - Perl Compatible Regular Expressions, http://www.pcre.org/pcra

Indices, Meaning and Topic Maps: Some Observations

Thea Miller[1] and Hendrik Thomas[2]

[1] Faculty of Information Studies, University of Toronto, Canada
thea.miller@utoronto.ca
[2] Chair of Information and Knowledge Management,
Faculty of Economic Sciences, Technische Universität Ilmenau, Germany
hendrik.thomas@tu-ilmenau.de

Abstract. Topic Maps were initially developed as an indexing tool, and many of the subsequent issues addressed by Topic Map research has reflected this initial focus. However, in regard to the semantic aspects of Topic Maps, indexing appears to have fallen by the wayside, replaced largely by formalised techniques, typically first-order logics. To some extent, this is supported by the literature on indexing itself, where treatment of semantic aspects is generally minimal, or completely absent; even when discussion does occur, it tends to be flawed by the adoption of a perspective inappropriate to the communicative situation which characterises the *raison d'être* of any index. On the other hand, philosophers and semioticians have long recognised the importance of indices as semantic devices. By examining two key discussions on the nature of indices: C.S.Peirce's account of the index within the context of his theory of signs, and Martin Heidegger's account of signs and *Verweisung* within the context of his unfolding of being-in-the-world, it is possible to begin plotting how a deeper understanding of the nature of indices can assist in developing the semantic potential of the Topic Maps technology.

1 Introduction

Starting in the early 1990's Topic Maps were initially developed to model back-of-the-book indices [1,2]. The goal was to allow the interchange of index information and provide a model where indices of different sets of information resources could be merged and navigated in an intelligent manner [3]. To some extent, indices as the basic model have continued to play a determining role in the development of Topic Maps. For example, Pepper realised very early that the potential of Topic Maps lay in making the creation and maintenance of traditional indices much easier and more flexible [3,4]. Also in the "TAO", still one of the best introductions to the Topic Map paradigm, he discusses common indexing techniques from library science (such as glossaries, taxonomies and thesauri) [2], and shows how, based on these techniques, the core components and functionalities of Topic Maps have been derived. Garshol gives a good overview of the connections and dependencies between Topic Maps and indexing techniques [5],

L. Maicher, A. Sigel, and L.M. Garshol (Eds.): TMRA 2006, LNAI 4438, pp. 130–139, 2007.

which can be modelled in Topic Maps as they are [6]. Ahmed presented detailed design patterns for this purpose [7]. Indeed, not only can Topic Maps replicate the features of printed indices, but they can also generalise them, and through their expressive power go far beyond traditional indexing solutions in providing a significant improvement of information retrieval [2,6,5].

Nevertheless, in developing this expressive power, the orientation towards indices appears to have fallen by the wayside. In recent work on the standard, for example, one searches in vain for any reference to indices, even in the central definition of "subject". This is odd, given the acknowledged importance of indices as communication devices, and it raises the question as to whether a thorough understanding of the nature of indices really has nothing to contribute to the further development of Topic Maps. We do not intend to answer this question here, but aim rather to address it by pointing out what it might be about the semantic nature of indices which should, at the very least, be taken account of.

2   Meaning and the Indexing Literature

We turn first to the literature on indexing, where two observations can be made in regard to semantics. First, there is a clear trend towards limiting discussion to the practical aspects of indexing, including subject analysis, classification, thesauri, automatic indexing and so forth; in other words, semantics is, in most cases, not visible as an issue. Second, where semantics is discussed, there is a marked tendency for this to be conducted from the perspective of index construction (as opposed to, for example, better understanding the nature of indices), with rather unfortunate consequences for the resulting accounts of meaning. This second observation bears some explanation.

Keeping in mind that indices are a kind of communication tool, it is clear that the issue of meaning relates to the receiver of the information, and not to the transmitter. In other words, in the case of any particular index, its meaning derives from how the user understands it, not from how it was constructed. To put this more forcefully: one can construct an index as artfully or in as sophisticated a manner as possible; while this may facilitate the interpretative process for the user, it cannot cause the user to understand (the meaning of) the individual entries in the index, any more than someone can force or compel another to understand (the meaning) of what she or he is saying, or referring to. In light of the literature on semiotics this point appears almost trivial, however in view of how most writers on indexing theory account for meaning, it is clear that, in the present context, it deserves some explicit attention.

Take, for example, Fugmann's "Concept Triangle" [8].[1] This figure has its genesis, as Fugmann himself states, in a diagramme used by Ogden and Richards to illustrate "the three factors involved whenever any statement is made, or understood" [9].[2] For Ogden and Richards, it is apparent that in the resulting triangle there is a direct (causal) relationship between "thought" and "symbol"

---

[1] pp. 14ff.
[2] p. 11.

(for Fugmann, "concept" and "expression"), a "more or less" direct relationship between "thought" and "referent", but only an indirect relationship between "symbol" and "referent". In other words, there is no way of determining how any given symbol, or index expression, refers to any given referent. In Fugmann's account, however (and following Dahlberg), it is nevertheless possible to craft the concept (thought) in such a way as to capture essential characteristics of the referent. What is overlooked, in this account, is that it is irrelevant whether it is possible to do this or not, in the end, it is the user who determines whether the concept (or the expression of the concept) is meaningful, not the indexer, who, in this case, (merely) acts as transmitter.

This is why, as Lancaster points out, writers on indexing who "enter into a philosophical discussion" have "failed to clarify the situation, at least as far as the task of subject indexing is concerned" [10].[3] In our opinion however, the problem lies not in engaging in a philosophical examination of how indices come to be meaningful, or function semantically, but in how that examination is directed. This can be demonstrated by a philosophical excursus. We present first a brief discussion of the analysis of the indexical situation as given by C.S.Peirce, a philosopher not unknown to many in the Topic Map field. This is followed by a similar analysis offered by M.Heidegger, a choice motivated to some extent by Sowa's discussion of the basic categories identifed by Peirce [11].[4]

3   Peirce on Indices

Peirce's account of indices is well known and needs here only to be summarised. As he describes it, the index is one of three important types of signs, the other two being icons and symbols.[5] In general, the essence of signs is to represent, so much so that Peirce also referred to signs as 'representamens': "A sign, or representamen, is something which stands to somebody for something in some respect or capacity."[12].[6] The three types of signs differ only in the manner they represent: icons accomplish this by resembling what they stand for, symbols represent through established conventions, and indices represent through sharing some quality with their object.[7]

Peirce provides many and varied examples of indices, including personal appearance and behaviour, instruments such as clocks and barometers, alphabetic characters used in scientific formulae, rapping on the door, thunderbolts, yardsticks and so forth [13]. [8] Only some of these, however, enable us to understand the nature of a genuine index, which is to forcibly draw attention to the object by being directly associated with it. Thus a yardstick is directly associated with

---

[3] p. 13.

[4] p. 65ff.

[5] Peirce eventually came to distinguish 10 classes of signs, of which the group icon-index-symbol forms one trichotomy (the 2nd).

[6] p. 135.

[7] ibid.

[8] pp. 160-161.

the "bar in London called the yard",[9] as a direct physical comparison of the two lengths will demonstrate. This "direct association" is particularly clear in Peirce's example of the weathercock:

> A weathercock is an index of the direction of the wind; because in the first place it really takes the self-same direction as the wind, so that there is a real connection between them, and in the second place we are so constituted that when we see a weathercock pointing in a certain direction it draws our attention to that direction, and when we see the weathercock veering with the wind, we are forced by the law of mind to think that direction is connected with the wind.[10]

As Peirce's example makes clear, there are actually two kinds of associations, or connections, involved with indices. On the one hand, there is the connection between the object, and the indexical sign; on the other hand, there is a connection between the sign and the idea of it in the mind of the observer. The latter connection bears examination, because for Peirce, that is precisely the site of the meaning of the index.

Unlike icons and symbols, which do not require the factual existence of the object of the sign (that to which it refers), in the case of indices, the reverse is true: the index does not require that there be an idea of it. As Peirce explains:

> An index is a sign which would, at once, lose the character which makes it a sign if its object were removed, but would not lose that character if there were no interpretant. Such, for instance, is a piece of mould with a bullet-hole in it as sign of a shot; for without the shot there would have been no hole; but there is a hole there, whether anybody has the sense to attribute it to a shot or not.[11]

In other words, wherever there is an index, there is an object to which it refers, necessarily. We may not understand the index, we may not even notice it, but that does not impinge on the factual nature of its object. Looking at this situation from a slightly different perspective, we can observe that indices, on Peirce's account, are always meaningful, because they always represent a true state of affairs.

One might, at first, suppose that this kind of meaning is not really very meaningful; especially in our everyday communication, we need to understand more than that any message we have received indexes an actual transmitter of some kind. When we take into account Peirce's fundamental pragmatic approach to meaning, however, the value of this insight becomes more clear. In recalling the meetings of the "The Metaphysical Club", Peirce warmly describes one member who frequently urged that belief is "that upon which a man is prepared to act", to which pragmatism is "scarce more than a corollary" [14].[12] In fact,

---

[9] ibid., p. 161.
[10] ibid.
[11] ibid., p. 170.
[12] p. 7.

Peirce constructed his logical and semiotic edifice on the foundational belief that it would best serve the practical needs of living in general, and scientific activity in particular; it accomplishes this by facilitating the understanding of the consequences of our thinking about matters. As Peirce describes this:

> Such reasonings and all reasonings turn upon the idea that if one exerts certain kinds of volition, one will undergo in return certain compulsory perceptions. Now this sort of consideration, namely, that certain lines of conduct will entail certain kinds of inevitable experiences is what is called a "practical consideration". Hence is justified the maxim, belief in which constitutes pragmatism, namely, *In order to ascertain the meaning of an intellectual conception one should consider what practical consequences might conceivably result by necessity from the truth of that conception; and the sum of these consequences will constitute the entire meaning of the conception.*[13]

Or, as Misak paraphrases "The pragmatic maxim is, roughly, that a person does not have a complete grasp of a predicate F if she is unable to say what would be the consequences of hypotheses of the sort 'a is F'." [15].[14] As a simple example relating to indices: a loaf of bread is finished baking when rapping on its bottom produces a hollow sound; the sound is an index of the bread's condition of being fully baked: the sound cannot be produced otherwise. That a baker understands the meaning of this sound is equivalent to saying that she knows the consequences which result from believing that the bread is done (because of the sound produced), namely, that it can be eaten.

To summarise: signs represent; of the three kinds of signs (icons, indices, and symbols), indices are especially important because their very existence indicates a factual state of affairs. Because of this, they acquire meaning within the context of acting by providing a means of gauging the certainty of our beliefs.

4 Heidegger on Signs

It is not usual to regard Heidegger as having contributed anything significant to semiotic theory.[15] Nevertheless, in *Sein und Zeit*, he provides an account of signs and meaning within the context of how individuals understand their life worlds, vis-à-vis the various tasks they carry out. Heidegger unfolds this account in four steps, explaining first referencing, then signs, then "availability", and finally, meaningfulness.

While Heidegger lays out the formal character of referencing (*Verweisen*) as a relationship, he is careful to distinguish this from subsuming the concept of 'referencing' under that of 'relationship', that is, from making referencing a kind of relationship. As he expresses this, "every reference is a relationship, but not

---

[13] p. 6; emphasis in original.

[14] p. 4.

[15] Dreyfus, for example, refers to Heidegger's contribution as an "implicit critique of semiotics", [16], p. 101.

every relationship is a reference" [17].[16] To understand this better, it must be recalled that Heidegger's *Dasein*, which is always interpreting its situation in order to pursue its particular life projects, needs to be able to make connections and establish contexts. The ability to perceive an instance of referencing is thus functionally crucial to an individual's action (in a way perceiving a simple relationship is not). This is why Heidegger can also characterise referencing with expressions such as "serviceable for", "harmful for" or "useful to"; for example, X references Y because X is useful to Y.

Signs, for Heidegger, simply provide an easy way of illustrating this phenomenon of referencing. His one detailed example of a sign is worth studying closely:

> Recently a movable red arrow has been installed on automobiles, in order to indicate, for example at an intersection, which direction the auto will take. The position of the arrow is manipulated by the driver. This sign is a device which is not just present-to-hand for the driver's action (steering) alone. Also those who are not in the car – and especially these – make use of this device by way of keeping to the appropriate side or by stopping. This sign is innerworldy present-to-hand in the whole of the device context of traffic vehicles and traffic regulations. As device, it is constituted as a sign device through referencing. It has the character of the "in order to", it has its particular service, it is for indicating. This indication of the sign can be understood as "referencing".[17]

Two things are to be noted here: first, the sign is only relevant because it is useful to the actions of the various individuals involved; the same arrow on a parked car would only have a factual presence, but no function as a device.[18] Second, its function as a sign is due to the context within which it is used: it is the context which enables not only the driver to use it correctly, but also all others in this particular traffic situation to respond appropriately.

This point is important, because it is the basis for the availability of the device. As referent, the device, as Heidegger observes in his example, has its *um-zu* ("in order to"). In any actual situation, what follows the "to" is determined by the context of action: the arrow on the car is for showing the direction the driver intends to steer; it is not for predicting the weather, it is not for indicating the mood of the driver, and so forth. In other words, the sign device, as referent, is available as a device within a specific context.

Availability, in turn, is the key to understanding the nature of meaning. This is because once availability is perceived, the context is revealed, which is to say,

---

[16] p. 77.

[17] ibid., p. 78, trans. TM.

[18] In Heidegger's terminology, it would only be *vorhanden*, not *zuhanden*. Wittgenstein makes the same point: "'I set the brake up by connecting up rod and lever.' – Yes, given the whole of the rest of the mechanism. Only in conjunction with that is it a brake-lever, and separated from its support it is not even a lever; it may be anything, or nothing." [18], no.6.

the other devices and individuals within that context which are relevant to the individual's purpose of action. For Heidegger, this revelation of the context is, at the same time, the disclosure of a "relational whole". To return to the example: the arrow on the car is perceived as a sign device, because of its "in order to"; this "in order to" calls to mind traffic regulations, other automobiles, streets and intersections; these devices in turn call to mind urban living, industrialisation, and so forth in a chain of associations which ends at the very being of the individual.

In summary, Heidegger develops his concept of sign around the notion of referencing (*Verweisen*). For referencing to function, there must be a context; this context is provided by the perceptions "in order to", "useful for" etc. which occur as part of the process which every individual goes through in determining their course of action (on the everyday, micro-level). By thus connecting the nature of the sign to individual action, Heidegger simultaneously is able to account for its semantic characteristics.

5   Discussion

In comparing the approaches of Peirce and Heidegger, we can begin by noting that there are significant similiarities between the two. First is their fundamental pragmatic approach to philosophical issues: in the end, for both any account of signs or meaning must accord with how individuals go about their practical activities. Second is the importance which both assign indices in regard to human action: for Peirce, the index is crucial for the pragmatic maxim, for it plays a key role in "determining the consequences" of one's actions; for Heidegger, on the other hand, indices, by revealing their contexts, also reveal a part of the world to each individual, thus helping to provide a foundation for deciding and acting. Finally, both view the index as having an especially close relationship with its object; for Peirce, as we have seen, the relationship is so close that one could speak figuratively of it being "torn off" the object; for Heidegger the connection is almost as physical: the directional arrow on the car has its functional identity as part of traffic devices, the leather the shoemaker uses comes from a cow, and so forth.

There are, nevertheless, some obvious dissimilarities. First is their perception of the nature of relationships; for Peirce, relationships have an existence independent of human cognition, a relationship is perceived, because it is there to be perceived; for Heidegger, on the other hand, a relationship only exists relative to the needs of the acting individual: where one person might perceive a relationship of a specific kind, another might perceive a relationship of a different kind, or not perceive any relationship at all, because the situation lacks relevance. A second difference relates to how indices are perceived: for Peirce, this occurs in a quasi-physical, almost law-like manner: the mind is forced to acknowledge the object which the index references; for Heidegger, however, the index is constituted by the situational context within which the individual acts.

Finally, and most important, is the difference between the two accounts in regard to the nature of indices. For Peirce, it will be recalled, an index is a sign, and signs *represent*; according to Heidegger, all signs are indices, and all indices *reference*, rather than represent. The implications of either position are far-reaching: conceiving one object as representing another implies a certain kind of ontological relationship between the two; one can ask, for example, "Does it really represent?"; or, "Is it a faithful representation?", or "Is it an adequate representation?" This is clearly not the case for referencing, especially as discussed by Heidegger (and Wittgenstein): the ontological relationship is constituted by the specific activity of the individual acting within their life world; if the "in order to" or "is useful for" is not perceived within the context of this action, there is no sign at all, and hence, no referencing (no index).

Given this significant disparity between the two accounts of the nature of indices, between representation and referencing, and at the same time, reflecting on the similarities between the two accounts, one is tempted to conclude that Peirce, at least in his description of indices, is somewhat less than consequent. After all, because his approach, as Heidegger's, is fundamentally pragmatic, he in fact comes to the conclusion that indices are meaningful because *they are useful to* human action (albeit in a manner different than that described by Heidegger). Indeed, on at least one occasion, he lapses into langauge rather similar to Heidegger's when describing what an index is:

> A sign, or representation, which *refers* to its object not so much because of any similarity or analogy with it, nor because it is associated with general characters which that object happens to possess, as because it is in dynamical (including spatial) connection both with the individual object, on the one hand, and with the senses or memory of the person for whom it serves as a sign, on the other hand.[19]

Based on this admittedly brief analysis, it appears that there are at least strong grounds for giving more consideration to a referential, as opposed to a representational, view of indexical meaning.

6   Implications for Topic Maps Research

Returning to Topic Maps, the most obvious implication of this discussion concerns the association element. If the semantics of an index has more to do with referencing, rather than representing, then this will clearly make associations the semantic backbone of topic maps, in so far as they are modelled on indices. Up to now, however, associations have tended to play only a secondary role in how Topic Maps are conceptualised. This is especially evident in the discussions concerning subject identity, which generally proceed from the viewpoint that subjects are discreet, identifable entities, from and to which various relationships with other (subject) entities can be plotted. As should be clear from the discussion of Heidegger, however, this is not necessarily the case. The turn signal on the automobile only becomes a subject when it is seen within a certain relational network of referencing. This is as much as to say that the subject *per se* is constituted by its perceived relationships with other subjects, and accordingly derives its identity from these relationships.

---

[19] [13], p. 170, my emphasis.

We suggest that the best way to build on this insight is to begin to take logics other than the first-order predicate variety into account in the effort to develop the Topic Map model. Attention has already been drawn to the need to consider alternative logics for Topic Maps [19]. What these logics might be, is as yet not clear. Possible candidates include logics which are better at accounting for semantic nuances, such as possibility, relevance, and temporality. Of particular interest, we feel, is the logic which Heidegger himself used to underpin his work in hermeneutics. As Øverenget has shown in a recent study[20], Heidegger was deeply influenced by Husserl's theory of wholes and parts (Logical Investigations, 3rd Investigation), without ever discussing this, however. Nevertheless, it is clear that, once it is established that a relationship part/whole or part/co-part obtains between any two given subjects, the enquiring user can come to a number of valid and meaningful conclusions about these subjects.

7   Conclusion

Topic maps, as a technology, emerged in alignment with the practice of indexing. We have shown in this paper that any exploration of the semantic aspects of topic maps should take into account the semantic nature of indices, not simply because this pertains to the genesis of topic maps, but especially because indices themselves are such semantically rich devices. Like ontologies, indices appear to play a fundamental role in how people navigate through their practical worlds of everyday activity.

Leveraging this fundamental – one is tempted to say, 'primordial' – significance of indices is a provocative challenge for topic map research. One needs to stand back a bit, and develop a critical stance to the notion of topic maps as a representational device (as implied by the very name, 'maps'). In particular, there is a need to pay more attention to the everyday phenomenon of referencing and its role in how we find the information we need to guide and support our activities. By cultivating the indexical qualities of topic maps, especially in regard to referencing, it should be possible to enhance the contextual environment within which the search for information is conducted.

References

1. Freese, E.: So Why Aren't Topic Maps Ruling the World? In: Proceedings of the Extreme Markup Languages conference (EML 2002), Montreal, Canada. http://www.mulberrytech.com/Extreme/Proceedings/html/2002/Freese01/EML 2002Freese01.html
2. Pepper, S.: The TAO of Topic Maps - Finding the Way in the Age of Infoglut. (2002) http://www.ontopia.net/topicmaps/materials/tao.html
3. Pepper, S.: Euler, Topic Maps, and Revolution. (1999) http://infoloom.com /tm-sample/pep4.htm
4. Pepper, S.: Navigating Haystacks and Discovering Needles - Introducing the New Topic Map Standard. Markup Languages: Theory and Practice 4 (1999) 41-68

5. Garshol, L.M.: Metadata? Thesauri? Taxonomies? Topic Maps! Making Sense of it all. Journal of Information Science 30/4 (2004) 378-391
6. Rath, H.H.: Topic Maps: Introduction and Allegro. (1999) http://www.ontopia.net/topicmaps/materials/allegro.pdf
7. Ahmed, K.: Beyond PSIs - Topic Map Design Patterns. In: Proceedings of the Extreme Markup Languages Conference (EML'03). Montreal,Canada (2003). http://www.mulberrytech.com/Extreme/Proceedings/html/2003/Ahmed01/EML/2003 Ahmed01.html
8. Fugmann, R.: Subject Analysis and Indexing: Theoretical Foundation and Practical Advice. Indeks, Frankfurt a.M. (1993)
9. Ogden, C.K., Richards, I.A.: The Meaning of Meaning. Harcourt, New York (1967)
10. Lancaster, F.W.: Indexing and Abstracting in Theory and Practice. 3rd edn. University of Illinois, Champaign, Illinois (2003)
11. Sowa, J.F.: Knowledge Representation: Logical, Philosophical, and Computational Foundations. Pacific Grove, California, Brooks/Cole (2000)
12. Peirce, C.S.: Division of Signs. In: Hartshorne, C., Weiss, P. (eds.): Collected Papers of Charles Sanders Peirce, Vol. 2. Belknap Press of Harvard University Press, Cambridge, Massachusetts (1931), 227-273
13. Peirce, C.S.: The Icon, Index, and Symbol. In: Hartshorne, C., Weiss, P. (eds.): Collected Papers of Charles Sanders Peirce, Vol. 2. Belknap Press of Harvard University Press, Cambridge, Massachusetts (1931), 274-308
14. Peirce, C.S.: Preface. In: Hartshorne, C., Weiss, P. (eds.): Collected Papers of Charles Sanders Peirce, Vol. 5. Belknap Press of Harvard University Press, Cambridge, Massachusetts (1934), 1-13
15. Misak, C.J.: Truth and the End of Inquiry: A Peircean Account of Truth. Clarendon Press, Oxford (2004)
16. Dreyfus, H.L.: Being-in-the-World: A Commentary on Heidegger's "Being and Time", Division I. The MIT Press, Cambridge, Massachusetts (1991)
17. Heidegger, M.: Sein und Zeit. 16th edn. Max Niemeyer, Tübingen (1986)
18. Wittgenstein, L.: Philosophical Investigations. 3rd edn. Prentice Hall, Englewood Cliffs, New Jersey (1958)
19. Maicher, L.: Topic Map Exchange in the Absence of Shared Vocabularies. In: Maicher, L., Park, J. (eds.): Charting the Topic Maps research and Applications Landscape. Lecture Notes in Artificial Intelligence, Vol. 3873. Springer-Verlag, Berlin (2006) 77-92
20. Øverenget, E.: Seeing the Self: Heidegger on Subjectivity. Kluwer, Dordrecht (1998)

The Impact of Semantic Handshakes

Lutz Maicher

University of Leipzig, Johannisgasse 26, 04103 Leipzig, Germany
maicher@informatik.uni-leipzig.de

Abstract. One of the key challenges for the breaking through of the semantic web or web 2.0 is global semantic integration: if two proxies in different subject-centric models represent the same subject in the "real world" they should become mergeable. The common top-down approach to semantic integration is the enforcement of centralised ontologies, vocabularies or PSI repositories. This top-down approach bases on an overly optimistic premise: the success of one universal vocabulary enforced by a central authority. This paper proposes a bottom-up approach. A semantic handshake is the decision that two terms from different vocabularies can be used to identify the same subject. If these local decisions are broadcasted, global integration can be achieved without any ontological imperialism. Within this paper this hypothesis is investigated by simulations. We show that if the majority of proxies describes its identity only by *two* different public known terms, global integration is almost achievable at the large scale.

1 The Challenge of Semantic Integration

One central challenge in each kind of modeling is this subtle identity relationship between a "thing" in the real world and it's proxies in the models. In subject-centric modeling this relationship has to be made explicit if models from different sources should become mergeable. If the identity relationship is made explicit, it could be decided whether two proxies from different models are representatives of identical "things" in the real world.

The general and widely adopted approach for creating mergeable models is the definition, evangelization and usage of global ontologies, vocabularies or PSI repositories. Such standardized vocabularies can be used to express the identity relationship between a proxy and the thing it represents in the real world, the proxy's subject. If two different proxies in different models should represent the same subject, the model creators can use the identical term provided by the central ontology to express the identity relationship. In the case all model creators use the same ontology, global integration is achievable. Global integration means, that all proxies in diverse models representing the same thing become mergeable.

We assume that this terminological standardization approach bases on an overly optimistic premise: the success of a top-down approach, the definition and enforcement of a universal vocabulary by a centralized authority. We expect that in practice global integration is not achievable by trying evangelizing one centralized vocabulary.

L. Maicher, A. Sigel, and L.M. Garshol (Eds.): TMRA 2006, LNAI 4438, pp. 140–151, 2007.
© Springer-Verlag Berlin Heidelberg 2007

In this paper we will discuss a bottom-up approach to come closer to the goal of global integration. The premise of our approach is that for expressing the same relationship a lot of different "terms" are defined in diverse ontologies or vocabularies. In practice these different terms are used simultaneously. Instead of evangelizing one universal term out of the universe of terms, our approach bases on the usage of local integration decisions. A local integration decision is the commitment of the model creator that term *A* and term *B* from different vocabularies can be used to express the same identity relationship. If this local integration decision is broadcasted, all proxies originally only using term *A* become mergeable with all proxies originally only using term *B*. This paper investigates the impact of these distributed local semantic agreements which we will call *semantic handshakes*.

In Topic Maps the advent of exchange protocols (like TMRAP [Ga06], TMIP [Ba05] or systems like Topincs [Ce07]) allows the request and exchange of proxies having the same identity from distributed, heterogeneous models. A peer requests from a remote peer whether proxies with the same identity are available. In that case, the remote peer responds with the appropriate proxy and the requesting peer can merge (parts of) the received model in its local model. If the network is requested the next time, new terms for expressing the identity learned from the requested peers can be used to improve the request.

We will show by simulations, that if the majority of proxies describes its identity by *two* different public known terms (i.e. two different results from swoogle [1]), the existing terminological diversity can be preserved and global integration is almost achievable. We assume that the bottom-up approach of semantic handshakes does even better fit the requirements of the practice as the enforcement of centralised vocabularies.

The remainder of this paper is the following. In section 0 the theoretical background for the simulations is given. It bases on the identity approach introduced in Topic Maps [TMDM, DNB06], the international industry standard for information integration. In the section 0 the simulation design is described in full detail. In section 4 different experiment series based on the simulation design are described and discussed. In section 5 related research is described and section 6 summarizes the findings of the experiment series.

2   Theoretical Background

Topic Maps are a subject-centric modeling method which enforces the disclosure of the identity relationship of each proxy [DNB06, DN07]. This means if a proxy should represent "Bernd Hilfreich" (facts assigned to this proxy are statements about the person which is called Bernd Hilfreich) the proxy has to disclose its identity by at least one string.[1] According to the theory two proxies have to be merged, if they have the same identity. (In Topic Maps terms they represent the equal subject.)

Decisions about subject equality are straightforward: if two proxies have at least one pair of strings representing the identity in common, both are considered to have the same identity and both have to be merged. Merging of two proxies is well defined

---

[1] The following description of the identity mechanism in Topic Maps is a mixture and a simplification of the TMRM [DNB06] and one of its legends, the TMDM [TMDM].

and leads to one proxy having the union set of all properties of the original proxies. The following example illustrates the identity approach:

[id = "id1"; identity identifiers = {"I1", "I2"}; names = {"Bernd Hilfreich"}]
[id = "id2"; identity identifiers = {"I2", "I4"}; names = {"Bernd"}]
[id = "id3"; identity identifiers = {"I5"}; names = {"Meyers, Jim"}]

According to the rules defined above, the first two entities are considered to have the same identity and both have to be merged. The third entity is considered to have a different identity and rest untouched:

[id = "id1,id2"; identity identifiers = {"I1", "I2","I4"};
                        names = {"Bernd Hilfreich", "Bernd"}]
[id = "id3"; identity identifiers = {"I5"}; names = {"Meyers, Jim"}]

For the simulations a slightly different identity and merging mechanism will be used: a proxy does not have any other properties than one proxy identifier (to refer to the proxy as object of the model) and a set of *comparable* identity identifiers for disclosing the identity of the proxy. Subject equality of two proxies holds, if the intersection of their sets of identity identifiers is not the empty set. In that case, the set of identity identifiers of *both* proxies will become the union of their sets of identity identifiers. In contrast to the integration model above, all proxies continue to exist and only the sets of their identity identifiers will be merged and will grow in time. Global integration is achieved, if all a proxies representing the equal subject have the identical set of identity identifiers.

To illustrate the impact of the local semantic handshakes, the example given above should be viewed from a distributed perspective. All three proxies *id1*, *id2* and *id3* should be considered to be part of different distributed subject-centric models. All of these proxies request all known remote models, whether proxies with the equal identity are available. As result, the set of identity identifiers of *id1* and *id2* become merged. Thus the local decision that the identity of *id1* can be described by "I1" and "I2", and the independent local decision that the identity of *id2* can be described by "I2" and "I4" will be broadcasted then. The next time *id2* will request remote models, the request can be improved by "I1". In the next sections, the enormous impact of this simple effect towards a bottom-up standardization through distributed, local semantic handshakes is investigated with simulations.

3 Simulation Design

This section describes the simulation design in detail. The simulation setting is implemented in Java and well documented. Both, implementation and documentation are available at [2] and can be used for further experiment series. The remainder of this section is organised as follows. The first parts define some terminological specifications. In the subsequent parts the process implemented in the simulation setting is described in more detail.

Experiment Series, Experiment, Test, and Merge Roundtrip

Each simulation is an experiment series, which consists of a sequence of parameterised experiments. Each experiment is a sequence of tests. Each test is a sequence of merge roundtrips. In this document these terms are used according the following definitions:

Experiment Series. An experiment series is a sequence of parameterised experiments. Usually, one parameter iterates (in example the number of different identity identifiers which are "known" in the world) in a given range.

Experiment. An experiment is a sequence of tests. Because the setup of a test environment is a stochastic process, the results of experiments are means of measures observed in a sequence of tests.

Test. A test is one process as described below. According to the given parameters, all proxies are created and identity identifiers are assigned. Within a test a specified number of merge roundtrips is executed.

Merge roundtrip. A merge roundtrip is the following process: for each proxy in E it is decided whether there are other proxies available in E which have to be merged with the given proxy.

Terminological Specifications

We will define E as a set of proxies e_i which have by definition the same identity. For example E might be the set of all available proxies of the type "person" or E might be the set of all available proxies of the individual "Bernd Hilfreich". Each proxy e_i has a unique proxy identifier which is used to refer to this proxy[2]. Additionally, each entity e_i discloses its identity by a *non empty* set I_i of identity identifiers. Identity identifiers are comparable: it is always decidable whether two identity identifiers are equal or not. The set T_i of a proxy e_i consists of the proxy identifiers of all proxies which are considered to have the same identity as e_i (identity equality has already hold).

Equality Rule: Two proxies e_i and e_j will be considered as equal (identity equality holds) if

(1) $e_i = e_j \Leftrightarrow I_i \cap I_j \neq \emptyset$

Merging Rule: If proxy e_i is equal to proxy e_j (identity equality holds) merging will create two proxies e_i' and e_j' in E' with the following characteristics:

(2) $I_i' = I_j' = I_i \cup I_j$

(3) $T_i' = T_j' = T_i \cup T_j$

The premise of the simulation design is that all proxies in E have the same identity. But this can only be globally exploited by information systems, if identity equality is detected between all entities in E. In terms of the simulation design, *global integration* is achieved if T_i of all entities e_i in E is equal to E[3]:

(4) $\nexists e_i \in E \mid card(T_i) < card(E)$

---

[2] For clarity, the value of the index i will be the value of the proxy identifier. In example, e_{id1} is the proxy with the proxy identifier *id1*. The same holds for all variables, like I_i and T_i.

[3] This holds iff e_i is contained in T_i (otherwise T_i should consist of *card(E)-1* proxies). The comparison of the set cardinality is allowed because T_i only consists of elements from E.

After these terminological specifications, in the following the process implemented in the simulation setting is described.

Initialisation of a Test

In the first step of a test, E has to be initialised. The variable[4] *cardE* defines the number of proxies which have to be created.[5] To each proxy a unique proxy identifier is assigned. The variable *distributionNbrOfII* defines the distribution of the *numbers* of identity identifiers which will be assigned to the proxies. (In the section "Defining Distributions" of [2] the definition of a distribution is described in detail; additionally see the example for a distribution definition below). According to this variable, for each e_i the number of identity identifiers which have to be assigned to it is calculated stochastically.

Afterwards, a value for each identity identifier has to be created. This will be done stochastically according to the distribution defined by the variable *distributionII*. The variable *nbrOfDifferentII* is the number of different identity identifiers which are known in the world. Therefore, the *value* of an identity identifier is a number in [1,*nbrOfDifferentII*].

> ***Example for distribution definition.*** The distribution for the values of the identity identifiers might be defined as follows [{0.8,1.0},6]. This is equivalent to the lottery that with a probability of 80% an identity identifier gets the value 1, 2 or 3. In the same time, with a probability of 20% an identity identifier gets the value 4, 5 or 6. This means, that half of the six possible identity identifiers are widely used and the other half of the six possible identity identifiers is rarely used.

Executing a Merge Roundtrip

A test is a sequence of merge roundtrips (the number of merge roundtrips is defined by the variable *nbrOfMergeRoundtrips*[6]). In a merge roundtrip for each proxy e_i in E identity equality to all other entities in E is decided according to (1). If identity equality holds e_i' and e_j' will be created in E' according to (2) and (3). After the merge roundtrip all e_i in E which have counterpart in E' will be replaced by this e_i'.[7]

Analysing an Experiment Series

To get statistically valid measures, each experiment is a sequence of tests with the same instantiation parameters. This is necessary due to the stochastic nature of the initialisation process. The number of tests in an experiment is defined by *nbrOfTests*.

---

[4] A full overview of all variables is given by [2].

[5] Experiments have shown, that *cardE* partially influences the result. If *cardE* is less then a threshold both *card(T)* and *clouds(E)* changes simultaneously with *cardE*. In the case *cardE* exceeds this threshold both values are not significantly influenced by its changes. In all cases, the threshold is less then *cardE*=100. Therefore, in all following experiments *cardE* is set to 100.

[6] Through the connectedness of all proxies, the result does not change after the second merge roundtrip. If the connectedness of proxies would become a stochastic process, too, more merge roundtrips become necessary.

[7] The separation of E and E' is necessary to avoid further merging within one merge roundtrip. For example, if a proxy gets a new identity identifier through merging, new merging opportunities might occur. Through separating E and E' these new opportunities will be executed in the next merge roundtrip.

For comparing the influence of parameters within an experiment series different measures have to be calculated. These measures specify the size and nature of the *integration clouds* which emerge in the tests. An integration cloud is a set of proxies within E where identity equality is considered. Global integration is achieved, if there exists only one integration cloud. This cloud has the size *cardE*.

card(T). This measure depicts the average size of an integration cloud in E after a test. Formally, it is the weighted average cardinality of T_i of all e_i in E. The algorithm is implemented in `Simulation.getAverageCardT()` [2].

> *Note.* This measure favours large integration clouds because the size s of a cloud is the weight for the weighted average. Given three integration clouds (one of size 98, and two of size 1) *card(T)* is 96,06.

clouds(E). This measure depicts the number of different integration clouds in E. Formally it's the maximal number of T_i in E which have empty intersections. The algorithm is implemented in `Simulation.getNbrOfClouds()` [2].

To evaluate an experiment, the mean of all tests' *card(T)* and the mean of all tests' *clouds(E)* are the appropriate measures. Within an experiment series, these measures for parameterised experiments are compared.

4   Results of the Experiment Series

This section introduces and discusses different experiment series. Starting from a scenario where a global ontology is enforced, different parameters influencing the global integration are investigated. Besides the implementation and the documentation of the simulation setting, [2] provides the protocols of all experiment series. We urgently recommend the consultation of this additional material.

Global ontology

If the overly optimistic premise holds and global ontologies, global vocabularies or global PSI repositories are enforceable, further experiment series might be not necessary. In that case, I_i of all e_i will consist of only one element: the globally unique identity identifier. After *one* merge roundtrip *card(T_i)* of each entity e_i is *cardE* and *clouds(E)* is one. Global integration is reached. But the premise of our research is that this top-down approach is an overly optimistic one.

A completely heterogeneous world without any semantic handshakes

The counterpart of the enforcement of global ontologies, global vocabularies or global PSI registries is a completely heterogeneous world. In that case, each e_i gets its own *globally unique* identity identifier and no semantic handshakes are done. Obviously, the global integration defined by (4) can never be achieved. After each merge roundtrip, *card(T)* will be always 1, and *clouds(E)* will be always *cardE*.

A partly heterogeneous world without semantic handshakes

In a first step, the constraint of *globally unique* identity identifiers for each proxy will be softened. In the following experiment series, to each proxy e_i only one identity identifier will be assigned. But, instead of being globally unique, the identity identifier assigned to each e_i is a randomly chosen value (according to a uniform distribution $distributionII=\{1.0\}$) in the range [1, $nbrOfDifferentII$]. (From a given set of identity identifiers one identity identifier for each proxy is drawn.) As a result, two different proxies will get the same identity identifier with a certain probability (depending on $nbrOfDifferentII$). In the experiment series $exp01$[8] shown in Fig. 1 $nbrOfDifferentII$ iterates from 5 to 100.

In the experiment series $exp02$[9] shown in Fig. 1 the parameter $distributionII$ is set to $\{0.8, 0.9, 0.95, 1.0\}$. This means, that the identity identifiers are not drawn according to a uniform distribution. Instead of, some identity identifiers are more popular than others.

The results of the experiment series $exp01$ show, that for small $maxII$ the number of resulting integration clouds $clouds(E)$ is equal to $nbrOfDifferentII$. If five different identity identifiers are available in the world, five separate clouds of nearly identical size will appear.

The more $nbrOfDifferentII$ increases, the more the average number of $clouds(E)$ is less than $nbrOfDifferentII$. This has a simple rationale: if for 100 proxies an identity identifier has to be chosen, this is similar to a hundredfold repetition of drawing an identity identifier from the given set of identity identifiers. If the cardinality of this set is 5, $clouds(E)$ is only less than five in the case, if after 100 trials one of the five given identity identifiers is not drawn one time. This is not expectable. But if the cardinality of the set of identity identifiers is i.e. 80, there is a significant probability that one of these 80 identity identifiers is not drawn in 100 trials.

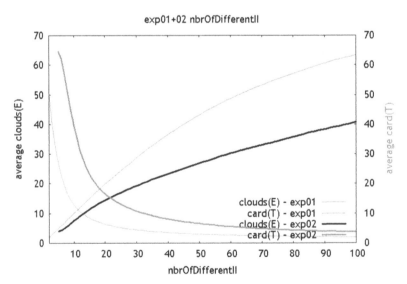

Fig. 1. exp01+02 Iterating $nbrODifferentII$ in [5,100] **general parameters:** $cardE=100$, $distributionNbrOfII=\{1.0\}$ **specific parameter exp01:** $distributionII=\{1.0\}$ **specific parameter exp02:** $distributionII=\{0.8,0.9,0.95,1.0\}$

---

[8] The detailed protocol of experiment series $exp01$ is available at [3].
[9] The detailed protocol of experiment series $exp02$ is available at [4].

The experiment series *exp02* shows the influence of the distribution of the identity identifiers. In this series the identity identifiers are drawn according to a distribution with some popular and a lot of unpopular identity identifiers. The results improve significantly. The size of the resulting clouds increases due to the fact that popular identity identifiers imply bigger clouds. But even the number of clouds *clouds(E)* decrease significantly due to the strengthening of the effect discussed related to experiment series *exp01*. Nevertheless, great fragmentation rests in *E*. (This is problematic because we assume that experiment series *exp02* reflects the current state in the practice: there are a lot of different terms, some of them are more popular and all of them are used simultaneously.)

The impact of semantic handshakes in a partly heterogeneous world

In the following the impact of semantic handshakes will be investigated in detail. A semantic handshake is done, when two different identity identifiers are assigned to one proxy. In that case, the distribution of the *number* of identity identifiers which will be assigned to proxy have to be changed. Changing *distributionNbrOfII* to [{0.3,1.0},2] means, that 30% of all proxies will get one identity identifier randomly drawn from the universe of identity identifiers and 70% of all proxies will get two randomly drawn identity identifiers. Starting the iteration of *distributionNbrOffII*={a,1.0} with *a*=0.0 means, that all proxies will get two different randomly chosen identity identifiers. In contrast *a*=1.0 means, that to all proxies only one randomly drawn identity identifier will be assigned. (This situation is equal to experiment series *exp01*.)

Experiment series *exp03*[10] shown in Fig. 2 bases on the assumption that the assigned identity identifiers are uniformly distributed (*distributionII*={1.0}). If all proxies get two different identity identifiers (*distributionNbrOffII*={0.0,1.0}), the results are very impressive: average *clouds(E)*=4 and average *card(T)*=92. Due to the semantic handshakes, more than 92% of all proxies are accumulated within one cluster. Around a maximum of 3 further semantic handshakes are sufficient to achieve global integration.

Furthermore, in the experiment series *exp04*[11] shown in Fig. 2 the existence of popular identity identifiers is assumed. The value of the variable *distributionII* is changed from {1.0} to {0.8,0.9,0.97,1.0}. In that case, both values improve significantly: *clouds(E)*=2.5 and *card(T)*=97.0. In fact, more than 97% of all proxies are integrated within one integration cloud. Only around 1.3 further semantic handshakes are sufficient to gain global integration.

It is remarkable, that these results are similar to reducing the number of possible identity identifiers (*nbrOfDifferentII*) to a very small number (according to the findings of *exp01* and *exp02*). Whereby reducing the number of possible identity identifiers have to be enforced by a centralised authorisation, the concept of semantic handshakes is based on decentralised, autonomous decisions.

We assume that only a part of all proxies will barrow a semantic handshake. Therefore, the results for *distributionNbrOfII*={0.0,1.0} should be a interpreted as a best world scenario. To be more realistic, a view to the development of the result quality during the iteration is necessary.

---

[10] The detailed protocol of experiment series *exp03* is available at [5].
[11] The detailed protocol of experiment series *exp04* is available at [6].

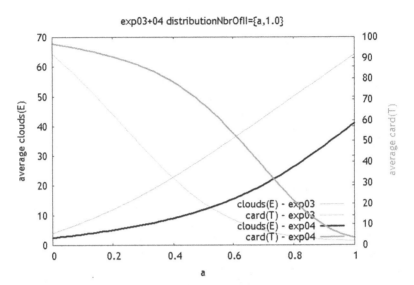

Fig. 2. exp03+04 Iterating *a* in *distributionNbrOfII={a,1.0}* in [0.0,1.0] ***general parameters***: *cardE*=100, *nbrOfDifferentII*=100 ***specific parameter exp03***: *distributionII*={1.0} ***specific parameter exp04***: *distributionII*={0.8,0.9,0.97,1.0}

From this perspective, Fig. 2 does reveal the influence of popular identity identifiers in experiment series *exp04*. In the case, where only to the half of all proxies a semantic handshake is assigned (*distributionNbrOfII*={0.5,1.0}), the results are still impressive: *clouds(E)*=10.7 and *card (T)*=75.9. This means, that there still exist an integration cloud which consists of more than 75% of all proxies. In contrast, in experiment series *exp03* with uniformly distributed identity identifiers the results are less convenient: *clouds(E)*=14.0 and *card (Ti)*=28.8.

The influence of the diversity of identity identifiers

When investigating the impact of semantic handshakes in the experiment series *exp03* und *exp04*, the diversity of the available identity identifiers was big (*nbrOfDifferentII*=100). As already shown in the experiment series *exp01* and *exp02* (by iterating over *nbrOfDifferentII*), a lower diversity of the available identity identifiers has a significant impact to the quality of the results. In the following the connection of semantic handshakes and the diversity of the available identity identifiers should be investigated.

In the experiment series *exp05*[12] shown in Fig. 3 semantic handshakes are assigned to the majority of proxies: *distributionNbrOfII*={0.2,1.0}. The results are very impressive: even if 40 different identity identifiers exist, global integration will be achieved. It has to be outlined, that the top-down approach using centralised ontologies tries to achieve this global integration by evangelising one universal identity identifier. These findings illustrate the impact of semantic handshakes very well.

---

[12] The detailed protocol of experiment series *exp05* is available at [7].

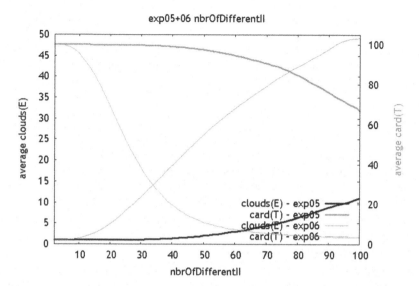

Fig. 3. exp05+06 Iterating *nbrOfDifferentII* in [2,100] *general parameters: cardE*=100, *distributionII*={1.0} *specific parameter exp05: distributionNbrOfII*={0.2,1.0} *specific parameter exp06: distributionNbrOfII*={0.8,1.0}

But even if semantic handshakes are only assigned to a minority of proxies, the quality of the results increases significantly. In the experiment series *exp06*[13] the variable *distributionNbrOfII* is set to {0.8,1.0}. In the case only 40 different identity identifiers exist, the results are: *clouds(E)*=18.9 and *card(T)*=16.0. This is a dramatic decline in contrast to *exp05*. But in contrast it is a significant improvement in contrast to *exp01*, where (ceteris paribus) no semantic handshakes are assigned: *clouds(E)*=36,9 and *card(T)*=3.5.

5   Related Research

The problem of scaling shared vocabularies is part of the research field called emergent semantics [ACC+04]. From the perspective of our research, a relevant work in the context of emergent semantics is [ACH03]. While Aberer et al. focus on the problem of achieving the decision about the semantic handshakes, this paper evaluates the premise of approaches like emergent semantics: the suitability of bottom-up approaches.

The idea of semantic handshakes is influenced by Gladwells "The tipping point" [Gl00]. He revealed that local interactions can have significant global impact if a certain threshold is exceeded. The similarity to semantic handshakes is obvious. If a majority of proxies does disclose local semantic handshakes, global integration can be achieved without centralised authorization.

The web 2.0. bases on distributed tagging using folksonomies. These folksonomies explicitly do not relay on central authorizations. However, using semantic handshakes

---

[13] The detailed protocol of experiment series *exp06* is available at [8].

these tags become mergeable at the large scale which allows a diversity of new applications using these tag data.

Semantic handshakes are means for terminological standardization and vocabulary evolution in a bottom-up fashion. The development of vocabularies in self-organizing systems is investigated by Steels [St96].

6 Discussion

The experiment series have shown that the semantic handshake approach might be appropriate to achieve the goals discussed in the introduction: preserving the existing terminological diversity and achieving global integration. To achieve these goals the following guidelines for proxy creators can be derived from the findings:

(a) add always at least *two* different identity identifiers to one proxy (disclosure of the semantic handshake) and

(b) use popular identity identifiers.

Both design rules are that much important that we propose to make them to a central part of subject-centric modelling engineering methods, i.e. a topic maps engineering [Ga07]. Spreading the idea of semantic handshakes around by evangelising these modelling techniques, a majority of proxies will disclose semantic handshakes and their impact becomes significant. Furthermore, using popular identity identifiers leads de facto to terminological standardisation. The results of *exp05* can be interpreted as follows: if a proxy uses one of the 40 most popular identity identifiers ($cardE=100$), it will be definitely part of the main integration cloud.

Otherwise it is obviously, that observed or created "specialities" (very seldom identity identifiers) should be made public by assigning it to a proxy which has already some public identity identifiers.

Naturally, the simulation design does represent a "best case" scenario in which all proxies are connected by communication channels and exchange their identity identifiers immediately. Due to this connectedness stable integration clouds are always established after two merge roundtrips. This speed does not reflect the real world, but we assume that if the simulation achieves global integration, real life applications will come close to it in finite time. We propose further experiment series where the existence and stability of communication channels between proxies become a stochastic and in time changing property.

Nevertheless, the proxies (or their creators) must be able to exchange information about their identity by any means. For example, making all public topic maps querable by TMRAP or TMIP, an enormous pool of identity identifiers occur and can be exploited for the purposes of semantic handshakes. We assume that this approach might be more practicable than defining and maintaining centralised PSI repositories. The same holds for RDF or other metadata repositories.

Naturally, if the semantic handshakes are incorrect the approach of broadcasting them implies problems. In this case, wrong but enormous integration decisions can be inferred (this is of great impact especially if two big complementary clouds of entities are touched). The main problem is, that semantic handshakes once submitted into E, might lead to a chain of new integrations. It will be complicated to trace back to the situation before the incorrect semantic handshake was done. To avoid incorrect semantic handshakes only identity information from trusted sources should be used. In that case, fraud will harder be broadcasted. This strategy does not avoid taking over incorrect semantic handshakes which were made accidentally by a trusted source.

Summarised, we assume that knowing and using the impact of semantic handshakes semantic integration on the large scale is achievable. It seems to be a more realistic way than the attempt of the evangelisation of one universal vocabulary by a central authority.

References

[ACC⁺04]   Aberer, K.; Catarci; T.; Cudré-Mauroux, P. ; et al.: *Emergent Semantic Systems.*

[ACH03]   Aberer, K.; Cudré-Mauroux, P.; Hauswirth, M.: *The chatty web: Emergent Semantics Through Gossiping.* Proceedings of the 12th International World Wide Web Conference, Budapest (2003).

[Ba05]   Barta, R.: *TMIP, A RESTful Topic Maps Interaction Protocol.* In: Proceedings of Extreme Markup Languages 2005, Montreal, (2005).

[Ce07]   Cerny, R.: *Topincs. A RESTful Web Service Interface for Topic Maps.* In.: Procs. of TMRA 2006, this volume (2007).

[DNB06]   Durusau, P.; Newcomb, S.; Barta, R: *Topic Maps Reference Model, 13250-5.* Available at: www.isotopicmaps.org/TMRM/TMRM-latest.pdf

[DN07]   Durusau, P.; Newcomb, S.: *The Essentials of the Topic Maps Reference Model.* In.: Procs. of TMRA 2006, this volume (2007).

[Ga06]   Garshol, L. M.: *TMRAP – Topic Maps Remote Access Protocol.* In: Proceedings of First International Workshop on Topic Maps Research and Applications (TMRA'05), Leipzig; Springer LNAI 3873, (2006).

[Ga07]   Garshol, L. M.: *Towards a Methodology for Developing Topic Maps Ontologies.* In.: Procs. of TMRA 2006, this volume (2007).

[Gl00]   Gladwell, M.: *Der tipping point. Wie kleine Dinge Grosses bewirken können.* Berlin-Verlag, Berlin (2000).

[St96]   Steels, L.: *Self-organising vocabularies.* In: Proceedings of Artificial Life V, (1996).

[TMDM]   ISO/IEC: Topic Maps – Part 2: Data Model. Latest version available at: http://www.isotopicmaps.org/sam

[1] http://swoogle.umbc.edu/
[2] http://www.informatik.uni-leipzig.de/~maicher/sh/sh.htm
[3] http://www.informatik.uni-leipzig.de/~maicher/sh/Protokolle/exp01.htm
[4] http://www.informatik.uni-leipzig.de/~maicher/sh/Protokolle/exp02.htm
[5] http://www.informatik.uni-leipzig.de/~maicher/sh/Protokolle/exp03.htm
[6] http://www.informatik.uni-leipzig.de/~maicher/sh/Protokolle/exp04.htm
[7] http://www.informatik.uni-leipzig.de/~maicher/sh/Protokolle/exp05.htm
[8] http://www.informatik.uni-leipzig.de/~maicher/sh/Protokolle/exp06.htm
[9] http://www.informatik.uni-leipzig.de/~maicher/sh/Protokolle/exp07.htm
[10] http://www.informatik.uni-leipzig.de/~maicher/sh/Protokolle/exp08.htm

The Essentials of the Topic Maps Reference Model (TMRM)

Patrick Durusau[1] and Steven R. Newcomb[2]

[1] Snowfall Software
Patrick@snowfallsoftware.com
[2] Coolheads Consulting
srn@coolheads.com

Abstract. The Topic Maps Reference Model (TMRM) defines the qualities of subject mapping that distinguish it from other information technologies. It defines subject maps very abstractly in order to avoid limiting the design choices that can be made when creating them. However, its high level of abstraction is not helpful to readers who need only to grasp its essential principles. Using commonplace examples,[1] this paper illustrates those principles. Briefly, they are that authors can determine what subjects they wish to represent in a subject map, how information about those subjects is expressed, and how, when two or more representatives represent the same subject, they should be viewed as a single representative. The TMRM provides requirements that disclosures of such design choices must meet in order to facilitate the interchange and exploitation of subject maps.

1 Whose Subjects?

The answer to the question, "Whose Subjects?" illustrates the starting premises of the TMRM.

There is no shortage of technologies and proposals for assisting users with modern information overload. All such systems reflect choices about, and therefore limit, how they allow their users to talk about subjects. Some systems are able to detect situations when two or more users are talking about the same subject (or, for that matter, when the same user talks about the same subject more than once). Some of those, including virtually all Topic Mapping systems, are able to make all of the information about each subject available from a single perspective that is uniquely dedicated to that subject. Such systems also always reflect design choices about how subjects can be identified, and about how their identity information is supposed to be compared. All subject maps that conform to the TMRM necessarily reflect such choices.

---

[1] The examples are drawn from fictitious subject maps that reflect design choices that were presumably made by their (nonexistent) authors. Except as otherwise noted, none of the constraints expressed in or implied by the examples are imposed by the TMRM.

L. Maicher, A. Sigel, and L.M. Garshol (Eds.): TMRA 2006, LNAI 4438, pp. 152–160, 2007.

It is possible to integrate information about a subject by transposing all the information into a single system. The TMRM approach is to understand what represents and identifies subjects in different systems and then to map those representatives together, while preserving the separate identifications of the same subject.[2]

The TMRM follows from the following premises:

1. **All information, when understood, is information about specific subjects.**
2. **For any given subject, there is no single way of identifying it that can meet all requirements, in all contexts.**
3. **No one system or methodology for identifying subjects, or even for associating information with them, can meet all requirements in all contexts.**
4. **No subject is owned by any user for purposes of identification or to determine its properties.**
5. **Users are uniquely qualified to identify their subjects and their properties.**
6. **Users are uniquely qualified to judge when others have spoken of the same subjects.**
7. **Merging user identifications of subjects capitalizes on the abilities of those most interested in those subjects.**

The designs of information systems vary widely, and the requirements that inform those designs vary widely, too. Before an information system can be implemented, decisions must be made about how information about subjects will be handled. If it's a subject-centric system, decisions must also be made about how to determine whether two or more sets of information will be deemed to be about the same subject, and what to do when they are.

Even more diversity comes from users. As already noted, the subjects they choose, the ways they identify them, and the information they associate with them is endlessly variable.

Even if a universal system or means of identifying subjects were to emerge, the question of how to handle existing systems and historical information about subjects would remain.

However, certain critical aspects of subject-centric information can be seen as common to all systems and all users. One such universally-required understanding is how, in each diverse information resource, the properties of each subject are represented. Another is how to detect when two or more subject representatives should be treated as representing the same subject. In the absence of these understandings, information about subjects cannot be integrated.

---

[2] The TMRM deliberately avoids proposing any system or methodology for integrating information about subjects. Instead, the TMRM provides a list questions about a subject map, the answers to which must be disclosed in order to allow others to integrate the information that it contains about its subjects with information that other subject maps contain about those same subjects.

In order to allow it to talk about subjects and their representatives in information resources, the TMRM begins by abstractly defining the term *subject proxy*.

2   Subject Proxies and Subject Maps

Subjects are represented in a *subject map* by *subject proxies*, or, more simply, *proxies*. Each proxy consists of one or more *properties*, and each property is a *key/value pair*. As the name *key/value pair* implies, each property consists of a *value* (some data), and a *key* that establishes the semantic(s) of the value.

A *subject map* is a collection of subject proxies accompanied by a *legend* that provide the rules for interpretation of the subject map. Briefly, legends specify, among other things, the rules that govern what properties proxies must, should, and may have, and when two or more proxies are deemed to represent the same subject.

There is no express or implied methodology in the TMRM for the implementation or expression of proxies, properties, subject maps, or even legends, despite the fact that the latter are its primary focus. In order to discuss semantic integration without favoring one implementation technique over another, the current abstraction was developed for discussion of the issues.

To illustrate the application of this abstraction, consider an entry in a relational database for the subject Eric Miller, a human being who serves as the Activity Lead for the World Wide Web Consortium's 'Semantic Web' initiative.

The results of a query of a relational database might result in the following information:

ID	firstName	lastName	email
001	Eric	Miller	em@w3.org

The first question that must be answered is which of these properties are properties of the subject Eric Miller? All systems contain information for the management of information that is not information about subjects. Use of such information for comparison or access is certainly useful, even for subjects, but it is of little use when integrating information between different systems.

We assume that the key/value pair ID/001 is not going to be relevant for inter-system comparison of information about the subject (Eric Miller, the human being). Three key/value pairs, firstName/Eric, lastName/Miller and email/em@w3.org, remain, all of which really are properties of the subject.

In the TMRM abstraction, all three of the keys, firstName, lastName and email are references to other subject proxies in the same subject map. The subjects of those proxies have properties, just as does the proxy for Eric Miller. Even if another system used different ways to identify the same "key" subjects (firstName, etc.), it would be possible to merge the properties of the representatives of those subjects into a single representative – a single proxy – in which the identifiers used by both systems could appear as property values.

For example, let's assume that we have queried another relational database with the following result:

ID	givenName	familyName	employer
001	Eric	Miller	W3C

Treating the strings `givenName` and `familyName` as references to proxies which have been merged, respectively, with the proxies referenced by the strings `firstName` and `lastName` seen in the prior example, can, given appropriate rules, require the merging of the information from these two different information sources into a single representative for Eric Miller.[3]

The most obvious method for comparing the values of `firstName`/`givenName` and `lastName`/`familyName` is string equality, but the nature of such tests is left to the discretion of the creator of the subject map. Once the two proxies for Eric Miller have been merged, the resulting single proxy might appear as follows:[4]

```
{
  firstName   = Eric
  lastName    = Miller
  email       = em@w3c.org
  givenName   = Eric
  familyName  = Miller
  employer    = W3C
}
```

In the above proxy, all the information, as originally expressed, has been preserved, with the result that Eric's first and last names each appear twice. If such redundancy is considered undesirable, and if the merged proxy appears in a subject map whose legend provides two additional keys (`firstName`/`givenName` and `lastName`/`familyName`), and if there is no need to retain the original key/value pairs, the result could be a more compact proxy:

```
{
  firstName/givenName   = Eric
  lastName/familyName   = Miller
  email                 = em@w3c.org
  employer              = W3C
}
```

---

[3] Subject maps can be implemented using relational database systems as well as other storage mechanisms. The relational nature of this example allows the operation of the abstraction to be illustrated using a familiar data structure and paradigm.

[4] The properties are a set; their order of appearance in the example is not significant. The notation used here was invented for this paper, and is purely for purposes of illustration. Any resemblance to any known notation is coincidental. (By design, the TMRM says nothing about the notations that can or should be used to interchange subject maps. Other parts of ISO 13250 provide suggested notations, and other notations exist, as well. Each such notation is necessarily associated with certain specific ontological commitments.)

Which result is preferred is left in the hands of the author of the merging rules in question.

2.1   More Subject Proxies

But what if yet another data source listed the employer of Eric Miller as 'World Wide Web Consortium'? After merging, the result might be:

```
{
  firstName/givenName   = Eric,
  lastName/familyName   = Miller
  email                 = em@w3c.org
  employer              = W3C
  employer              = World Wide Web Consortium
}
```

Such a result is certainly possible, but another possibility should be considered. Since subject map authors can decide which subjects should be represented in their subject maps, the possibility of representing the World Wide Web Consortium by means of a subject proxy should be considered.

In the TMRM, the *values* of key/value pairs may *also* be references to subject proxies. Obviously, such proxies may reflect multiple ways of identifying their subjects.

```
{
  firstName/givenName   = Eric,
  lastName/familyName   = Miller
  email                 = em@w3c.org
  employer              = (reference to the proxy for
                          the World Wide Web Consortium proxy)
}
```

The use of such reference is not compelled but one advantage to it is that other information, besides simply the name of the organization, may be recorded at its subject proxy. In this particular case, for example, the proxy for the W3C might read:

```
{
  organizationName      = World Wide Web Consortium
  shortName             = W3C
  internetDomainName    = w3c.org
  employs               = (reference to the proxy for
                          Eric Miller)
}
```

Given the appropriate merging rule(s), proxies whose name (or name-like) properties contain the strings 'W3C' or 'World Wide Web Consortium' can be merged with the above proxy, so that everything known about the W3C can be made available from the perspective of that single proxy.

It is important to note that nothing compels the use of a proxy to represent the W3C. Creators of subject maps have the authority *not* to represent subjects, as well as to represent them.[5]

3   Absent Subjects

A subject map represents the opinion of an author as to what subjects exist, what properties they have and the basis on which representatives of those subjects can be compared to other representatives of subjects. Since the universe of possible subjects is infinite, of necessity, authors will omit some subjects from being represented in their subject maps.

The omission of a subject from a particular subject map means that, in that subject map, there is no collection of properties (i.e., no subject proxy) for that particular subject. The subject cannot be referenced, and no proxy for that subject can be compared to other proxies for that subject. In other words, an author's decision to omit from a subject map a representative for any particular subject is consequential.

Returning to the relational database example from above, if no proxy exists for the `firstName` key, for example, then there is no proxy to consider merging with a proxy for the `givenName` key. There is no explicit, principled basis on which to compare it to any other subject representative. Of course, another subject map author may create a proxy to represent the `firstName` key, and the subject map that contains that proxy could be used by anyone in order to guide the merging of proxies that contain `firstName` properties, ultimately resulting in combining whatever various sources may know about Eric Miller into a single subject proxy for Eric Miller.

4   Legends

In any given subject map, its *legend* provides a principled basis for "subject-sameness detection" and, as a consequence, for merging.

The term *legend* is used by the TMRM in the same sense as it is used in cartography. In any city, subway or topographical map, its legend indicates how to interpret the symbols that appear in the map as features of the mapped territory. In a subject map, the "legend" defines, among other things, the semantics of the keys.

The TMRM requires each subject map legend to disclose certain choices that must be made by its author. Even though those choices are not limited by the

---

[5] However, if a subject, such as the W3C, has a representative in a given subject map, and if the semantics of a key/value pair are such that the W3C is what they are referring to, then it's probably a good idea for the value to be a reference to the proxy for the W3C, rather than being the string "W3C" or the string "World Wide Web Consortium".

TMRM, and the manners in which legends may be expressed are unconstrained, all legends must answer the following questions:

- What properties (key/value pairs) must, should, or may occur in any subject proxy?
- What properties of subject proxies should be compared in order to determine whether they represent the same subject?
- What rules should be enforced when subject proxies are determined to represent the same subjects?
- What other rules are in effect?

The TMRM does not prescribe any particular form or manner of implementing legends.

A legend can be thought of as the equivalent of **good** documentation that details how to interpret an information resource in terms of the subjects represented therein, and on what basis to compare representatives for those subjects for merging. When two or more subject maps are to be merged together, the resulting subject map, too, has a legend that explains how to interpret it.

5   Illustration with Proxies

Let's consider the need to merge information from different data sources concerning the same subject.

The subject in this case is the gene for the chemokine lymphotactin.

This gene was cloned and named by three independent groups as SCM1, ATAC and LTN, in addition to the official name, XCL1. Each of the three groups used their names for this gene until the official name was established.[6]

The problem posed is a typical one. Researchers tend to use their favorite names for genes, and even if they later adopt the 'official' name, the problem of retaining convenient access to previously published literature remains.

The initial temptation is to create a subject proxy along the following lines:

```
{
  gene    = chemokine lymphotactin
  aliases = SCM1 | ATAC | LTN | XCL1
}
```

Future problems are lurking in that approach, because 'ATAC,' for example, is already the name of many things. A quick search of the WWW returns Aftermarket Technology Group, Air Transport Association of Canada, Aids Treatment Activist Coalition, the transit system in Rome, Italy, etc. etc. Clearly, we cannot afford to presume that *any* proxy that says that one of the aliases of its subject is 'ATAC' necessarily represents the gene for the chemokine lymphotactin.

---

[6] The success (or not) of HUGO nomenclature, Javier Tamames, and Alfonso Valencia, Genome Biology 2006, 7:402 doi:10.1186/gb-2006-7-5-402.

Even so, maybe there's a solution. We can exploit the fact that researchers tend to use the names that they use, whatever they are, consistently. We can also take advantage of the fact that people who write papers tend to follow the naming conventions of the works that they cite. One approach might be to add the researchers who have written articles about this gene to the proxy for the gene in one subject map:

```
{
  geneName    = SCM1 | ATAC | LTN | XCL1
  researcher  =  Yoshida T | Imai T | Muller S
}
```

In another subject map, one with proxies for genes cited in periodical literature, proxies are created that have the properties, geneName, author, and authorCited.

Let's assume the following two proxies were created from a search of the literature for the gene for the chemokine lymphotactin.[7]

When proxies are created from published sources for genes cited in publications, each proxy has among other properties:

```
{
  geneName       = SCM1
  author         = Yoshida T
  authorCited    = Imai T
}
```

```
{
  geneName       = ATAC
  author         = Muller S
  authorCited    = Dorner B
}
```

In order to merge the proxy for the gene with the two proxies from the literature, one rule to achieve that result would be:

1. If match on any geneName and,
2. If author matches researcher, or authorCited matches researcher,
3. Then merge the proxies.

Note that the identification of the subject, that is the gene for the chemokine lymphotactin, is no longer a matter of simple string matching but also matching other information, such as the author of the paper where the gene name appears or an author being cited in such a paper.

A system can be imagined in which, as articles are added, new authors are added to the proxy for matching in subsequent searches. Not to mention that

---

[7] Proxies can have any number of properties but for purposes of this example, only three are used.

articles and authors should also be represented by proxies which would allow those to be merged as well. The ultimate result would be one listing for each article under any of the names or aliases for this gene, such that a user who knows only one name or alias, can locate all of the literature on this particular gene. And does so without having to change current information systems or practices of other users.

There is no guarantee that any particular approach to subject-sameness detection will always yield good results. However, the "ATAC" example is intended to show that a sufficiently-nuanced approach, developed by sufficiently well-informed people, can yield results whose aggregate value to their users far exceeds the cost of achieving them. And, just as importantly, that such results can be achieved and exploited without changing current practices or information systems, without relying exclusively on any new kind of centralized naming authority, and without disenfranchising any naming authorities.

6   Conclusion

Just as different communities identify their subjects differently, so will they choose different paths for integrating information about those subjects. The disclosure model of the TMRM enables users to meaningfully discuss how to integrate information from inside and outside their communities, about whatever subjects concern them.

Towards Converting the Internet into Topic Maps

Lars Heuer

Semagia
Markt 1, 27777 Ganderkesee, Germany
heuer@semagia.com
http://www.semagia.com/

Abstract. This paper describes Semants, a work-in progress framework that uses the Wikipedia as focal point to collect information from various resources. Semants aims at developing several specialized applications (the ants) that are used to convert a resource into a topic map fragment that is merged into a bigger topic map.

1 Motivation

Wikipedia [6] has proven to be useful for humans; in June 2006 the English Wikipedia website provides over one million articles. These articles (topics) are frequently used by humans, but the Wikipedia system lacks of an interface that can be used by machines to gather information from it. Each article is written from humans for humans.

In conjuntion with Topic Maps, Wikipedia is mainly used as valuable source for Published Subject Identifiers (PSIs) because the majority of the articles provide stable information resources. Wikipedia contains many non-addressable subjects and the burden to create a PSI is taken from the topic map author because she can simply use an article from Wikipedia that describes the subject (i.e. http://en.wikipedia.org/wiki/John_Lennon for the person John Lennon). Using Wikipedia as PSI collection eases the distributed authoring of topic maps if the authors agree to use Uniform Resource Locators (URIs) from Wikipedia to identify non-addressable topics.

Wikipedia seems to be useful to generate topic maps, but one problem remains: An application cannot retrieve more information of a particular topic from Wikipedia. The aim of the Semants framework [10] is to use Wikipedia as information resource for a topic map that offers more than just a collection of PSIs. Semants is using Wikipedia as focal point to merge in other information resources (i.e. using the Internet Movie Database [1]).

2 Wikipedia Overview

Wikipedia is probably the largest knowledge repository on the Web and is available in dozens of languages. It is based on a Wiki [2] and the authors write the

L. Maicher, A. Sigel, and L.M. Garshol (Eds.): TMRA 2006, LNAI 4438, pp. 161–165, 2007.

articles in a simple text format, called "Wiki markup". This plain-text format is converted into a HTML representation.

The Wikipedia community offers templates for some kind of articles, which help to provide a common article structure. These templates assist the author to remember which information should be provided. An article about a person should contain the forename, surname, birthday, date of death etc. For the HTML representation, the template content is rendered as information box outside the narrative information and provides a summary of common properties.

2.1 Wiki Markup and Templates

Since natural language processing is a major problem for computer programs, the Semants framework uses only the well-formed Wiki markup and the Wikipedia templates as input. An analysis of the Wikipedia template structure has shown that it is simple enough to be parsed by an application and that valuable content can be extracted by computer programs. The HTML representation of an article and its narrative information is completely ignored.

The analysis of different Wikipedia language versions has shown that each language uses a different set of templates with their own conventions. Especially the English version uses a lot of different templates: While the German website uses the template "`Personendaten`" for all articles about people, the English version uses a template "`Infobox_Biography`" for persons, but also the template "`Infobox_Philosopher`" for a peson who is a philosopher. The usage of these heterogeneous templates was the reason to opt for the German Wikipedia version as entry point for the Semants framework.

3 Semants

One design objective of the framework was simplicity and programming language independency. For these reasons the framework is divided into different layers:

- Semants
  A Semant is a resource converter that takes an information resource and transforms it into a topic map fragment. A Semant is capable to provide a topic mappish view on a resource. It uses an ontology and converts the resource into a Topic Maps syntax (i.e. XTM [11]). The kind of Topic Maps syntax is determinated by content negotiation and depends on the preferences of the client which initiates the resource convertion.
- Crawler
  A crawler is used to walk through a collection of resources. A crawler instance instructs a particular Semant to provide a Topic Maps view on the resource and delivers this view back.
- Mediator
  This layer is used to mediate between crawlers and a Topic Maps server. The mediator collects the Topic Maps views from a crawler uses a communication protocol to store the fragments.

- Communication protocol
  To create, maintain and query topic maps a variation of the Topic Maps Interaction Protocol (TMIP [7] is used. This protocol was chosen because of its simplicity and the RESTful [9] approach.
- Topic Maps server
  The Topic Maps server is hidden behind the communication protocol. The prototype implementation uses a TMAPI [5] compatible Topic Maps engine. The server is responsible for merging the topic map fragments into a topic map.

This layered approach provides the advantage that the Semants which convert the information resources may be kept small and a developer of a Semant can ignore the other layers. The resource transformation process is transparent for the crawlers which act as clients for the Semants. A crawler knows how to walk through a collection of resources and how to send a request to a Semant. Specialized crawlers may walk through a local filesystem and instruct Semants to convert particular files into a topic map fragment.

The Topic Maps server is used to provide the "big picture": The topic map fragments from different resources are collected into a topic map. If one Semant delivers, for example, a topic map fragment which describes the city Liverpool and another Semant provides a fragment that describes the musician John Lennon who was born in Liverpool, these fragments are automatically connected through the common subject identifier "http://en.wikipedia.org/wiki/Liverpool".

3.1 Converting Wikipedia Articles

In the following an exemplary article transformation is shown; for illustration purposes the English Wikipedia version is used.

As stated above, a Wikipedia Semant uses the Wiki markup and the information provided by the templates. Figure 1 shows an excerpt from the Wikipedia page about the musician John Lennon.

```
{{Infobox_Biography
|subject_name='''John Lennon'''
[...]
|date_of_birth=[[October9]], [[1940]]
|place_of_birth=[[Liverpool]], [[England]]
|date_of_death=[[December8]], [[1980]]
|place_of_death=[[NewYork City]], [[USA]]}}
```

Fig. 1. Excerpt from the Wikipedia article about John Lennon

The excerpt shows only a subset of the provided information. Words which are enclosed in brackets (i.e. [[Liverpool]]) represent links to other Wikipedia articles.

A Semant which is dedicated to articles about persons parses the page and enriches the information with its own ontology. The result of this process is shown in figure 2 (using AsTMa= [8] syntax).

```
http://en.wikipedia.org/wiki/John_Lennon isa person
tn: John Lennon
birthday: 1940-10-09
date-of-death: 1980-12-08
[...]
http://de.wikipedia.org/wiki/John_Lennon
http://fr.wikipedia.org/wiki/John_Lennon
[...]

born-in(person: http://en.wikipedia.org/wiki/John_Lennon,
        place: http://en.wikipedia.org/wiki/Liverpool )
[...]
```

Fig. 2. Topic map fragment created from the John Lennon article

The first line shows the URL of the article which is used as subject identifier and the enriched information that subject indicated by the URL is a person. The next lines assign a name and two occurrences of type "birthday" and "date-of-death" to the topic. Additionally, the Semant has extracted the links to other Wikipedia language versions and uses these links as subject identifiers. These subject identifiers ensure that the Semants can operate on an arbitrary Wikipedia website and generate the same set of subject identifiers which enhances the interoperability between independent Semants.

The last statement shown creates a "born-in" association, where the players are indicated by the article URLs. As laid down above, the Semants are specialized applications and the instance that is capable of converting articles about persons cannot parse a page about a city. But the interoperability is kept because the Semants use the Wikipedia URLs as subject identifiers. Once another Semant provides a topic map fragment about the city Liverpool, the information is automatically merged with the existing data.

While the result looks promising it should be stated that the Semants only extract a small subset from the Wikipedia articles. Staying at the John Lennon example, it is difficult to infer that he was member of The Beatles and that he played together with Sir Paul McCartney, George Harrison and Ringo Starr.

4   Conclusions and Further Work

The basic concepts of converting a Wikipedia article into a topic map fragment have been outlined above. While converting Wikipedia into a topic map is an interesting task of its own, more advanced applications can be created if other information resources use Wikipedia as source for PSIs as well. It would be desirable to use the subject indicator of John Lennon to receive his discography from an online music trader. Wikipedia provides an excellent source for non-addressable subjects and can be used as focal point to integrate other information resources.

While the Semants architecture allows the developer to integrate new information resources easily (using any programming language she likes), it can be a tedious task to convert an information resource created for humans into a topic map fragment. The recent efforts to integrate metadata directly into the articles [4] will ease the information retrieval from Wikipedia for machines.

Referring to the provocative title of this paper it should be stated that the Semants framework is not limited to the exemplified transformation of Wikipedia articles. The framework will be extended to provide Semants that are capable of converting E-mails and other information resources into topic map fragments.

References

1. Internet Movie Database. http://www.imdb.com/.
2. MediaWiki. http://mediawiki.org/.
3. Ontoworld. http://wiki.ontoworld.org/.
4. Semantic MediaWiki. http://sourceforge.net/projects/semediawiki.
5. Topic Maps API. http://www.tmapi.org/.
6. Wikipedia. http://en.wikipedia.org/wiki/.
7. R. Barta. TMIP, A RESTful Topic Maps Interaction Protocol. http://www.mulberrytech.com/Extreme/Proceedings/html/2005/Barta01/EML2005Barta01.html.
8. R. Barta and L. Heuer. AsTMa= 2.0 Language Definition. http://astma.it.bond.edu.au/astma=-spec-2.0r1.0.dbk.
9. R. Fielding. Architectural Styles and the Design of Network-based Software Architectures. http://www.ics.uci.edu/ fielding/pubs/dissertation/top.htm.
10. L. Heuer. Semants. http://www.semants.org/.
11. International Organization for Standardization, Geneva, Switzerland. ISO/IEC JTC1/SC34, Topic Maps - XML syntax, 2007. http://www.isotopicmaps.org/sam/sam-xtm/.

Topic Map Objects

Graham Moore, Kal Ahmed, and Andrew Brodie

Networked Planet, Oxford Centre for Innovation, Mill Lane, Oxford, England
{Graham.Moore, Kal.Ahmed, Andrew.Brodie}@networkedplanet.com

Abstract. This paper presents a framework that provides domain specific classes for accessing and updating topic map data structures in a distributed environment. While work on Topic Map Web Services (TMWS) [1][2][3][4][5] have begun to provide developers with SOA type patterns for interacting with Topic Map data there is still a need for developers to be able to work with higher level views of the topic map data. TMAPI [6] has been the de-facto mechanism by which developers have accessed and updated topic map data. Topic Map Objects marries the advances in TMWS development with advances in modern language features of Java and C#. The result is a framework that allows developers to work with classes and objects that are relevant to the problem domain at hand. The expected contribution from this development is that developers can more easily use and work with topic maps with only a limited amount of knowledge about the full Topic Map Data Model (TMDM)[7]. In addition, developers will spend less time writing specific access code in order to construct domain specific applications.

1 Introduction

The Topic Map Data Model is a complex and heavy piece of machinery for developers to understand and use. In addition, TMAPI provides very little support for higher level abstractions and behavior. We consider these higher levels as aspects that are less generic than TMAPI and closer to the problem being addressed.

In the absence of these higher level abstractions developers are forced to build these themselves on top of TMAPI in order to help them complete their tasks. Topic Map Objects is a way to provide developers with this capability with minimal amounts of effort on their part. With a firm understanding of topic maps, TMAPI and also an understanding of the kinds of patterns developers will use in developing applications we are able to build the Topic Map Objects Framework.

The Topic Map Objects provides a framework that allows developers to create a set of classes and then using declarative attributes define how this set of classes map onto instances of a given topic map ontology. In addition to this data binding feature the framework also supports the construction of new topics and the updating of existing associations, names and occurrences by making changes to the objects used as representation proxies.

The approach is based on several key components; a topic map web service that supports high granularity of update, declarative property decorations on language classes, the use of subject identifiers for topic map ontology topics, and that the topic map system will provide persistent and long lived item identifiers for all topics.

L. Maicher, A. Sigel, and L.M. Garshol (Eds.): TMRA 2006, LNAI 4438, pp. 166–174, 2007.

The paper first presents the framework from a high level architectural perspective. The role of each component of the architecture is described as are its dependencies with other components. Subsequently there are sections on each of the components along with examples of use where relevant.

We conclude with future directions this work can take and the upcoming key challenges.

2 Topic Map Objects Framework

2.1 Overview

The Topic Map Objects framework consists of two key services. We use the term "service" to mean a SOAP or HTTP service that exposes a number of named capabilities. One service is the Topic Map Web Service, a generic service that supports transactional updates to a topic map. The other is the Object Manager Service, which is able to create domain specific objects based on topic map data and return them serialized to a calling application.

The Object Manager Service is able to build domain objects because of information passed to it as part of the client request, but also from declarative information contained in class definitions. These declarations describe how a given instance of the class should be constructed from topic map data.

All domain specific classes inherit from a common base class or mix-in that provides support for making changes and additions to the localized model. These changes are recorded in such a way that they can be posted to the update capability of the Topic Map Web Service. This effectively closes the loop from initial request, to constructed object, to serialized object, to object on client, to changes to local model and then changes posted back to the update capability of the Topic Map Web Service.

2.2 The Object Manager Service

The object manager service is a web service that provides a capability that given a topic identifier and a class name it will return a serialized collection of objects. The reason for a collection of objects to be returned is that the initially constructed object can be related to other objects and these may also become instantiated and returned by the service.

The abstract definition of the service capability is as follows:

```
capability: conjureobject   // the operation
parameter : topicidentifier // a topic identifier
parameter : classname       // name of class to bind
```

An example of invoking the service using a HTTP service implementation is as follows:

```
GET
/tmobjs/conjureobject.aspx?topicidentifier=2324&classna
me=D.Person
```

What is returned from this service is a serialized form of the object(s) that are instantiated as a result of the request. This framework does not impose any restrictions on the format or organization of this representation. This provides flexibility and openness for developers to choose how the objects are serialized and de-serialized. There is an implicit expectation that the collection of classes that comprise the domain model is available to both the Object Manager Service and the client application. It is required on the client in order to deserialize and reconstitute the objects provided by the Object Manager Service capability.

The main semantics of the Object Manager Service are the interpretation of the different annotation types. The object construction process consists of first locating the topic specified in the request, constructing a single instance of the class requested and then proceeding to introspect all of the properties of the object. If the property is to be populated from the topic map it will have been decorated using one of the decoration types described. Decoration is a generic term for the annotation of class level properties in languages such as Java[8] and C#[9].

Annotation based applications, such as Topic Map Objects, define a set of Annotation classes. An annotation class is just as any other except the context in which it is used. An instance of an annotation class is used to 'say more' or add metadata about a property of another class.

Below, as an example, is the definition of one of the annotation classes from the Topic Map Objects library.

```
public class TopicPSIAttribute :TopicMapObjectAttribute
{
}
```

The thing to notice is that these annotation classes (in C# called Attribute classes) are many cases simply markers. They mark or decorate a property in a class such that some other process can know which properties to operate on and in what way. However, some annotation classes also have additional properties that can be populated when used. The TopicNameAttribute, shown below, is an example of this.

```
public class TopicNameAttribute : TopicMapObjectAttribute
{
    private string _scopePSI;
    public TopicNameAttribute(string scopePSI)
    {
        _scopePSI = scopePSI;
        if (_scopePSI==null) _scopePSI = "";
    }

    public TopicNameAttribute()
    {
        _scopePSI = "";
    }

    public string ScopePSI
    {
        get {return _scopePSI;}
        set {_scopePSI = value; }
    }
}
```

The following section on Annotation Types describes all of the annotation types that form the Topic Map Objects library. These annotation classes are, in a way, a description of the different ways that an object can be constructed from topic map data.

One the topic map service has constructed the object in line with the semantics associated with each Annotation type it serializes the structure and returns it to the calling application.

2.3 Annotation Types

The annotation types are the set of classes that allow the mapping of topic map data into a domain specific object. This section describes all of the annotation classes that comprise the Topic Map Objects library, and specifically, the interpretation of each class by the Topic Map Objects Service 'conjure' capability.

For each of the annotation types we provide its name, a description of any properties it has the interpretation of it as made by the Object Manager service.

TopicObjectIdentityAttribute

This attribute class is used to convey that a given class property should assume the value of the *ObjectID* of the topic object it is being bound to. The type of the class property must be a string. This attribute is rarely used explicitly by a solution developer as a base class called TopicMapObjectBase automatically maps this property using this decoration.

This attribute class has no additional properties.

TopicPSIAttribute

This attribute class is used to convey that a given class property should assume the value of the PSI (subject identifier in TMDM) that belongs to the topic object it is being bound to. The type of the class property must be a string. If more than one PSI exists then one is selected at random.

This attribute class has one additional property called RegExp. If this property is defined then the selected PSI must match the regular expression provided. If more than one PSI matches then one is chosen at random. The random selection in the case of more than one may seem dangerous, but subject identifiers are used for identity and all of them are equal, therefore it is not an issue to pick one from a bunch as they all resolve to the same subject.

TopicNameAttribute

This attribute class is used to convey that a given class property should assume the value of a name of the topic object it is being bound to. If the scope property is defined then the name selected will be the topic name value that is valid in that scope. The property type of the target property must be a string. If there is more than one name value then one is chosen at random.

If the class property type is an Array then all names that match the criteria will be added into the array.

TopicOccurrenceAttribute

This attribute class is used to convey that a given class property should assume the value of the occurrence that belongs to the topic object it is being bound to. The type and scope parameters are used to decide which occurrence value should be used.

If the class property type is defined as being an Array then all matching properties are added into the Array. If it is a singular property then one of the matching values is selected at random.

It has been seen in many applications that quite often there is only one property of a given type, i.e. age, height, weight. Thus the default of mapping just one property is an intuitive outcome.

TopicAssociationAttribute

This attribute class defines that the IList property belonging to the class will contain a list of objects. Each object is bound to one topic in the set of related topics as defined by the source role type, association role type and target role type PSIs properties of the annotation class. The name of the class defines which C# class is to be used in the binding process. The IsLazy property indicates that this collection should be constituted only when accessed on the client.

This annotation class contains the full definition of the relationship between the focus topic (this object) and the related topics. This is to enable the client to create an update that can add and remove associations based on changes to the local model.

There is scope, in a read only mode to enable the related topics to be defined via a TMQL query. The reason this would need to be read-only is that it would be semantically ambiguous what to do if a new object were to be added to the collection or removed.

When the Object Manager Service traverses an association then it will construct a new object based on the class name and then re-apply the same semantics for building that instance. The IsLazy property allows developers to ensure that circular models, long lists or deep trees are not pulled down in one large lump. However, there may be certain times when a client application would want to load the entire model into memory.

Example Annotation

The following example shows how two classes are annotated. The classes involved are Person and Skill. The model that is to be utilized is the fact that a Person will have several skills.

```
[TopicTypeAttribute("http://www.networkedplanet.com/person")]
public class Person : TopicMapObjectBase
{
    private string m_name;
    private string m_age;
    private string m_homepage;
    private IList m_skills;

    [TopicNameAttribute()]
    public string Name {
```

```
      get { return m_name; }
      set {
        OccurrenceSet(this, "Name", value);
        m_name = value;
      }
    }

[TopicOccurrenceAttribute("http://www.networkedplanet.com/octype
s/age")]
    public string Age {
      get { return m_age; }
      set {
        OccurrenceSet(this, "Age", value);
        m_age = value;
      }
    }

[TopicOccurrenceAttribute("http://www.networkedplanet.com/octype
s/homepage")]
    public string HomePage {
    get { return m_homepage; }
    set {
      OccurrenceSet(this, "HomePage", value);
      m_homepage = value;
    }
}


[TopicAssociationAttribute("http://www.networkedplanet.com/atype
s/personhasskill",

"http://www.networkedplanet.com/roletypes/person",

"http://www.networkedplanet.com/roletypes/skill",

"NetworkedPlanet.TopicMapObjects.TestData.Skill,TopicMapObjectTe
stData", true)]
  public IList Skills {
    get { return m_skills; }
    set { m_skills = value; }
  }
}

// The Class Skill
[TopicTypeAttribute("http://www.networkedplanet.com/skill")]
public class Skill : TopicMapObjectBase {
  protected string m_name;

[TopicNameAttribute("http://www.networkedplanet.com/scopes/engli
sh_name_scope")]
  public string Name {
    get { return m_name; }
    set {
      OccurrenceSet(this, "Name", value);
      m_name = value;
    }
  }
}
```

Variants

Variants are generally considered to be a complex and messy aspect of the topic map model. Thus is important as variants do not map easily to a single object property, but instead have a dependency on another value. To this end they are not included in the Topic Map Objects framework, although creating an annotation class for them would be possible.

2.4 Topic Map Objects Client

The a client of the Topic Map Object service in general doesn't need to do anything different from using a normal set of objects. When actions occur on the object model internally the TopicMapObjectBase class creates topic map update events. When an occurrence is changed a delete and create occurrence event are created. When a new topic is added to a collection of topic map managed objects then a new object is created and in the topic map transaction, a new topic with a GUID along with a new association is defined.

When a client application has made a collection of changes then it can instruct the client object to post the update transaction back to the server.

Topic Map Objects has been engineered to make use of optimistic locking. To this end, if a change has occurred to any topic since the client made a read, then any changes by the client will result in a concurrent modification exception. The version information is stored in the TopicMapObjectBase object. This means that it is hidden from developers.

If a collection is defined as 'IsLazy' then upon a user accessing such a collection a new request is sent to the Topic Map Object Service to construct the required objects.

2.5 Example Usage

This example shows a client conjuring a Person instance, iterating a set of skills, deleting one skill and creating a new skill *and* adding it to the skills of the person.

```
object o =
tmom.Conjure("http://www.networkedplanet.com/people/gdm",
typeof(Person));

Person p = o as Person;
System.Console.WriteLine(p.HomePage);
System.Console.WriteLine(p.Age);
System.Console.WriteLine(p.Name);

foreach (Skill s in p.Skills)
{
   System.Console.WriteLine(s.Name);
}

// remove the relationship between a skill and a person.
// Note the skill is not deleted.
p.Skills.Remove(p.Skills[0]);

// add a new skill
Skill nskill = new Skill();
```

```
nskill.Name = "sql";
p.Skills.Add(nskill);


// look at txn
TopicMapTransaction txn =
TopicMapTransaction.GetTopicMapTransaction();

UpdateServiceClient usc = new
UpdateServiceClient("http://localhost/updateservice/tmupdateserv
ice.aspx");

XmlDocument xdoc = new XmlDocument();
xdoc.LoadXml(txn.XML("tmobjects"));
usc.PostUpdate(xdoc);
```

2.6 The Topic Map Web Service Update Capability

The Topic Web Service Update capability supports a number of operations to update, add or remove topic map data. The full capability of this service goes beyond the scope of this paper.

However, to complete the picture in the context of Topic Map Objects it should be noted that the transaction consists of delete and add operations for Topics, Names, Occurrences and Associations. All of these operations occur by value and occur within a single atomic transaction.

If any aspect of the transaction fails then the whole transaction is rolled back. This is to ensure that the topic map is always preserved in a consistent state. If an exception occurs in update then the client is required to re-fetch the objects it needs to ensure that it has the latest version which it can then begin modifying.

2.7 Packaging and Deploying the Different Components

The Topic Map Objects can be grouped into a number of different libraries. The reason for having a number of libraries is to ensure that client applications can be light weight modules that do not have a binary dependency on any of the server, Topic Map Objects service libraries or dependencies.

This approach supports a fully distributed model with no server dependencies. It also enables a heterogeneous environment with different language servers supplying different language clients.

3 Applications of Topic Map Objects

3.1 Data Transformer

Topics Maps is a powerful technology for integrating data sources. However, one of the problems is how to easily map data into the topic map model. Using Topic Map Objects allows developers to use their existing sets of classes and with some schema bound annotation map their data into that of the topic map.

The vision is that multiple models that before were not mergeable become so when each is mapped into a topic map using this technology.

An example of this is to integrate different XML languages into Topic Maps Objects and then into a topic map as a way to merge different XML vocabularies without needing to develop a bespoke merger for each combination of XML vocabularies.

3.2 Multiple Views on Data

The truth, or usefulness of a topic map can vary based on who is looking at it and in what context. The dynamic and late binding of the objects to the data means that developers can map a data and behavioural model to topic map data based on the application and the context. In addition, they are not forced to use one definitive model.

This freedom of expression enables developers to create patterns of code that can be bound to topic map structures in ways that best solve the problem to hand.

3.3 Hibernate on Steriods

One of the interesting aspects of Topic Map Objects, is that it is very similar to efforts such as Hibernate[8]. However, we see the dynamic and late binding, as well as the fundamental flexibility of the Topic Map Model as unique features that are not present in Hibernate.

4 Conclusion and Future Work

Future work will look at new patterns of attribute classes that can add more expressiveness and support other common patterns. Also, the use of TMCL to generate a starting set of classes would also be a valuable and worthwhile research activity. This would also lead to an extension of set of attribute classes.

However, without further development the Topic Map Objects Framework is a powerful and exciting addition to the toolset of all topic map application developers.

References

1. Moore, G.; Ahmed, K: Networked Planet Topic Map Web Service.: http://www.networkedplanet.com/ technology/webservices/intro.html
2. Schwotzer, T.; Moore, G.: SNAPI – Semantic Network API, http://sourceforge.snapi.org
3. Moore, G.; Pepper, S.: TMRAP – Submission to SC34
4. Barta, R.: TMIP – Topic Map Interaction Protocol, Bond University
5. Moore, G.: Semantic Web Servers. In: Proceedings of Extreme Markup Languages 2004
6. Ahmed, K.; Garshol, L. M.; Moore, G.: TMAPI – Topic Map API, http://sourceforge.tmapi.org
7. Garshol, L. M.; Moore, G. (eds): Topic Map Data Model, ISO13250 part 2.
8. Hibernate, http://www.hibernate.org/.

Topincs - A RESTful Web Service Interface for Topic Maps

Robert Cerny

In der Klauer 27, D-55128 Mainz, Germany
robert@cerny-online.com
http://www.cerny-online.com

Abstract. Topincs is a RESTful web service interface for retrieval and manipulation of topic maps. It allows the creation and publication of information in a way that is understandable by humans as well as computers. To accomplish this, it uses the Topic Maps Data Model and overcomes the weakness of HTML documents where most of the meaning is buried in natural language and invisible for computers to act upon. The items of a topic map are exposed and identified through URLs and manipulated with the HTTP methods. The Topincs Interface is implemented in a software product for authoring, storing and publishing topic maps, called the Topincs Server which comes with a web based editor.

1 Motivation

The World Wide Web was built around the Uniform Resource Locator (URL), the HyperText Transfer Protocol (HTTP), and the HyperText Markup Language (HTML). It started as a system for information management within the European Organisation for Nuclear Research, CERN [2]. HTML was easy to learn, documents were quickly published and whoever was interested could access them. As a matter of fact, it was so easy that it quickly spread outside CERN into the realms of science, business, and government administration, making it one of most successful computer systems to date. With the majority of the information in a document being in natural language, it requires a person to extract the meaning. This is the reason why a search engine cannot distinguish between *Topincs*, the software product and *topincs*, the misspelling of *topics*.

With computers and the Internet changing many aspects of our lives, the density of information has increased dramatically leaving however the individual with the same information processing capabilities they were equipped with some thousand years ago. A scientist has to keep track of publications, new ideas, and their source, not to mention the content of the field he is working in. A software developer has to keep up with new languages, standards and technologies, products and companies, web sites, and many more topics that he encounters during his work. A project manager has to gather information from various sources, encode, transform, and distribute it. Last but not least she has to ensure that the information she is spreading is understood.

L. Maicher, A. Sigel, and L.M. Garshol (Eds.): TMRA 2006, LNAI 4438, pp. 175–183, 2007.

Many positions that were created in the last 30 years deal with gathering, transforming, and distributing knowledge. For most people it becomes evident that the software products that are installed on their computer today do not enable them to manage their personal and organizational knowledge. It rather keeps them within the boundaries of natural language and additionally confronts them with artificial constructs like programs and file systems, leaving them with frustrating, endless searches through mailboxes and hard drives.

With the fore mentioned situation in mind a software system was sketched to allow a more effective approach to personal knowledge management. The first intention was to build a sophisticated notebook, which allows programmatic manipulation and retrieval of its content. Access to this notebook should not be restricted to one location or one device, but should be possible at home, work, and eventually on the road. The administration of the software should be simple and inexpensive.

These requirements led to a Client-Server Architecture consisting of a user interface running in a web browser and a web server for processing requests for Creation, Retrieval, Update, and Deletion (CRUD) of entities in a RESTful manner. This eliminates the need for installing and updating clients and allows fine grained access control to knowledge based on the URL. The blessings of modern web technology should also allow more comfort than an ordinary web page, creating an almost application like feeling within the browser. A first version of the software was presented by the author at the Open Space Session of TMRA 2005 [12].

2   Status

Topincs is mature enough to allow for the creation of topic maps in collaboration over the Internet or an intranet, allowing individuals or groups to share, publish and exchange their knowledge. One Topincs Server can be used to host many *topic map stores*, which are identified by an URL path prefix and have independent content and users. The *Topincs Server* is set on top of Apache, PHP and MySQL. The *Topincs Editor* requires the Firefox or Opera web browser. Content is served in JTM (see below), XTM 1.0, XTM 2.0, and XHTML, for viewing in any browser.

Topincs can be facilitated for Content Management, as a semantic Wiki or a Personal Information Manager. It brings humans and computers in the same starting position in the Web, simplifying the production of structured web content for humans and enabling processing for computers. If you put focus on software as a consumer of web content, Topincs can be used for Web services, since the semantics of the resources is interpretable by a machine.

Topincs was used during the course of TMRA 2006 as a knowledge logging tool. Every participant was equipped with an account to join the collaborative effort to create a conference topic map. The result of this endeavour, which was driven by the author and the conference organiser Lutz Maicher, is available at http://www.topincs.com/tmra/2006. Currently, access to the store is limited to the participants of the conference. The interested reader can request an account from the author.

The remainder of this paper introduces a new notation for topic maps (JSON Topic Maps), describes the web service interface and discusses the Topincs Server and Editor. An outlook for future extensions closes this paper.

3 JSON Topic Maps (JTM)

The JavaScript Object Notation (JSON) is a built-in JavaScript feature that allows literal notation of objects in programs. It fulfills a similar need as XML, the expression of structured data and the storage in human readable form. Douglas Crockford calls JSON *the fat-free alternative to XML* [6]. Parsers and generators are available for many popular programming languages [5]. The ratio between content and markup is better in JSON than in XML which the following example illustrates.

This XML document lists a few movies:

```
<collection>
  <movie year="1993"><title>Short Cuts</title></movie>
  <movie year="1999"><title>Magnolia</title></movie>
  <movie year="2004"><title>Crash</title></movie>
</collection>
```

Writing this data structure in JSON below not only reduces its size, but also yields a better content to markup ratio:

```
{"movies" : [
    {"year": 1993, "title":"Short Cuts"},
    {"year": 1999, "title":"Magnolia"},
    {"year": 2004, "title":"Crash"}]}
```

Since Topincs exposes a RESTful web service interface, it can support many representations of topic map items. While being a more compact format than XML, the parsing of a JSON string on a web browser is done by simple evaluation. The created object can then be augmented with JavaScript functions. This very small gap between data and program creates many straight forward solutions and is very comfortable to work with.

The Topics Map Data Model (TMDM) is the container a topic map can be filled into. [11] defines the structure of topic maps independent of any syntax. The notation of the TMDM in JSON is quite simple. An item is enclosed by braces. The properties of the item are written down as a comma separated list of the form *"name" : "value"*. Arrays are enclosed by square brackets.

One big advantage of Topic Maps is that the only thing that can be referred to is a topic. A topic has three means of being referred to: subject identifiers, subject locators and item identifiers. Wherever the TMDM does define a reference to a topic, e.g. the type of occurrences, an URI identifying the topic can be mentioned directly.

The following topic map shall illustrate the JSON Topic Maps (JTM) format. It states the existence of a movie entitled *Dear Wendy* released in 2005.

```
{"topics":[
  {"subject_identifiers":[
    "http://psi.topincs.com/movies/dear-wendy"],
   "names":[
    {"value":"Dear Wendy",
     "type":"http://psi.topincs.com/title",
     "scope":[
       "http://www.topicmaps.org/xtm/1.0/country.xtm#US",
       "http://www.topicmaps.org/xtm/1.0/country.xtm#DE"]}],
   "occurrences":[
    {"value":"2005",
     "type":"http://psi.topincs.com/publication-year",
     "datatype":"http://www.w3.org/2001/XMLSchema#gYear",
     "item_identifiers":[
       "http://psi.topincs.com/movies/dear-wendy?pubyear"]}]}],
  "associations":[
   {"type":"http://psi.topicmaps.org/iso13250/model/type-instance",
    "roles":[
     {"player":"http://psi.topincs.com/movies/dear-wendy",
      "type":"http://psi.topicmaps.org/iso13250/model/instance"},
     {"player":"http://psi.topincs.com/movie",
      "type":"http://psi.topicmaps.org/iso13250/model/type"}]}]}
```

4   The Topincs Web Service Interface

This section might also be titled "To Rest!", in response to Lars Marius Garshols question "To REST Or Not to REST" in [10]. Given the requirement that the application has to run in an ordinary web browser installation without any additional modifications, the best proven possibility to communicate with a server is the HTTP protocol. Since this allows a very different way of working as the countless non RESTful web applications out in the World Wide Web demonstrate, a decision towards a RESTful API for the sake of clarity and simplicity was made. Representational State Transfer (REST) is the architectural style that guides the development of the World Wide Web [8].

The application of REST creates an interface which exposes a small number of verbs to manipulate an unlimited number of nouns. In the case of Topincs the nouns are the items of a topic map. Robert Barta already applied REST to Topic Maps [1], creating the Topic Map Interaction Protocol (TMIP). This approach is fundamentally different from TMIP, but both should be able to coexist peacefully on one server.

4.1   Addressing Items

The Topincs Server segments the URL space into stores, which are identified by a unique prefix to the path. The store is a container for topic maps. A store of the imaginary movie reviewer Thomas V. could be located at `http://www.topincs.com/thomasv`. The items of a store are located in separate spaces, e.g. the topic representing the subject *Director*, might be located at `http://www.topincs.com/thomasv/topics/621`. This URL has two functions: it exposes the resource to be retrieved and manipulated with HTTP in different representations and it functions as an item identifier within the TMDM. The movie topic map of Thomas V. would be addressable under `http://www.topincs.com/thomasv/topicmaps/movies`. The item identifiers are kept independent of their location within the topic map. This way topics and associations can be moved from one map to another within the store without rendering URLs that were distributed in topic map exports broken. Consumers of such topic maps can still use the item identifiers to contact the server for updated information.

4.2   Creating Items

To create a resource, which in our case is an item of the TMDM, a client must know the parent of the item. The TMDM defines a parent for every construct except for topic map. For topics and associations the parent is a topic map, names and occurrences belong to topics, variants to names and roles to associations. In Topincs the parent of a topic map is the store it resides in.

An item is created by sending a POST request with a representation of the item to its parent-to-be. The representation of the topic map item may hold children. This way topics, associations and complete topic maps can be created in one request.

This procedure for creating new resources is in accordance with [7], which specifies the usage of the POST method for creating resources as subordinate of the resource identified by the Request-URI in the Request-Line. It further enumerates some examples, one of them being the extension of a database through an append operation.

The representation format used in the examples of this paper is JTM. Yet, the Topincs interface is not limited to any specific format. To illustrate the creation of an item, we shall add the name "Regisseur" in the scope German to the topic representing the subject *Director*.

```
POST /thomasv/topics/621 HTTP/1.1
Host: http://www.topincs.com
Content-Type: application/json

{"value":"Regisseur",
 "type":"http://psi.topicmaps.org/iso13250/model/name-type",
 "scope":["http://www.topicmaps.org/xtm/1.0/language.xtm#de"]}
```

The Topincs server will process this request and in case of success return the following response:

```
HTTP/1.1 201 Created
Location: http://www.topincs.com/thomasv/names/1978
```

The URL in the *Location* header of the response is functioning as the item identifier of the created name, but allows its retrieval and manipulation as will be shown shortly.

4.3   Reading Items

To retrieve an item, the client must send a GET request to its identifier. HTTP requires a GET request to be *safe* and *idempotent*. A request is *safe* if it does not have side effects and *idempotent* if numerous identical requests have the same side effects as one. The safe methods are GET and HEAD, the idempotent methods are GET, HEAD, PUT and DELETE. Furthermore, HTTP supports the retrieval of different representations of a resource [7]. To specify which representation a client can deal with, the *Accept* header is used. To communicate a certain scope the client is set in, an *Accept-Scope* header is used [1].

In case of the Topincs Editor, items are requested as *application/json*. If the client retrieves the topic *Director*, it sends the following request to the Topincs server:

```
GET /thomasv/topics/621 HTTP/1.1
Host: http://www.topincs.com
Accept: application/json
```

The server will respond:

```
HTTP/1.1 200 OK
```

```
{"subject_identifiers":["http://psi.topincs.com/director"],
 "names":[
   {"value":"Regisseur",
    "type":"http://psi.topicmaps.org/iso13250/model/name-type",
    "scope":[
      "http://www.topicmaps.org/xtm/1.0/language.xtm#de"]}]}
```

4.4   Updating Items

An update request is sent directly to the item to be updated. The HTTP method for sending a new version of a resource to the server is PUT. If the orthographical rules for the German language change once more, the following request might become necessary:

```
PUT /thomasv/names/1978 HTTP/1.1
Host: http://www.topincs.com
Content-Type: application/json
```

```
{"value":"Reschisoer",
 "type":"http://psi.topicmaps.org/iso13250/model/name-type",
 "scope":["http://www.topicmaps.org/xtm/1.0/language.xtm#de]}
```

On successful completion of the update the server will respond:

```
HTTP/1.1 200 OK
```

4.5 Deleting Items

If a resource becomes obsolete, the DELETE method allows us to remove it from the server. The identifier of the item to be deleted must be known to the client in order to accomplish the removal. It becomes the Request-URI of the DELETE request. To delete the German name for director the following request must be sent:

```
DELETE /thomasv/names/1978 HTTP/1.1
Host: http://www.topincs.com
```

On successful deletion the server will respond:

```
HTTP/1.1 200 OK
```

With a name all its variants are deleted. In general, the deletion of an item results in the deletion of all children. Furthermore, after deletion, the item can no longer be referred to within the store, e.g. if a topic that represents the role type *Director* is deleted, all roles of that type will be deleted. Programs that encounter the item identifier within a topic map and subsequently contact the server, will receive a response stating 404 Not Found.

5   The Topincs Server

Currently there exists one implementation of the Topincs Interface. This Topincs Server is written in PHP and requires Apache. For persistance it uses MySQL. For every store that is maintained on the server there is one MySQL database instance. This implementation supports XTM 1.0 and 2.0, JTM, and a generic XHTML representation. The last one can be retrieved by pointing a web browser to an item identifier.

6   The Topincs Editor

The Topincs Editor is a browser based application, which is at the time of writing the only human interface with editing capabilities to the content of a store on a Topincs Server. It is written in JavaScript and makes use of the XMLHttpRequest object to send HTTP requests to the Server. This technique is also referred to as Ajax, a term coined by Jesse James Garrett [9]. It makes use of the Topincs Interface to manipulate and retrieve resources on the Server.

Any number of users with valid credentials can point their web browser to the URL of a Topincs Store and collaboratively edit topic maps. The Editor has a simple ontology browser, a search function, and a journal to see the development over time. It supports editing of all features of the TMDM except for Reification and Variants and allows exporting to XTM 1.0, XTM 2.0 and JTM.

When the user creates individuals, the Topincs Editor offers support by making suggestions regarding occurrence types and association types. This is done by examining the type of occurrences and associations of topics of the same type as the individual. For example if a user creates a new occurrence for a movie, a list of all occurrence types that movies have in the store is displayed. On selecting one particular type the datatype of the first occurrence of this type is looked up and suggested to the user.

This *ontological prototyping* combined with suggestions provides some guidance to avoid deviation in the usage of typing topics. An example for a deviation is, if one user uses *Director* as a role type and another uses it as a topic type. This might lead to unrecoverable situations for programmatic consumers and to confusion for human consumers. Another form of deviation, which probably affects only machines, is occurrences of the same type having different data types.

The Topincs Server and Editor are currently distributed together under a proprietary license. For both products the source code is available. The distribution can be downloaded at [4].

7   Outlook

Topincs can provide infrastructure for a semantic domain, where users and groups work in separate stores on the same domain, but have the option to publish topics with a PSI, a name and description, so that users in fellow stores in this domain can start talking in the same terms. There should be an easy way for users of the Topincs Editor to publish and to search already published PSIs to see if a topic already exists that represents the subject one wants to talk about.

Topincs needs an import hub so that legacy data following a rigid structure (like an Internet message according to RFC 822) can be easily imported into a map.

Topincs can be used as a tool to communicate across language boundaries. Typing topics need to be translated once and then people can easily start communicating.

The ontological burden and freedom that the Topincs Editor offers is too overwhelming for everyday use. Topincs will receive another client, which will work very similar to a Wiki. It will limit the user in its expressibility and at the same time offer a stronger ontological guidance, so that a deviation in the usage of typing topics can be omitted and a larger user base can be targeted. The current Editor will stay in place to provide unlimited expressibility for creating the ontology by prototyping. In another step, the possibility of forms, which will fill a topic map template, will be provided. This way even stronger restrictions on the ontology can be realized.

References

1. Barta, R.: TMIP, A RESTful Topic Maps Interaction Protocol. Available at: `http://www.mulberrytech.com/Extreme/Proceedings/html/2005/Barta01/EML2005Barta01.html`
2. Berners-Lee, T.: Information Management: A Proposal. Available at: `http://www.w3.org/History/1989/proposal.html`
3. Berners-Lee, T., Hendler J., Lassila, O.: The Semantic Web. In: Scientific American, 284(5):34–43, May 2001
4. Cerny, R.: Topincs. Available at: `http://www.cerny-online.com/topincs`
5. Crockford, D.: Introducing JSON. Available at: `http://www.json.org`
6. Crockford, D.: JSON: The Fat-Free Alternative to XML. Available at: `http://www.json.org/xml.html`
7. Fielding, R., Mogul J.C., Frystyk, H., Masinter, L., Leach, P., Gettys, J., Berners-Lee, T.: Hypertext Transfer Protocol – HTTP/1.1. Available at: `http://www.ietf.org/rfc/rfc2616.txt`, Internet Engineering Task Force, 1999
8. Fielding, R.: Architectural Styles and the Design of Network-based Software Architectures. Doctoral Dissertation, University of California, Irvine, 2000
9. Garrett, J.J.: Ajax: a new approach to web applications. Available at: `http://www.adaptivepath.com/publications/essays/archives/000385.php`
10. Garshol, L.M.: TMRAP — Topic Maps Remote Access Protocol. In: Charting the Topic Maps Research and Applications Landscape, Heidelberg, 2006
11. ISO/IEC FDIS 13250-2: Topic Maps — Data Model, 2005-12-16, International Organization for Standardization, Geneva, Switzerland. `http://www.isotopicmaps.org/sam/sam-model/2005-12-16/`
12. Sigel, A.: Report on the open space sessions. In: Proceedings of the First International Workshop on Topic Maps Research and Applications (TMRA'06) Leipzig; Springer LNCS, 2006

TopiWriter -
Integrating Topic Maps with Word Processor

Rani Pinchuk[1], Richard Aked[1], Juan-Jose de Orus[1], David De Weerdt[1],
Georges Focant[1], Bernard Fontaine[1], and Mikael Wolff[2]

[1] Space Applications Services, Leuvensesteenweg 325, B-1932 Zaventem, Belgium
{rani.pinchuk, richard.aked, juan.jose.de.orus, david.de.weerdt,
georges.focant, bernard.fontaine}@spaceapplications.com
http://www.topiwriter.com/
[2] European Space Agency, European Space Research & Technology Centre
Keplerlaan 1, Postbus 299, 2200 AG Noordwijk, The Netherlands
Mikael.Wolff@esa.int
http://www.esa.int/

Abstract. While authoring topic maps using knowledge extracted from technical documentation, it was realized that the actual process of authoring topic maps can contribute to the quality of the documents. This has led to the idea of integrating Topic Maps technology with a word processor. It was found that such an integration provides advantages for document authors and topic map authors, alike.

The integration, resulting in a product called TopiWriter,[1] has been made with MS Word.[2] Three types of objects have been introduced in MS Word: bi-directional placeholders of topic map content, containers and sequential containers. These objects together with the ability to define constraints in the topic map, assist the author to produce consistent, high quality documentation. In addition, TopiWriter provides a set of features which can assist documentation authors as well as Topic Maps authors and users.

1 Introduction

Today, much knowledge is contained in documents. However, documents have known disadvantages - it is not always easy to find information within documents, they do not always follow a clear standard and structure, document content is not easily reusable and the knowledge contained in documents is not always clear and explicit. In addition, many documents include inconsistencies and are incomplete which degrades their quality and usefulness.

Topic Maps technology is a novel medium for representing knowledge. It provides the ability to browse knowledge through associations, to define constraints

---

[1] An application has been filed with the Benelux Trademark Office to register the TopiWriter name as a Benelux trademark for goods and services in several classes.
[2] MS Word is a registered trademark of Microsoft Corporation.

L. Maicher, A. Sigel, and L.M. Garshol (Eds.): TMRA 2006, LNAI 4438, pp. 184–191, 2007.

on the knowledge in order to keep it consistent and complete, and to exchange, share, merge, filter and query the knowledge.

This paper describes work that has been done to integrate documents and topic maps, enabling the creation and use of knowledge within a word processor environment. The work is implemented as a product called TopiWriter.

2   Why TopiWriter

Integrating Topic Maps with a word processor meets several needs.

2.1   From Topic Map to Document - Reporting Tool

A topic map can be seen as a cloud of knowledge without start or end. Although it can be very useful in finding knowledge while browsing through the cloud, sometimes a document about subsets of the knowledge is needed, for example an introduction document or a scientific report ("give me all the earthquakes that occurred in this region in the last 15 years").

Actually, such a reporting tool is needed by the Topic Maps users in the same manner as reporting tools are used for getting data from a Relational Data Base Management System (RDBMS).

2.2   Assisting in Topic Map Authoring

Unlike a document that has a clear order with start and end, a topic map has a much more complex structure. This means that authors of topic maps might have a conceptual difficulty during the authoring process because there is no clear progress line while authoring such a cloud. When the author stops his work at the end of the day, he might have difficulty to continue from the same place the next day. It is not clear which parts of the cloud are complete and which parts should still be worked on. By mapping the topic map to a document, a certain order can be attached to the topic map. The document can be used as a clear path throughout the cloud.

2.3   From Document to Topic Map

During the work on the AIOBCT project,[3] topic maps describing different systems of the Columbus laboratory[4] were authored. It was found that inconsistencies, mistakes and incompleteness's could be found in the documentation solely by the process of authoring the topic maps.

Consistency - technical documentation should be consistent:

 — *Consistency of knowledge.* For example, names should be consistent - a certain subject should be referred to by the same name and if there are aliases to that name those should be listed.

---

[3] A Question/Answering system over Topic Maps done as a study for European Space Agency (ESA).

[4] The Columbus laboratory is the European module of to the International Space Station (ISS).

– *Consistency of the document structure.* Layouts of different yet similar sections should look alike. For example, all sections describing devices of the same type should look alike.
– *Consistency between documents.* Knowledge in one document should not contradict knowledge in other documents.
– *Consistency over time.* Document maintenace should ensure consistency over time.

Completeness - technical documentation should be complete. This means that *all* relevant topics are *fully* described. For example, all devices of a certain type should be listed and adequately described. And for each device, all its relevant characteristics should be provided (mass, dimensions, location, etc.).

Correctness - simple mistakes can be avoided by having the knowledge organized. For example, if the content of the document is related to the knowledge in the topic map, different occurrences of the same content are all fixed when one occurrence is fixed.

Re-usability - the resulting topic map can be *reused* for creating an improved version of the document, but it can also be used for authoring other related documents. This means that the document becomes reusable when it has a topic map which contains the knowledge in it. For example, the knowledge in a document describing a certain space vehicle system could be reused to write maintenance documents, training documents, and even for the process of designing a new similar system.

2.4   Authoring Documentation and Topic Maps in Parallel

If the creation of a topic map from a document can increase the quality of the document, the next obvious step is the process of writing the document in parallel with the authoring of the topic map containing the knowledge of the document. This means that the during the writing process, the author is reminded about inconsistencies and missing parts. Some of the text can be generated and the knowledge that is authored can be browsed.

3   What is TopiWriter

TopiWriter is an integration of Topic Maps technology with a word processor - MS Word. This integration is done by adding three kinds of objects generally called TopiObjects: TOMECs, TOMATOs and Content Generators.

3.1   A TOMEC is a Bi-directional Placeholder for Topic Map Content

TOMEC - (**TO**pic **M**ap **E**mbedded **C**ontent) is the most simple TopiObject and is a placeholder for knowledge from the topic map.

A TOMEC is defined by two Toma[5][1] excerpts and parameters. The two Toma excerpts are combined together to build Toma statements that are used to refer to a specific characteristic of a topic or association of the topic map. The following example describes a TOMEC which holds an occurrence of type *description* of a certain topic.

The Toma excerpts that are needed are:

```
$topic.id = '&p1'
```

and

```
$topic.oc(description)
```

The excerpts may include parameters. A parameter can be configured to hold a topic id. In the example above, the first excerpt includes a parameter: &p1.

TopiWriter uses the first excerpt to find the id of the topic the TOMEC refers to:

```
select $topic.id where $topic.id = '&p1';
```

If the above parameter &p1 is configured to hold the topic id *cpu*, the statement becomes:

```
select $topic.id where $topic.id = 'cpu';
```

This selects the topic *cpu*.

Now, using the second excerpt and the topic id that is found, TopiWriter can generate INSERT, SELECT, UPDATE or DELETE Toma statements:

```
insert 'new value' id('found_id').oc(description);

select $topic.oc(description)
 where $topic.id = 'found_id';

update $topic.oc(description) = 'new_value'
 where $topic.id = 'found_id';

delete $topic.oc(description)
 where $topic.id = 'found_id';
```

When the Toma excerpts are defined, but the parameters of the TOMEC are not yet configured, the TOMEC is said to be unconfigured. Such a TOMEC can be seen as a template for many TOMEC instances, and indeed TopiWriter allows to define and store such TOMEC templates and to instantiate them (that is, to insert and configure them) at different places in a document.

---

[5] Toma is a Topic Map Query Language (TMQL), Topic Map Constraint Language (TMCL) and Topic Map Manipulation Language (TMML).

As mentioned above, a TOMEC parameter can hold a topic id. However, the user could define, in advance, that a certain parameter can get only topic ids of a certain type. In the example above, if we define that the parameter *p1* can get only topic ids of type *device*, when we configure that parameter, the list of possible values for the parameter will contain only the ids of the topics of type *device*.

When the TOMEC is instantiated and configured, it shows the value it retrieves from the topic map using the generated Toma statement. Moreover, if the user now changes the value of the TOMEC, that change will also be reflected in the topic map.

The user can create a TOMEC that refers to a topic that does not yet exist. In this case the new topic can be created by using TopiMaker. TopiMaker is a Topic Maps editor that is integrated into TopiWriter. In addition, if the user selects text prior to the creation of the TOMEC, that text will be inserted in the topic map as the initial value of the TOMEC. If there was already a value in the topic map for that TOMEC, the user will be asked to select the valid value.

Thus, a TOMEC keeps a bi-directional link with the topic map - meaning that a piece of text can be changed in place in MS Word and the underlying topic map is automatically and transparently updated. Correspondingly, a change in the topic map is automatically propagated to all relevant TOMECs in the document.

A TOMEC may hold only a single value. However, in some Topic Maps, a query such as the following might give more than one result:

```
select $topic.bn where $topic.id = '&p1';
```

That is, if the selected topic has more than one base name. TopiWriter considers this as an error, because there is no correct way to choose one of the items in such a sequence. This is an inherent characteristic of Topic Maps. However, the Topic Maps standard provides mechanisms to avoid the problem, such as the use of scopes. Therefore, users are encouraged to use scopes and to design the topic map and their TOMECs in such a way that only one result is returned by a query that is used in a TOMEC.

TOMECs can be configured to show text, images or hyper-links. A mix of those three types is not allowed within one TOMEC - i.e. an image followed by text must be shown by two TOMECs. This is due to the way the content of the TOMEC is kept in the Topic Map - as text, or as a textual reference.

If required, read-only TOMECs can be used to prevent changes in the underlying topic map. In addition, an aggregation TOMEC can be defined as a TOMEC that gets a value of a Toma SELECT statement that uses aggregation functions (such as *count*, *sum* or *concat*). For example, a TOMEC that presents the total mass (occurrence of type *mass*) of all the parts of a certain type. Aggregation TOMECs are always read-only.

TOMECs assist the author in keeping the document consistent. In addition, they provide ways to reuse knowledge. For example, a TOMEC that contains a description of a certain device can be used in more than one place.

The fact that the TOMECs are bi-directional means that while the author authors the document, the topic map is authored as well and vice versa. Moreover, the ability to select text in the document and insert it into the topic map provides a way to harvest knowledge from existing documents.

TOMECs and Toma. TopiWriter provides built-in TOMEC templates. However, any author can create his own TOMECs using Toma. This is the reason that Toma was extended to become a TMML[6] - the use of a framework such as TMAPI[2] is intended for programmers and not for end users, and we could not see how to provide a user interface to such a framework. An interface based on Toma is much less complex to provide and target also end users who are not programmers.

3.2   A TOMATO is a Composite and a Skin

A TOMATO is a Composite[3] as it can contain any of the other TopiObjects - TOMECs, TOMATOs and Content Generators (Content Generators are explained hereafter in section 3.3). It is also a Skin[4] as it defines the way that knowledge is presented while the knowledge itself is kept separately in the topic map.

A TOMATO (**TO**pic **MA**p **T**emplate **O**bject) is a template which can contain text, the usual MS Word objects and, in addition, can contain TopiObjects such as TOMECs, other TOMATOs and Content Generators. However, the configuration of the contained objects is done in one place by configuring the TOMATO itself. That is, the parameters of the TOMATO are the distinct union of the parameters of all the contained TopiObjects. For example, if a TOMATO contains two TOMECs which refer to the same parameter, those two TOMECs are configured only once in the TOMATO, by configuring that common parameter. This way, we can create a TOMATO that contains, for example, TOMECs holding the name, description and address of a company. Afterwards, instances of this TOMATO can be configured in different locations in the document to present different companies, in a standard manner.

As with TOMECs, unconfigured TOMATOs can also be kept as templates. Later, these templates can be used to instantiate TOMATO instances in different places in the document.

After a TOMATO is instantiated, it can be edited. The user can keep the changes to the TOMATO in the template of that TOMATO, or as a new template. On the other hand, the user can choose to get rid of those changes by re-instantiating the TOMATO again from the original template.

TOMATOs, therefore, let us reuse document structures in addition to the ability of generating text from the knowledge kept in the topic map.

3.3   A Content Generator is a Sequential TOMATO

A Content Generator is a TOMATO wherein one parameter expands to a sequence.

As explained above, a TOMATO has parameters which are the distinct union of all the parameters of the contained TopiObjects. Each of these parameters can

---

[6] TMML - **T**opic **M**ap **M**anipulation **L**anguage.

be configured to a scalar value - that is, an id of a topic. A Content Generator is a TOMATO where one of its parameters is configured to be a sequence of topic ids.

For example, one can extend a TOMATO which describes a company by including it inside a Content Generator. In this way a topic id which represents a specific company can be extended to a sequence of topic ids by defining a Toma query which selects, for example, all the companies:

```
select $topic.id where $topic.type = 'company';
```

When the Content Generator is instantiated, multiple configured TOMATOs are added automatically to the document. Each contains the name, description and address of a different company in that sequence.

A Content Generator provides additional features which help the user manage these kinds of sequences. Adding or deleting items in the sequence can be managed from within the word processor. In the example above, adding a new company topic can be done by adding a new item to the Content Generator. By correctly defining the Content Generator, the new topic will automatically receive the right type, and can automatically be associated to other topics.

With Content Generators, TopiWriter becomes a Topic Map reporting tool that can generate documents by going over sequences of topics.

Moreover, by using Content Generators, the author can create a skeleton representation of the topic map in a document and afterwards author the document, hence populate the topic map, in a clear sequential way. For example, the user might create a topic map with empty topics, each representing a company. Then the user can list all those topics in a document using a Content Generator and edit the TOMECs to add the description and the address of each company.

3.4   Constraints in All Their Glory

The Topic Maps technology includes the concept of constraints - the ability to define, for example, that each topic of type *device* will be associated with a topic of type *location* and will have an occurrence of type *mass* and an occurrence of type *dimension*.

When authoring a document using TopiWriter, the author can define a TOMATO and then define constraints to ensure that the TOMATO will be populated correctly. The constraints are defined using the Topic Maps editor (TopiMaker), which is integrated with TopiWriter. When a constraint is broken, the user is shown which topic, and if available, which TOMEC is at fault. This way the constraints contribute to the consistency and completeness of the resulting document.

4   Conclusion

Integrating Topic Maps technology into a word processor is a novel and maybe revolutionary usage of the technology. Not only does it bring the Topic Maps promise to new users - document authors, it also provides extra tools for authoring Topic Maps.

Acknowledgment. The TopiWriter project has been developed by Space Applications Services as a co-funded activity with the European Space Agency (ESA contract number 19077/05/NL/PG).

References

1. Pinchuk R.: Toma - TMQL, TMML, TMCL. Procs. of TMRA 2006, this volume (2007).
2. Common Topic Map Application Programming Interface, http://tmapi.org/
3. Gamma E., Helm R., Johnson R., Vlissides J.: Design Patterns, Elements of Reusable Object-Oriented Software. 1st edn. Addison-Wesley Publishing Co. (1995) 163–174
4. Pinchuk R., Sharon Y.: The Skin Design Pattern. PLoP^{TM}2000, USA http://jerry.cs.uiuc.edu/plop/plop2k/proceedings/Sharon/Sharon.pdf

Synchronizing Topic Maps with External Sources

Lars Marius Garshol

Ontopia AS, Oslo, Norway
larsga@ontopia.net
http://www.ontopia.net

Abstract. Topic Maps hold out great promise as a way to simplify data integration and presenting an easy-to-use interface to integrated data sets. Through merging, it is easy to build an integrated data set; the challenge is keeping the merged data set up to date.

This paper provides a procedure by which a subset of one topic map can be automatically synchronized by a subset of another topic map, in such a way that all updates to the source topic map will make their way into the target topic map. The procedure is flexible, and can meet a large variety of use cases. This effectively solves the update problem in a generalized way.

1 Introduction

Topic Maps are being used in a variety of different kinds of applications today, and it is very common for parts of the information in topic maps used in applications to originate in external systems. The information will in most cases continue to be maintained in the original system, which means that the Topic Maps application will need to be updated automatically as the data in the external system changes.

Normal conversion and merging, however, would only be sufficient if the topic map only contained information from external systems. However, in most cases the topic map is modified directly by human beings, which means that it is necessary to update the parts of the topic map that originate externally while leaving the other parts unchanged. This, however, generally requires substantial amounts of custom programming.

This paper describes a generalized mechanism for synchronizing a subset of a topic map against a subset of another topic map. The subsets to be updated must be specified by the user, while the algorithm itself is independent of these specifications. This makes the algorithm very general, and suitable for a large range of use cases and situations. The full, general mechanism can be relatively complex to use, but a number of default options exist that can in many cases remove the need for any configuration at all.

The algorithm is deliberately limited to the case where the external data source is also a topic map. It is still possible to use the algorithm when the external data source is not a topic map, provided a Topic Maps view of the data source exists. As a result the algorithm should be able to handle the vast ma jority of synchronization needs.

L. Maicher, A. Sigel, and L.M. Garshol (Eds.): TMRA 2006, LNAI 4438, pp. 192–199, 2007.

1.1   Algorithm Overview

The basic TMSync algorithm is quite simple. It takes two topic maps known as S and T , where S is the source topic map and T is the target topic map. After each application of the algorithm T should informally be a superset of S.

The algorithm runs as follows: Extract the subset of topics in T for which S is the source (known as t_T), and compare it with the set of topics in S (known as t_S). Any topics in t_T but not t_S must be deleted. Any topics in t_S but not t_T must be created, and all characteristics copied over. This leaves the topics in both sets, where in each case the subset of characteristics for which S is the source is extracted from the target topic, and then synchronized in a similar way against those from the source topic.

This is the entire algorithm, informally understood. What makes it applicable to most real-world uses is the use of subsets against which to synchronize, and that it allows the subsets to be specified by the user of the algorithm.

1.2   An Example

An example may make both the applications of the algorithm as well as the algorithm itself more understandable. Imagine a Topic Maps-based web portal containing articles classified against a taxonomy. The taxonomy is maintained as a topic map by an external authority outside the organization that owns the portal. The challenge is to enable the portal's topic map to remain in sync with the taxonomy while at the same time allowing the portal topic map to be updated independently.

Figure 1 shows a simple sketch of the portal topic map, where "transport", "subway", and "bus" are categories from the taxonomy and the two articles are specific to the portal.

Synchronization is done by including only the topics of type category in the subset of the target topic map to be synchronized. This ensures that articles are left alone, even though they do not exist in the source topic map. Similarly, only the names and "broader-narrower" associations are included in the subset of characteristics to be synchronized. This ensures that the "is-about" associations are retained despite not being found in the source topic map.

Finally, the deletion algorithm used (which deletes all associations in which a topic participates) ensures that when a category is removed from the taxonomy

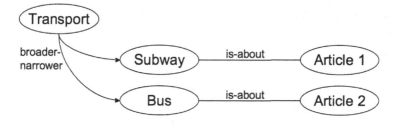

Fig. 1. Ontology sketch

all "is-about" associations to articles classified against that category are also removed.

2   The Update Algorithm

In order to define the algorithm formally a formal model for Topic Maps is needed. The definition given here uses the TMRM [Barta06] and the TMDM mapping to it currently being defined by ISO [Garshol07]. The update algorithm itself is mathematically a function of six parameters: $u(T, S, t_S, t_T, c_S, c_T)$ which produces the updated topic map. The T and S parameters are the target and source topic maps, respectively, while the t functions select the subsets of topics to be synchronized on either side, and the c functions select the characteristics to be synchronized.

2.1   Background

The TMDM mapping to TMRM [Garshol07] has not yet been published, and so an overview of it is presented here. It uses normal set and tuple syntax to represent proxies and properties. It also uses + to represent required and repeatable properties, * for optional and repeatable properties, and ? for optional properties.

The TMRM representation of TMDM primarily consists of proxies representing either topics or statements. (Statements in TMDM are associations, occurrences, topic names, and variants.)

Statements. The proxies for statements have the following form:

```
{(type,      ____),
 (scope,     ____),
 (roletype1, ____),
 (roletype2, ____),
 ...}
```

Of course, topic names, occurrences, and variants don't have role types in TMDM, but in this representation they have been extended so that they do.

The statements for occurrences take the following form:

```
{(type,     ____),
 (scope,    ____),
 (subject,  ____),
 (resource, ____)}
```

The value of `subject` is here the topic the occurrence is attached to, and `resource` is the actual occurrence.

The statements for topic names take the following form:

```
{(type,     ____),
 (scope,    ____),
 (subject,  ____),
 (value,    ____)}
```

Again, the `subject` is the topic, and `value` is the actual name.
The statements for variant names take the following form:

```
{(type,     variant),
 (scope,    ____),
 (subject,  ____),
 (value,    ____)}
```

Here the `subject` is the topic name the variant is attached to. The `type` is hard-wired because variant names do not have any type, and we need to identify this somehow as being a variant.

Supporting machinery. In addition, a function $topics(M)$ is defined which finds all topic proxies in a given map. The function is defined as follows:
$$topics(M) = \{x | x \in M \wedge x \downarrow \cap \{itemid, subjid, subjloc\} \neq \emptyset\}$$

2.2 Translation

An issue in the specification of the algorithm is that the topic proxies for the same subjects in the source and target topic maps need not be equal. This is because it can happen that the topic proxy in the source topic map is, say, $\{(subjid, a), (subjid, b)\}$, while that in the target topic map is $\{(subjid, a), (subjid, c)\}$. That is, the target and the source need not have the same identifiers, they need only share a common subset of identifiers.

This makes it very difficult to specify the update algorithm directly, as equivalent proxies in the source and target topic maps need not be equal, which again implies that the normal set operations are not sufficient. The solution is to first translate the source and target topic maps into new topic maps where equivalent proxies are guaranteed to be equal.

To be able to do this we need to define what it means for two topic proxies to be equivalent, which we do by defining the $\sim$ relation, as follows:
$$t \sim s \Leftrightarrow t \cap s \neq \emptyset$$
There are different translation functions for different kinds of proxies. The following function translates topic proxies:
$$\theta_t(t, M) = \left(\bigcup_{x \in \{t' \in M | t' \sim t\}} x \right) \cup t$$
The following function translates all other types of proxies:
$$\theta_c(c, M) = \{(k, v) | \exists (k', v') \in c \wedge k = \theta_*(k', M) \wedge v = \theta_*(v', M)\}$$

Using these we can define the general translation function, which works for all values that can appear in a map:
$$\theta_*(x, M) = \begin{cases} \theta_t(x, M) & x \in topics(M) \\ x & x \in \mathcal{V} \\ \theta_c(x, M) & otherwise \end{cases}$$

Given this we can now define the translation function for entire topic maps as follows:

$$\theta_m(T, S) = \{x | \exists x' \in S \land x \in \theta_*(x', T)\}$$

From now on we will refer to T' as $T' = \theta_m(S, T)$ and S' as $S' = \theta_m(T, S)$.

2.3 Additional Functions

We are still not quite ready to formulate the algorithm, as we need some more supporting functions first. These should eventually be replaced with TMRM path expressions, but these are not fully stable yet, and so we instead make this paper self-contained by defining some additional functions here.

We need an operator which given a general TMRM proxy produces all values in the proxy for all keys. TMRM only defines this operator for specific keys, and so we define a more general version here.

$$t \to * = \{v | \exists (k, v) \in x\}$$

The following function produces all statements about a given topic. This includes its names, occurrences, and the associations in which it participates.

$$s(t, M) = \{x \in M | t \in x \to *\}$$

The following function produces all statements about all topics in a set:

$$s_*(T, M) = \{x | \exists t \in T : x \in s(t, M)\}$$

2.4 The Algorithm

We are now ready to formulate the algorithm itself. The output of the function is essentially the union of five different sets minus the statements about deleted topics. (By "deleted" we mean topics that are in the synchronized subset of T, but which are no longer in S.) The five sets in question are:

- Topics in T that are not synchronized.
- Statements about these.
- Topics in T that are synchronized, and which are in S.
- Unsynchronized statements about these from T.
- Synchronized statements about these from S.

Below is the corresponding formal definition of the algorithm, where the order of the five first lines of the definition match the order in the list above, for ease of comprehension.

$$\begin{aligned}
u(T, S, t_T, t_S, c_T, c_S) = & (topics(T') - t_T(T') \cup \\
& c_*(topics(T') - t_T(T')) \cup \\
& t_S(S') \cup \\
& c_*(t_T(T')) - \{x | \exists t \in t_T(T') : x \in c_T(t)\} \cup \\
& \{x | t \in t_S(S') : x \in c_S(t)\}) - \\
& c_*(t_T(T') - t_S(S'), T')
\end{aligned}$$

2.5 Observations

One obvious constraint on u is that if we are updating the entire target topic map against the entire source topic map the result afterwards must be the translated source topic map. This is because there is nothing in the target topic map that is not synchronized, and nothing in the source topic map that is not included.

Formally, if c is the function that returns all characteristics of a topic, then the following equation must hold:

$$u(T, S, topics, topics, c, c) = S$$

It is relatively simple to see that u as formulated above satisfies this constraint.

3 Practical Use

In order to use this algorithm in practice implementations will need to be provided with the six parameters of the u function in some way. In addition, they will need to be configured to apply updates at preconfigured intervals, or when the source data is known to have changed. Specifying T should be easy in any Topic Maps system, and S may in many cases simply be specified as the URL (or web service endpoint) from which the updated topic map in XTM format can be retrieved from. The specification of the four last parameters can simply be done either as TMQL query expressions, or as sets of types.

3.1 The Example Use Case

The example use case in 1.2 on page 193 can be solved quite simply, if we assume that the taxonomy is published in XTM at a fixed URL. The four remaining parameters can then easily be given as follows:

- t_T is defined using a query that selects all instances of category.
- t_S is defined the same way. (This avoids including ontology topics, which most likely have more information attached to them in T than in S, and for which we do not want updates.)
- c_T is defined using a query that selects all names, all occurrences, and all associations except the "is-about" ones.
- c_S is defined as a query which selects all characteristics.

This means that whenever any of the following changes occur in S they will be correctly transferred into T:

- A new category is added as a leaf. This requires discovering the new topic and its name and association.
- A leaf category is deleted. This requires detecting the deletion, and removing all statements about the category.
- A category is moved from one parent to another. This requires detecting that the category's "broader-narrower" association has changed.
- A category has changed its name.

Other changes are possible, but they are likely to consist of an accumulation of changes like the above over time, since most changes to classification systems are quite conservative. However, more dramatic changes should also be transferred correctly.

3.2 Extending the Example

In practice, the portal would most likely want to be able to extend the taxonomy by adding new categories, but while still retaining the ability to get remote updates. The algorithm can deal with this additional complication easily provided that locally created categories are marked (for example with a unary association stating "is-created-locally"). If this is the case, the only thing that needs to change in the configuration is t_T, where the query must now select only topics of type "category" which do not have the "is-created-locally" association.

The only potential problem that can occur in this situation is that a category is deleted from the external taxonomy which has locally created sub-categories in the portal topic map. In this case the system will have orphan categories. This is best handled by periodically doing a query for such categories to warn the editors of their existence so they can update the topic map accordingly.

3.3 Performance

The main problem with the algorithm as currently specified is that it is necessary to scan both tT (T) and tS (S) fully. In other words, it is necessary for the algorithm to scan the entire data set in order to work out what the changes are. This approach will only be able to handle data sets of limited sizes.

Further work is necessary in order to design an approach that avoid the full scan and only look at topics which really have changed. This can be achieved by means of timestamps on changed topics in S (for creations and updates) and by means of an external list of deleted topics in S . However, although this is known, more work is necessary to create a full formal description of this algorithm.

4 Related Work

The author is not aware of any related work on Topic Maps, but there exists a synchronization algorithm for RDF, known as RDFSync [Tummarello06]. However, RDFSync differs in that it does not address the problem of updating only a subset of the target data set, which is the key to the utility of the approach proposed in this paper.

Similarly, many synchronization algorithms exist outside the domain of semantic technologies, but again the author knows of none that specifically address the issue of updating just a subset of the target data set.

References

[Barta06]   R. Barta, P. Durusau, S. Newcomb, The Topic Maps Reference
                Model, ISO working document, SC34 document repository, N0710,
                2006-02-26. URL `http://www.jtc1sc34.org/repository/0710.pdf`
[Garshol07]   L. M. Garshol, TMDM mapping to TMRM, ISO working document,
                SC34 document repository, currently being written.
[Tummarello06] Tummarello, Giovanni; Morbidoni, Christian: *RDFSync*, Università
                Politecnica delle Marche wiki: http://semedia.deit.univpm.it/tiki-
                index.php?page=RdfSync

Tagomizer: Subject Maps Meet Social Bookmarking

Jack Park

SRI International
jack.park@sri.com

All the world's a stage. –Shakespeare

Abstract. The CALO project at SRI International offers a unique opportunity to explore the boundaries of knowledge representation and organization in a learning environment. One goal is to develop methods for learning in the wild, the accretion of new knowledge by combinations of machine learning and recorded social gestures. Social bookmarking provides one kind of recorded social gesture that, when combined with machine learning techniques, avail learning in the wild opportunities. We explore the informal ontologies of social bookmarking processes as recorded in a subject map. We apply the same thinking to federation of formal ontologies. We will illustrate the opportunities gained through subject-centric knowledge representation and organization. In the larger picture, we are exploring techniques for federation of heterogeneous world views.

1 Background

SRI's CALO project is one of two projects funded under DARPA's "Perceptive Assistant that Learns" (PAL) program. The goal of the PAL program is to develop an enduring personal assistant that "learns in the wild" (LITW), evolving its capabilities as a personal assistant more and more through automated machine learning techniques rather than through code changes. We created Tagomizer to facilitate LITW for CALO and the program's users by installing a social bookmarking application designed specifically to interoperate with CALO through a web services interface. Tagomizer behaves in ways similar to the website known as "delicious", where, as described below, users create bookmarks using tags. A tag can be a word or word phrase. In the future, a tag could be, say, a Wikipedia URL, an image, or other symbol that serves the purpose. When a particular user tags (bookmarks, as explained below) some website and notices that others have also tagged the same website, one opportunity for LITW occurs when that user visits the bookmarks of others. The opportunity for learning is predicated on similarities in thinking patterns among users and the fact that some users might bookmark websites unknown to others. In this paper, we describe Tagomizer, subject maps, knowledge representation, and federation of knowledge through subject maps. We will show that LITW can be facilitated by what we call wormholes. We will show that wormholes emerge when subject-centric federation of different world views brings together ideas expressed in different world models. In some sense, subject-centric federation is a natural process inherent in social bookmarking websites.

Tagomizer is built as an application of a subject map. The term "subject map" refers to the name given to implementations of the Topic Maps Reference Model

L. Maicher, A. Sigel, and L.M. Garshol (Eds.): TMRA 2006, LNAI 4438, pp. 200–214, 2007.
© Springer-Verlag Berlin Heidelberg 2007

(TMRM). Subject maps have been claimed to add value to traditional knowledge representation (KR) methodology. Such claims call for proper explanation and justification. This paper sets out, by means of an explanatory use case, to articulate such claims and lay a foundation on which justifications can be built. Those claims, and their foundations, are not inventions of imagination; there is a rich history, a vision, if you wish, behind this work. In this paper, we will articulate some claims for the TMRM as we see them, and those claims will be discussed in light of the Tagomizer project.

The entire world is a stage; perhaps important portions of that stage can be federated. We believe federation is possible using subject maps; this belief is based on our past work [1], [2], much of which was based on frame or rule-based artificial intelligence (AI) systems. Later, during participation on the XTM authoring group, part of a dream came into focus; the indexical and organizational aspects of knowledge work would come together through topic maps. Most recently, subject maps, a new view into the topic mapping paradigm, offered the opportunity to seamlessly integrate— now called federate as discussed here—the work products of many people. There are obvious parallels in this work to that of the KR community that we will explore here in the light of subject-centric merging.

In this paper we describe a novel process of federation of representations of knowledge. We will first sketch an approach to the comparison of subject mapping to traditional KR techniques, and introduce Tagomizer as a focal point of our federation discussion. We then describe TopicSpaces as an instance of a subject map provider. We then discuss subject-centric federation of ontologies, and compare our work to some aspects of knowledge representation.

2 A Context for Discussion of Subject Mapping and Knowledge Representation

When comparing subject mapping to traditional KR methodologies for performing knowledge organization and representation, consider that there are at least two separate dimensions along which discussions occur, and from which the scenario presented here grows. At the most abstract level, I believe the two primary dimensions are

- Discussions of Problem-solving systems (i.e., question answering)
- Discussions of Understanding systems (i.e., federations of disparate world views)

Problem-solving systems are well known among the important work going on in the AI and KR communities. Understanding systems might be thought to be a subclass of problem-solving systems, and they can very well be modeled as such. For now, we think of these two separately.

An illustrative sketch: if one explores online resources with a personal medical problem in mind, a goal might be to find a diagnosis of symptoms entered into an online query form. That would be a problem-solving scenario where one is most interested in ridding oneself of some visitation, really just looking for a diagnosis and prescription. Another mindset, one frequently the case for students, curious people, and others, is that of understanding the field. A description of symptoms might lead to links to a variety of resources, some of which include research reports, books on medical topics, and other resources aimed at deriving deep understandings of the nature of a visitation. In this scenario, one might be less interested in a single, thought to be accurate answer to a question, and more interested in a range of world views. There is ample reason to believe that both mindsets are important and worthy of continued inquiry. Humans will always need answers and they will need understandings to go with those answers.

Aligned with the understanding dimension, it is valuable to find ways in which heterogeneous world views, as expressed in database schema, ontologies, stories of all kinds, can be federated. We label this process subject-centric federation and define that term below.

A starting point for our work on semantic integration, interoperability, and federation, is the Open Knowledge Base Connectivity (OKBC) project. In [17], page 1, a statement is made that suggests opportunities for future innovation:

> "The interoperability achieved by using OKBC is at the level of the OKBC knowledge model. For example, the OKBC knowledge model defines the concept of a class that has the same interpretation across all OKBC bindings. OKBC does not guarantee, however, that a particular class (e.g. Person) defined in the KBs residing in two different KRSs represents identical concepts."

The subject mapping paradigm takes conventions and practices such as OKBC as starting points and seeks to evolve means with which classes residing in different KBs expressed as subject maps can be compared for identity equality.

This paper lays out an illustrative example, and looks at related work, all of which supports a particular set of claims. The claims are these:

1. Subject-centric federation of heterogeneous information resources is useful and appropriate for understanding (as compared to specific question answering).
2. Subject-centric federation requires close attention to the details of subject identity and to the rules or axioms appropriate to merging same-subject resources.
3. Subject-centric federation leaves intact the messages or representations available in each federated resource.
4. Subject-centric federation is not a process of deriving semantic equivalence among federated resources; it is possible to federate resources that carry contradictory messages.
5. Subject maps, the paradigm, provide a working framework on which subject-centric federation can be facilitated.
6. Subject maps are an extension of any of a variety of traditional, well-developed KR methods.

We now turn to an illustrative use case, and build on that to describe subject-centric federation.

3 Tagomizer—Informal Ontology Federation

Tagomizer is a social bookmarking application implemented as an application of TopicSpaces , an open source Java implementation of the TMRM. Tagomizer exists as a test-bed for exercises in learning in the wild experiments with the CALO project at SRI. Figure 1 shows some of the author's bookmarks at Tagomizer.

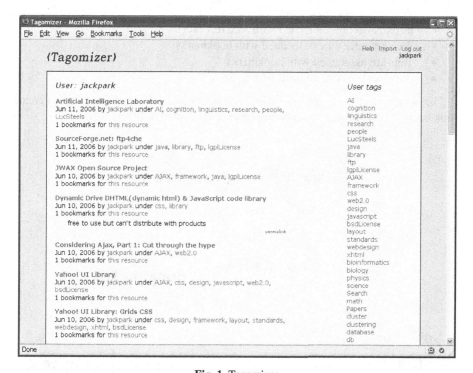

Fig. 1. Tagomizer

3.1 Social Bookmarking

Social bookmarking is facilitated through web-based portals that accept user-created tags in relation to specific web resources. Web resources are identified by the URL and by a brief descriptor of the resource (web page). Users link tags, typically in the form of single words or multiple-word phrases, to web resources through the medium of a bookmark. Thus, the ontology involved in social bookmarking includes the following ontology classes:

- Users
- Web resources
- Tags
- Bookmarks

The relationships entailed by the bookmarking process include

- Users create bookmarks
- Bookmarks are created by users
- Users create tags
- Tags are created by users
- Users select web resources to bookmark
- Web resources are selected by users
- Bookmarks are associated with web resources
- Web resources are associated with bookmarks
- Tags are associated with bookmarks
- Bookmarks are associated with tags

The subject map represents a variety of classes and relationships as users create bookmarks. These classes and relationships are illustrated in Figure 2

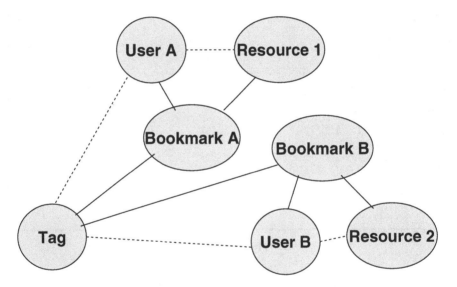

Fig. 2. Generalized View of Social Bookmarking

The process of social bookmarking typically follows these sequential events:

1. User visits a webpage
2. User decides to "bookmark" the page
3. User applies a bookmarklet to transport the chosen webpage and a brief description of it (the page's title and URL) to Tagomizer
4. At Tagomizer, user assigns some tags to the bookmark to serve as reminders for later search and retrieval, and as community links through those tags

In this scenario, there are several subjects at play. Those subjects are associated with the following:

- The created bookmark itself, which is identified by the pair: <user identity, bookmarked resource identity>
- The bookmarked resource itself, which is identified by its URL
- The tags themselves
- The user as a particular individual

To that list of subjects, we must consider other subjects. For instance, the user's intentions, as expressed in the choice of tags assigned to a bookmark, can imply other semantics, other subjects at play. The list of subjects grows.

- The subject(s) of the bookmarked resource; the intentions of the bookmarked resource are found in the subjects presented there.
- Implied semantics of the tags. Some tags might be simple random choices of words or phrases to suit the whims of individual users. Other tags might serve some intended ontology.

Given that there are subjects covered in the bookmarked resources that, in some cases, are reflected in potential semantics of tag names used, construction of a social bookmarking portal using the subject-centric representation system of subject maps has the advantage of providing a uniform framework into which additional subjects can be harvested and represented. To fill out this picture, consider, for instance, Resource 1 in Figure 2. Let us substitute some "real" values. Resource 1 is actually Matthew West's publications page . Of course, the lone tag in Figure 2 might be named, say "ISO18876". If that tag happens to carry a semantic meaning associated with those publications, then we might expect that Resource 2 just happens to be another resource that also deals with the same standard (Figure 3). Choice of tag names can have significant payoff as taggers evolve languages of reminding through semantic ties with the subjects they tag.

As Figure 3 illustrates, the specific subject of ISO 18876 appears in the graph. We will say, for illustration, that this subject was first harvested from Resource 1, then found to be one of possibly several subjects in Resource 2. We are able to surmise, again for purposes of illustration, that User A made the first tie through the tag to the ISO standard, and User B later found a different resource that covers the same subject (the ISO standard) implied by the tag; the tag was reused by User B to remind of the same subject.

By any of several means, it is possible to harvest new subjects from bookmarked resources. Harvesting methods include

- Fully automated harvesting using combinations of indexing, clustering, and text analysis tools
- Human-entered subjects by means of New Subject forms, perhaps along the lines of Wikipedia creation of new chapters
- Combinations of automated harvesting of subjects coupled with human refinement of subject identity properties, that is, collaborative filtering of harvested subjects.

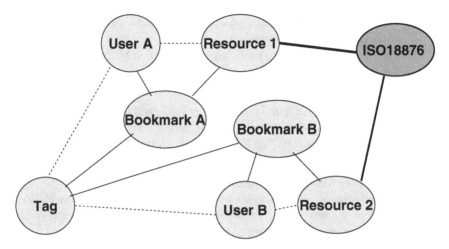

Fig. 3. Adding Subjects

Each new subject added to a growing subject map becomes, itself, a binding point for further harvesting, linking to other bookmarks and to resources not yet book-marked.

In the Tagomizer example, it can be said that some level of federation of the world views of users is happening through the semantics of tags chosen. Consider the case where User A notices that User B used the same tag to bookmark a related resource. There is a hint that User B might be thinking along the same or closely related lines of inquiry, so it might be useful to explore User B's other bookmarks. This is an instance of learning in the wild; in some sense, a wormhole has been opened between User A and the universe of thoughts of User B just through that single tag, which is a particu-lar subject in a subject map. In some sense, the personal ontologies of User A and User B were merged at that tag. User B, of course, enjoys the same opportunity to explore User A's bookmarks. We have more to say about wormholes below.

4 TopicSpaces—A Subject Map Provider

Figure 4 provides an architectural overview of TopicSpaces. TopicSpaces is a subject map provider (SMP) based on the TMRM, with a legend that specifies a kind of upper ontology that permits the creation of a range of subject maps, including those that can federate ontologies. The SMP includes a set of agents, each of which is engaged in some specific task. Tasks include subject-centric merging within the subject map, web harvesting to locate additional information related to specific subjects, and to provide content management services. We turn now to a sketch of how TopicSpaces repre-sents knowledge. We will show that the TMRM allows us to view KR in light of well-understood principles of frame-based methodologies. The TMRM dispenses with a predefined commitment to the ontology of XTM or the TMDM , and is neutral in terms of the means by which any subject map is constructed, so long as certain disclo-sure requirements are met.

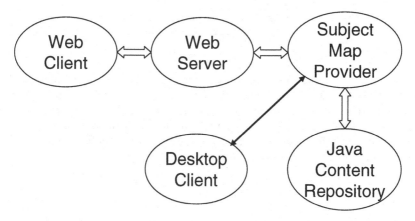

Fig. 4. TopicSpaces Architecture

4.1 Frame-Based KR in TopicSpaces

We provide a brief sketch of frame-based KR in order to establish working visual and textual vocabularies with which to describe subject-centric KR and to explore federation of world views. This discussion applies directly to the representation system implemented in TopicSpaces. In this discussion, the terms subject map and knowledge base are considered interchangeable.

In the most general terms, the objects (entities, concepts,...) of any universe of discourse are represented by statements describing properties (also called attributes) of the object, and the values those properties take. For instance, a particular person will have a name, a birth date, and various other properties, each of which has one or more values, depending on the type of the property.

Most KR projects take place within the context of some means by which the representative artifacts are persisted in some database. For that reason, there is another property of each object in the universe that is the identity of that object within the database. We call that property a locator and the value of that property must be unique at least within the database. We now describe a fragment of a knowledge base that contains entries regarding a particular person, and we will do so in a stylized frame-like representation. We will also represent a fragment of a taxonomy as it might appear in a real knowledge base. We first define three frames, one to establish a descriptor of a class of entities, and one to describe a subclass, and one to describe a particular instance of that subclass. Each frame contains properties and their values, also called slots. Slot values starting with "#" are local references to other frames within the database.

```
locator:    123455
   name:    Class
    psi:    http://www.topicspaces.org/psi#Class

locator:    123456
   name:        Person
   subClassOf:  #123455
```

```
locator: 58989859
  name:            Susan Sixpack
  instanceOf:      #123456
  birthdate:       01/21/1988
```

In each of these frames, the properties of the object, called slots, are noted by being indented from the base frame locator. In some frame notations, it is possible to express meta-properties, or properties of the properties. Typical meta-properties include cardinality of the slot, data types, domain, and range. There have been two distinct ways in which to define these meta-properties. One way is to define each slot with its own frame, as, for instance:

```
locator: 124767
name:              Slot

locator: 12469
  name:            date
  subClassOf:      #124767

locator: 124768
  name:            birthdate
  subClassOf:      #124767
  valueType:       #12469
```

Another approach has been to apply metadata directly to the slot, called facets. Let us illustrate facets by adding facets to the Susan Sixpack frame:

```
locator: 8989
  name:            marriedName

locator: 8990
  name:            maidenName

locator: 58989859
  name:            Susan Sixpack
    nameType:      #8989
  name:            Susan Jones
    nameType:      #8990
  instanceOf:      #123456
  birthdate:       01/21/1988
```

In this illustration, we note that this individual has two different names, the name she was given at birth, and the name she chose to take when she married. To establish a working vocabulary for this discussion, we call this particular kind of metadata scopes. Thus, we have scoped her two names with the context in which they are valid. Topic-Spaces applies this same representation scheme to the construction of subject maps.

4.2   Subject-Centric KR in TopicSpaces

Subject-centric KR posits that all entities existing within a particular universe of discourse are subjects. In the social bookmarking use case, the four enumerated classes are subjects, and each of the relationship kinds is also a subject. Each instance of each class is also a subject as is any individual relationship formed between each two class instances. Treating each entity as a unique subject requires that we provide for the unambiguous identification of each subject in the universe. Since users will continue to add instances to those subjects through bookmarking processes, subject identity processing takes a central role in maintaining the integrity of the growing knowledge base.

Establishment of subject identity properties is a requirement of the TMRM. In the trivial example above, a legend might specify that, for females, maidenName and birthdate are sufficient subject identifiers. A merging rule would compare those two values for detection of subject sameness. The same legend would specify that a psi (published subject indicator) is sufficient for identity of ontology entities such as Class, psi, and birthdate. In a subject map, all properties (slot types, in this case) are declared as subjects themselves.

5 Subject-Centric Federation of Formal Ontologies

Here, we consider federation of formal ontologies, but the discussion applies equally as well to the informal world of Folksonomies and less formal means of expressing world views. Implicit in this discussion is a contrast with ontology integration or semantic integration in the traditional sense where semantic equivalence is a goal. To anticipate, the achievement of semantic equivalence is not a goal of ontology federation as discussed here.

Subject-centric federation of world views is defined as the process where heterogeneous world views are brought together "under the same umbrella" (to use a metaphor). Federation involves this bringing together, and subject-centric federation demands that, where elements of different world views can be shown to be representations of the same subject, then those elements must be merged into a single knowledge base element that, alone, represents the particular subject, and that contains each of the merged statements in essentially its original voice. We use the term voice to mean that the re-representation process that occurs during merging does not alter the messages conveyed in the original representations.

In the simplest form of federation of two subjects, each representation (e.g., subject proxy, frame) is known to refer to the same subject, but each gave the subject a different name. Each representation is then merged into a single representation. If, for example, each representation is an ontology class from different ontologies, then each name in the merged representation is scoped to reference its source. In that manner, traceability to the original source is always preserved. Through that traceability, we say that wormholes emerge. Wormholes are hypothesized to be topological features in space-time that constitute a shortcut between regions. We believe that, when different world views are federated on a subject-by-subject basis, different stories captured in same-subject representations offer shortcuts, through scoping, out to other world views. Another way to look at federation is that of intersecting universes of discourse (Figure 5). The figure depicts scoping links into larger elements of each universe of discourse brought together in the subject proxy.

As far as subject maps are concerned, all elements of each universe of discourse are represented with subject proxies (Figure 6). That is, each element in an ontology is, in fact, imported into a subject map, where merging is performed on those subject proxies that are found to represent the same subject. In Figure 6, we see that the nodes labeled "C" and "N" happen to be merged, and wormholes out to nodes "D" and "M" are created.

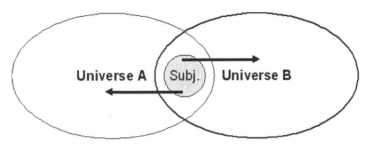

Fig. 5. Intersecting Universes

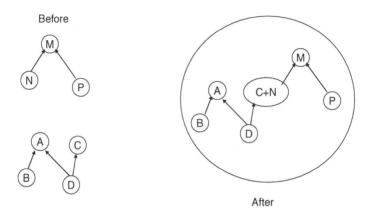

Fig. 6. Ontology Federation into a Subject Map

Following the import of several ontologies, it is reasonable to expect that disagreements will be voiced both for lack of merging where there is belief that two subjects are the same but which were not detected during merging, and where subjects were merged which are believed, by some, to not be representative of the same subject. New information always enters a universe of discourse when disagreements lead to thoughtful discussions. Any web portal assigned to federation of heterogeneous world views should be expected to facilitate thoughtful discussion and even revisions to the subject map where consensus is achieved.

Subject maps do not stand alone in the field of KR in the realm of semantic integration. We turn now to a look at work related to ours.

6   Related Work

We will draw from several references to understand relationships between the subject mapping contribution and prior and current work in the KR community. From those references, we can see that some workers are already following related paths where the nature of inquiry is closely aligned with understanding, and that some workers follow a path associated more closely with problem solving. We will see that many of the claims we are making have already been explored in past and in current work, in both the research and commercial worlds.

Knowledge federation on the web using topic maps is discussed in [14], where multiple topic map portals are interconnected. We first proposed our federation work in [3], "Just For Me: Topic Maps and Ontologies", related to our work on OpenIRIS as part of the CALO project. In [4], we present a vision, one among many, that articulates a mechanism for subject-centric federation of heterogeneous world views. In [5], Matthew West presents the results of his work with ISO 18876, co-extensive in history with ISO 13250 topic maps. I cast the 18876 work as a more-detailed look at both integration and federation. Subject-centric federation is not considered to be a process of integration, so aspects of ISO 18876 do not apply to the subject of this paper.

Our claim 2, that subject-centric federation calls for close attention to the details of subject identity, begs examination of subject identity practices in traditional KR. We find useful support in [6], "Object Co-identification on the Semantic Web":

> "For any two parties to exchange data about an object, they need to have a mutually comprehensible reference for that object. Common names (or URIs) are one kind of mutually comprehensible reference. Extant work on the Semantic web ([]) is based on the assumption that standardized ontologies will provide these common names, so that everyone can use the same name for everything. We believe that this assumption is overly optimistic."

The paper [6] then goes on to describe a kind of solution to the subject identity problem in the form of Discriminant Descriptions. A discriminant description is a formula constructed around keys and values. Opportunities for probabilistic matching are discussed.

In the commercial field, we find further interest in attention to subject identity. For instance, from [9]:

> "As we have seen, chunks of information that lack structure or have too rigid a structure tend to live in isolation, unable to discover and bond with others to create new information. What's required is a data-structure that provides unmistakable identity for every chunk of information but also facilitates flow and fusion."

We found evidence of interest in our claim 4 in the literature. From the abstract in [7], "Non-destructive Integration of Form-based Views":

> "The main idea of our approach is to keep the original views intact and to specify constraints between overlapping structures. For reasoning over constraints, we provide a set of inference rules that allows not only to infer implied constraints but also to detect conflicts."

A well-known dissertation in the AI field reveals the details of a system that appears to correctly anticipate, through implementation, some of our claims. Douglas Lenat's AM program [8] is an implementation of evolutionary programming techniques in a symbolic, frame-based system. For AM to "understand" the nature of concepts (frames) it would create, other classes (frames) were given slots that served as predicates to assess new concepts for subject sameness. These predicates served as an equivalent to the merge rules of claim 2.

The Harvard Law School has created H2O Playlist , a subject-centric tagging portal:

> "An H2O Playlist is a shared list of readings and other content about a
> topic of intellectual interest. It is a simple yet powerful way to group
> and exchange useful links to information–online and offline."

The process applied to tagging at H2O is slightly different from that of social bookmarking described above. At H2O, a user creates a "playlist" with a name, description, and some tags. The tags serve as reminders for search just as they do in other social bookmarking portals. The difference appears to lie in the fact that a subject-centric playlist is created, a binding point for bookmarks against the subject described by the playlist. In some sense, H2O Playlist appears to start with my Figure 3 above, where the subjects for which resources are to be bookmarked have been predefined. With Tagomizer, one can surmise that users who begin tagging as in Figure 2 already have in mind a particular subject and choose their tags accordingly. H2O appears to turn the tables and ask that the subject be declared first, together with tags appropriate to that subject. In the CALO exercise, users will mostly tag with specific tasks in mind.

Projects exist where tags are created automatically, and where creation of a subject for bookmarking is facilitated. Automated generation of tags based on semantic analysis of nouns extracted from web pages is the subject of a paper [10] "Browsing System for Weblog Articles based on Automated Folksonomy". Bookmarking with Annotea is discussed in [11], "Scenario: Organizing CML cancer research knowledge by using Annotea shared bookmarks", where methods are presented for de novo creation of topics to which bookmarks are associated.

The ScholOnto project [16] is an instance of semantic annotation worthy of comparison to social bookmarking. The project covers a wide range of technologies associated with annotation of research documents. The annotations made and the organizational means for marshaling those annotations are remarkably similar to social bookmarking with subject maps. From the project's website:

> "The ScholOnto Project is a 3 year effort (2001-2004) to build and deploy
> a prototype infrastructure for making scholarly claims about the signifi-
> cance of research documents. 'Claims' are made by making connections
> between ideas. Any claim is of course open to counterarguments. The
> connections are grounded in a discourse/argumentation ontology, which
> makes possible innovative services for navigating, visualizing and analyz-
> ing the network as it grows."

Outside the scope of this paper is the work associated with question answering and knowledge integration. Richard Fikes talks [12] about semantic integration associated with the Chimaera project at Stanford. Ken Murray produced a dissertation [13] on machine learning techniques in knowledge integration. Since we are not addressing the quest for semantic equivalence in federation, we mention those papers as representative of the semantic integration field.

7 Discussion

What is it in our claim set that constitutes a contribution to a vast and maturing knowledge representation community? A candidate answer to that question is to be found in the attention paid by the subject mapping paradigm to the details associated with subject identity. The attention to details is expressed in two separate ways

- Availability of any number of subject identity properties for identification
- No limits on means by which those subject identity properties can be used in merging processes

Closest to our claims is the Guha discussion [6] that articulates a means by which keys can be evaluated through discriminant descriptions and probabilistic tools. The TMRM is an abstract specification that leaves room for the application of a wide range of existing and new techniques for creation of subject identity properties and merging rules. Indeed, discriminant descriptions, conceptual graphs, any number of different frame-based representation schemes can satisfy the TMRM.

Is anything new proposed by the TMRM and our claims? Given that past and current work in KR already implements many of the claims, perhaps that which is new can be expressed in the core tenet of the TMRM itself, that the means by which subjects are to be identified in a given subject map must be disclosed, and that the ways in which representatives of subjects will be evaluated for subject sameness with other subject proxies must also be disclosed. The TMRM has named the document for disclosure a legend.

Tagomizer provides a platform for LITW explorations with CALO. Tagging of information resources turns those resources into knowledge assets through the process of attaching indexed symbols to the resources, and through semantic interpretations of those symbols. Taking queues from the ScholOnto playbook, it should be possible to extend Tagomizer into critical areas of human activities such as project management and design.

Acknowledgments

This work was supported by the Defense Advanced Research Projects Agency (DARPA) under Contract No. NBCHD030010. Any opinions, findings, and conclusions or recommendations expressed in this material are those of the authors and do not necessarily reflect the views of DARPA or the Department of Interior-National Business Center (DOI-NBC).

This work has benefited greatly from interactions with Patrick Durusau, Steve Newcomb, Vinay Chaudhri, Adam Cheyer, Simon Buckingham Shum, Douglas Bowden, Glen Haydon, Richard Fikes, Joshua Levy, Eric Yeh, and Mark Szpakowski. Joshua Levy collaborated on the design and fabrication of Tagomizer, and contributed the javascript web services interface to Tagomizer. Colin Evans has contributed to the TopicSpaces project.

References

[1] Abrams, Frances, Patrick Garrett, Thomas Lagnese, Steven LeClair, C. William Lee, and Jack Park, "Qualitative Process Automation for Autoclave Curing of Composites", AW-FAL-TR-87-4083, November 1987.
[2] Wood, Dan, and Jack Park, "Discovery Systems for Manufacturing", WL-TR-94-4008, January 1994.

[3] Park, Jack, and Adam Cheyer, "Just for Me: Topic Maps and Ontologies", in Lutz Ma-icher and Jack Park (Editors), Charting the Topic Maps Research and Applications Land-scape: First International Workshop on Topic Map Research and Applications, TMRA 2005, Leipzig, Germany, 6-7 October 2005, Revised Selected Papers, Springer LNCS Volume 3873/2006 pp. 145-159.

[4] Park, Jack, and Patrick Durusau, "Avoiding Hobson's Choice in Choosing an Ontology", teleconference to the Ontolog Community, 27 April 2006; http://ontolog.cim3.net/cgi-bin/wiki.pl?ConferenceCall_2006_04_27

[5] West, Matthew, "Integrating Data or Ontologies - A look at the ISO 18876 Architecture", teleconference to the Ontolog Community, 1 June 2006; http://ontolog.cim3.net/cgi-bin/wiki.pl?ConferenceCall_2006_06_01

[6] Guha, R., "Object Co-identification on the Semantic Web", http://tap.stanford.edu/CoIdent.pdf

[7] Hidders, Jan, Jan Paredaens, Philippe Thiran, Geert-Jan Houben, and Kees van Hee, "Non-destructive Integration of Form-based Views" in 9th East European Conference on Advances in Databases and Information Systems (ADBIS 2005); nr. 3631, pages 74–86, Springer.

[8] Lenat, D.B., "AM: An artificial intelligence approach to discovery in mathematics as heu-ristic search", Ph.D. Thesis, AIM-286, STAN-CS-76-570, and Heuristic Programming Project Report HPP-76-8, Stanford University, AI Lab., Stanford, CA.

[9] Harbor Research Inc. "Designing the Future of Information: The Internet Beyond the Web", A Harbor Whitepaper, September 2005; available at http://www.maya.com/web/infocommons/infocommons.mtml

[10] Ohkura , Tsutomu, Yoji Kiyota, and Hiroshi Nakagawa, "Browsing System for Weblog Articles based on Automated Folksonomy", 15th International World Wide Web Confer-ence, WWW2006, Edinburg Scottland, 23 May 2006.

[11] Koivunen, Marja-Riitta, "Scenario: Organizing CML cancer research knowledge by using Annotea shared bookmarks", on the web at http://www.w3.org/2003/cmlcase/cml.html

[12] Fikes, Richard, "Semantic Integration: Assuring the Coherence of Integrated Informa-tion", Powerpoint slides, November, 2003

[13] Murray, K, "Learning as Knowledge Integration", Ph.D. dissertation from The University of Texas at Austin, Department of Computer Sciences. Technical Report TR-95-41,. No-vember 1995.

[14] Pepper, Steve, and Lars Marshal Garshol, "Seamless Knowledge: Spontaneous Knowl-edge Federation using TMRAP",, Extreme Markup Languages Conference, 2004, Mont-real, Canada. Slides on the web at http://www.ontopia.net/topicmaps/materials/Seamless%20Knowledge% 20with%20TMRAP.ppt

[15] Abrams, Frances L., 1995. "Process discovery: automated process development for the control of polymer curing", PhD. Dissertation, School of Engineering. Dayton, OH: Uni-versity of Dayton.

[16] Shum, Simon Buckingham, "Semantic Scholarly Publishing and Discourse: Tools for Modeling Contested Knowledge Domains", webcast: Seminar on People, Computers, and Design, Stanford University, USA, 16 April 2004.

[17] Chaudhri, Vinay K., and Adam Farquhar, "OKBC: A Programmatic Foundation for Knowledge Base Interoperability", Proc. AAAI'98 Conference, Madison, WI, July 1998.

Semantic-Augmented Support in Spatial-Temporal Multimedia Blog Management

Sachit Rajbhandari[1], Frederic Andres[2], Motomu Naito[3], and Vilas Wuwongse[1]

[1] Asian Institute of Technology, Klong Luang, Pathumthani
12120, Thailand
sacheet@yahoo.com, vw@cs.ait.ac.th
[2] National Institute of Informatics, 2-1-2 Hitotsubashi, Chiyoda-ku,
Tokyo, 101-8430, Japan
andres@nii.ac.jp
[3] Knowledge Synergy Inc.3-747-4-203, Kusunokidai, Tokorozawa
Saitama 359-0037 Japan
motom@green.ocn.ne.jp

Abstract. Since the advent of blogging, this easy way to publish information has exponentially increased the data volume and its related complexity. Spatial-temporal information, contained inside multimedia postings, need to be better understood by search engines or by end-users as blogs still lack semantic management. The semantic web community has promoted Topic Maps as a technology which reduces the lack of semantics regarding the optimization of information creation, navigation, merging and dissemination. This paper introduces an innovative layer that combines web feed formats such as RSS 1.0 or 2.0 with the Topic Maps data model for semantic-augmented and interoperable information exchange support.

1 Introduction

Dissemination of information has become very fast and easy with social networking, wikis, blogs, and tagging tools, thanks to Web 2.0. Nowadays, enterprises, institutions, administrations, organizations, groups, families and individuals wish to have their own web presence and participate in communities that share personalized information over the web. Weblogs, popularly known as blogs, are a lightweight publishing paradigm for quick creation of web pages. With a blog, any individual is able to create a huge amount of user-centric information on different topics. These sets of postings can be characterized by different patterns and categorized accordingly. This helps in the subject-based creation of large corpora of data about people, places and times [10]. Blogs are created on specific topics containing spatial data that provide information about the physical world. Blogging acts as *a collaborative online journal including links and postings in reverse chronological order*, with the most recent posting appears at the top of the page. Multimedia postings include images, audio, video, graphics, and animation, which further increases the volume and complexity of information.

Because of this new opportunity to publish the information easily over the web, the amount of spatial information is increasing at a tremendously rapid pace. This is

L. Maicher, A. Sigel, and L.M. Garshol (Eds.): TMRA 2006, LNAI 4438, pp. 215–226, 2007.
© Springer-Verlag Berlin Heidelberg 2007

creating difficulty in the search and retrieval of specific information. Hence, there is a need for a new semantic blog layer to handle the increase in spatial data over time. Such a semantic layer will improve the effectiveness of discovery, automation, integration, and reuse of information across various applications, enterprises, and communities. In [3], the Semantic Web is seen as an extension of the current web in which information is given a well-defined meaning, better enabling computers and people to work in cooperation. Furthermore, it helps to define a machine understandable meaning for the published data on the web by associating formal descriptions so that relevant information can be easily retrieved when it is needed.

Any semantic layer requires metadata including annotations to describe the managed data. Indeed, the current blogging infrastructure supports annotation based on textual information. Annotations can be made from blogging attributes such topic of posting, length of posting, links to other resources, relation between posting and links, and the placement of the links in the post, blog rolls, comments and trackbacks [2]. Even images and other multimedia documents can contain additional information about the target subject. The new layer should also help to bridge the semantic gap by extracting the hidden semantics between the text and images.

Topic Maps (ISO/IEC 13250:2000) has emerged as an enabling technology for the Semantic Web [13]. Semantic blogging can benefit from using Topic Maps as it acts as an information-modeling technique that allows conceptual maps to be represented, linked, and shared [6]. Topic Maps improves the discovery and manageability of information in a large body of information. In addition, a topic is a proxy of some subject and topics can be identified not only by their name but by using a subject identifier (IRI: Internationalized Resource Identifiers). As a result, topics can be merged according to their subject.

Many experts, individuals or organizations are involved in the creation of spatial-temporal data with heterogeneous representations and formats, and this creates difficulties in sharing data among end-users. In such a collaborative environment, Topic Maps improves the semantic interoperability by allowing the exchange of information by defining complex semantic relations and maintaining indexes of knowledge. Composition of topic maps allows merging of two topic maps with the same subject or topics with the same name in the same scope [16].

Semantic ambiguities also are a problem affecting collaborative platforms. Different users may give different names for the same subject matter or may differ in the language they use. In such cases, a keyword-based search of the information may not be efficient or effective. Thanks to Topic Maps, using name associations allows portions of the information overlay to be scoped based on the user language preference of the information overlay to be scoped based on the user language preference" or "Thanks to Topic Maps, name associations can be used so that portions of the information overlay to be scoped based on the user language preference"?]. The identity and synonym problems are solved by using addressable and non-addressable subjects and multiple base names, respectively [7,17]. In addition, semantic distances between topics or between occurrences in Topic Maps can be used to reduce the semantic gap. Navigating through topic maps can be improved by using rich semantic topics [15].

Our paper proposes an innovative layer based on topic maps to enrich posting snippets with metadata and to extract semantic relationships between spatial-temporal multimedia information. Topic maps provide a new kind of knowledge structure for spatial-temporal data storage, data navigation, and visualization. These multimedia blogs can be represented as a collection of topics with topic names and related variances. Topic maps allow the use of different names for the same topics, which can help to solve the problem of synonymy.

In the remainder of the paper, section 2 describes the importance of semantics in spatial-temporal information. Section 3 describes how the semantic approach can increase the management of multimedia blogs. Section 4 introduces the architecture of the semantic-augmented layer for supporting spatial-temporal data. Finally section 5 concludes and addresses future work and assessments.

2   Overview of the State of the Art

In researches on Geospatial multimedia blogging management, semantic issues have been related to multimedia artifacts linked to temporal and/or spatial dimensions. Spatial semantics has been a very active research topic as reviewed in [18, 5]. Also, layered semantics has been pointed out as a key issue [9] in digital information systems. The upper-case "Semantic Web" research that has emerged in the past few years envisions a Web extended in an easy way for people to consume information but not so for computing machines. On the other hand, supporters of the semantic web (the lower-case semantic web) adopt a completely different philosophy. They extended the Web for people, and any introduction of web semantic solutions should be aimed to solve practical problems for the people, not for the computing machines. Multimedia spatial temporal data have become more and more real time as direct reflections of the Where and When about the geographic world. In this sense, they have various semantic interpretations within the large set of applications, as has been pointed out by the ECAI consortium's best practices.[1] As spatial temporal data are increasingly available over the Internet, GIS software is becoming more and more useful for understanding spatial and temporal dimensions of data for a wider range of disciplines. Google Earth[2] gained popularity with its simple functions (e.g. Explore, Search and Discover) for end-users. This tool combines satellite imagery, maps, and the power of Google Search to incorporate the world's geographic information in applications where semantic information is overlaid and temporally managed in TimeDrive.

Though the quality of its visualization function is good, Google Earth lacks an analytical functionality to deal with data semantics. Furthermore, it cannot be a substitute to professional GIS software until and unless it provides statistical and analytical features. A similar example is the research at the Environmental Systems Research Institute (ESRI)[3] that came up with ArcGis Explorer, another free application with analytical and visualization capabilities allowing users to create virtual digital globes over the net. Various other GIS applications are emerging that have both analytical strengths and visualization aids for easing use. One issue could be interoperability, as Google Earth uses a proprietary data format. On the other hand,

---

[1] http://www.ecai.org/

[2] http://earth.google.com/

[3] http://www.esri.com

ESRI promised to provide a compatibility feature by using a standardized data format issued by the Open Geospatial Consortium.[4] NASA also provides a similar type of application, called World Wind.[5] This open source application is designed to tailor the software as per the need of end-users. But its weak point as compared with Google earth is that it consumes much more memory and CPU usage [4].

In conclusion, the above systems have been built to provide spatial information but have not stressed much on the temporal aspect of the data. They lack the mechanism to deliver information that changes in time. Furthermore, their valuable geospatial data lack the interoperability to be integrated with other kinds of data such GXML or XTM. There is still a semantic gap between the available information, since previous researches did not consider methods to explore relationships among quantitative data.

3 Semantic Augmented Support Using Topic Maps

An innovative semantic-augmented support using the Topic Maps semantic model has been created as part of the blogging infrastructure. For semantic support, the system uses two categories of topic map: (1) structured topic maps and (2) content-based topic maps. Each structured topic map is created from different syndication standard formats of postings such as RSS or Atom. These standard formats contain different elements (e.g. title, description, link, date) which give to each posting a finite structure. They also add metadata semantics. Each RSS file is a dialect of XML which can become an occurrence of a topic map. The content-based topic map represents a collection of topics under different subject categories. These topics can be extracted from the elements of each structured topic map and associated with other topics. Before going through the procedure of semantic extraction from topic maps, let us formally introduce the resource algebra supported by the topic maps layer.

Resource Algebra

The resource algebra enables various users to share their documents as part of a collaborative platform. Resource semantic type and functions in the topic maps are directly represented using the appropriate data type and functions supported by the resource algebra. This algebra is the semantic interface between scientists to reduce the semantic gap and to strengthen the metadata bridge between them to enable a better understanding. Furthermore, his high level semantic algebra facilitates the collaborative works between scientists by using topic maps integrating high level semantics.

Let us remember the notion of many sorted algebra [7]. Such algebra consists of several sets of values and a set of operations (functions) between these sets. It consists of two sets of symbols called sorts (e.g. topic, pdf, rtf, lsi_sm) and operators (e.g. tm_transcribe, semantic_similarity); the function sections constitute the signature of the algebra. Second order signature [12] is based on two coupled many-sorted signatures where the top-level signature provides kinds (set of types) as sorts (e.g. DATA, RESOURCE, SEMANTIC_DATA) and type constructors as operators (e.g. set).

---

[4] http://www.opengeospatial.org/
[5] http://worldwind.arc.nasa.gov/

To illustrate the approach, we assume the following simplified many-sorted algebra, which is part of our full resource algebra [11]:

Kinds DATA, RESOURCE, SEMANTIC_DATA, TOPIC_MAPS, SET
Type constructor
  -> DATA   topic
  -> RESOURCE   pdf, rdt, htm, xml, cvs, jpeg, tiff // resource document type
  -> SEMANTIC_DATA   lsi_sm, mpeg7_sm, dc_sm, vra_sm, cdwa_sm,
                       ecai_sm, objectid_sm // Semantic and metadata vectors
  -> TOPIC_MAPS   tm(topic maps)

  TOPIC_MAPS ->SET   set

Unary operations

$\forall$ resource in RESOURCE, resource $\rightarrow$ sm: SEMANTIC_DATA,tm **tm_transcribe**
$\forall$ sm in SEMANTIC_DATA sm $\rightarrow$ set(tm)   **semantic_similarity**

The notion sm:SEMANTIC_DATA is to be read as "some type sm in SEMANTIC_DATA," and means there is a typing mapping associated with the tm_transcribe operator. Each operator determines the result type within the kind of SEMANTIC_DATA, depending on the given operand resource types.

Binary operations

$\forall$ tm in TOPIC_MAPS, (tm)$^{+}$ $\rightarrow$ tm **topicmaps_merging**

$\forall$ sm in SEMANTIC_DATA , $\forall$ tm in TOPIC_MAPS,
          sm,tm tm $\rightarrow$ tm   **semantic_merging**

$\forall$ topic in DATA, $\forall$ tm in TOPIC_MAPS,
     set(tm) x (topic $\rightarrow$ bool) $\rightarrow$ set(tm) **select**

The semantic merging operation takes two or more operands that are all topic map values. The select takes an operand type set (tm) and a predicate of type topic and returns a subset of the operand set fulfilling the predicate. From the implementation of view, the resource algebra is an extensible library package providing a collection of resource data types and operations for domain-oriented resource computation (e.g. cultural field).

The major research challenge is the formalization and standardization of cultural resource data types and semantic operations through ISO standardization.

Semantic extraction to enrich topic maps with additional semantics

Topic semantic extraction is automatically done in three steps as shown in Figure 1. New topics and associations are extracted from postings. These extracted local topic maps are merged with global topic maps. If similar topics exist in the global topic maps, the occurrences and associations are updated; otherwise they will be added as new topics and new associations.

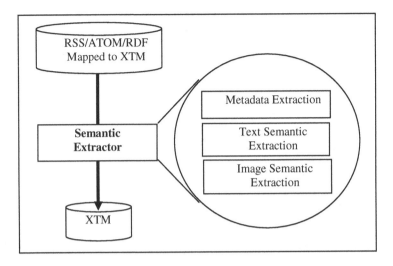

Fig. 1. Semantic Extraction of Topic Maps

Metadata Extraction. RSS and a taxonomy module such as Dublin Core are used to create the structural Topic Maps as mentioned in the previous section. Each RSS file is composed of channel elements and sub-elements including the Dublin Core elements. These standard metadata elements with some domain-specific elements can be mapped on the Topic Maps data model, thereby creating a structural topic map. Other additional elements such as latitude, longitude and height may be included, as the Dublin Core metadata field only contains title, description, category, creation date which may not be sufficient to describe the topics related to geospatial data. The title metadata acts as the topic name and the resource file like document, images, audios or videos related to this topic are assigned as occurrences. Elements such as published date and author are used as a separate topic having an associative relationship between resource's topic and elements such as category refer to a classification schema. Additional metadata elements such as latitude, longitude, and description can also be occurrences of topics. This kind of metadata provides information about the creator, format of the content, and created date but does not help to define the actual subject of the topics to develop content related topic maps.

Textual Semantic Extraction. Even using standard web document metadata such as Dublin Core is not sufficient to fill the semantic gap. Moreover, useful metadata information is hidden in other forms such as key words or in the message content itself. Latent Semantic Indexing has been widely used to resolve issues related to search and retrieval of information and overcome the deficiencies of term-matching. The LSI approach is implemented to address the problems of synonymy and polysemy in using the SVD (Singular Value Decomposition) approach [1, 21]. LSI techniques extract more information about existing topics and new topics from the blog contents. The new topics and relationships are mainly extracted from the titles, key words, message contents, blog rolls, permalinks, and comments of the postings.

4   Semantic-Augmented Layer Architecture

Based on the discussion in the previous sections, this section presents the overall architecture of our semantic augmented layer using Topic Maps. The high level architecture is represented in Figure 2.

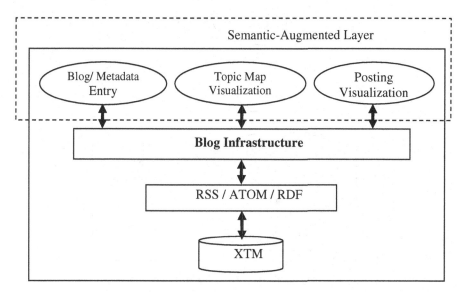

Fig. 2. High level Architecture of Semantic-augmented Blog

In the following, we will overview two key components regarding the semantic-augmented layer implementation: (1) its topic map-based storage component and (2) the related semantic viewer.

4.1   Topic Maps Storage Component

The topic map merging process integrates topic maps with similar topics collected from external environments. Topic maps are stored as mono-files, e.g., in XTM format, for simplicity in the current version. In addition, any option can used to choose a storage location from among different locations using external references.

The blog infrastructure usually syndicates its contents following a standardized format based on RSS or Atom. The framework makes use of these standard formats for data exchange. Figure 3 shows the steps involved in transforming and merging documents. The first step transforms an RSS file containing the posting message enriched with metadata into an XTM file by using the XSLT transformation. The XSL transformation is carried out by mapping RSS elements with the corresponding topic map elements.

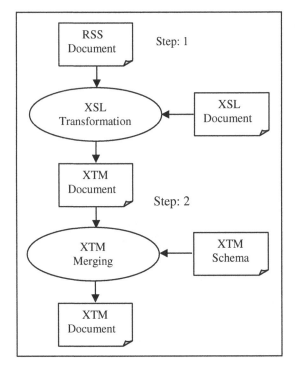

Fig. 3. Overall processes of XTM file creation

After the transformation, the new XTM file contains the topic maps structure of the blogs with different topics, association between topics, and the occurrences of resources. The XTM Schema file, provided by experts, contains the topics that define the associative relationships like whole-part, class-instance, Date-place, Name-Place, superclass-subclass, etc. In the second step, the schema file is merged with the created XTM file to mix topics and its occurrences with the global topic maps or create new topics if there is no topic related to that subject.

4.2 Semantic Viewer Function

Topics and topic associations provide a structured semantic graph above Geomedia information resources. In the following, we overview the visualization functions provided by our platform to display the semantic layer efficiently, which is a critical issue, as indicated in [8], especially when topic maps include millions of topics and associations.

Map Visualization. This function helps to visualize the locations by using maps. This kind of visualization allows the user to click on the map to get the geographical position of the place in time. The tool also provides a zooming feature to view higher resolution positioning.

Let us say that we post some information about "Madrasa Chahar Bagh Royal Theological College". First, let us use the zoom and the navigation functions provided by our semantic layer to point out the site we are looking for in the map. We are able to get the longitudinal and latitudinal location of the place by clicking on the map. The next step is to create a blog entry by inputting information about the target place with additional resources as such as images, audio/video, or any other document genre using the xml based form as shown in Figure 4. The triangular mark pointing out the target site enables the annotated information within the map to be visualized.

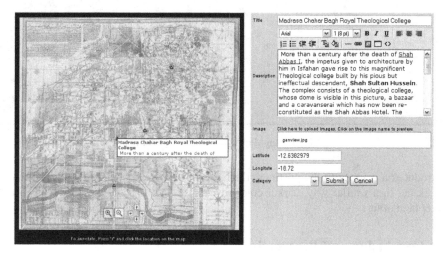

Fig. 4. BlogMap Visualization of Geospatial data

BlogMap Visualization. The BlogMap point of view is a 2D space-constrained visualization of hierarchical structures following the TreeMap research approach [20]. This kind of visualization is effective to show hierarchal categorizations as structural summaries in our semantic-augmented layer according to multidimensional topics such as size, time, and space. Also, using different colors, size metrics, and pattern schema, can improve the visualization's effectiveness. In Figure 5, the BlogMap shows the hierarchal structure of postings according to different categories (e.g. Geography, History and Education). The metric defining the size of each area can have three kinds of values: (1) the length of the content of each posting, (2) the number of postings associated with that specific topic or (3) the number of accesses to each posting. In addition, the color to display each posting represents the category under which each posting is classified. For instance, in Figure 5, history is one category which has a green background color to distinguish it from other postings. In the same way, the intensity of the color of each posting gives temporal information visualizing the time elapsed from the published date. A tool tip with the detail of the posting is displayed when a mouse is moved on the top of it.

Showing the hierarchical categorization of postings is a way to visualize the above information posted under the Education category (purple). The size variation

Fig. 5. BlogMap Visualization of postings

introduces a priority to the postings: the largest size corresponds to the most popular message. In a similar way, darker color reveals the fact that the message was posted later than others.

5 Conclusion and Perspectives

The key result of our semantic augmented layer is to provide a mechanism to enrich the multimedia blog framework with semantic metadata management. The implementation demonstrated the key role of geospatial semantics associated with a temporal dimension in the improvement of accesses in multimedia blogs. In this paper, we pointed out:

→ The essence of the semantic web in the field of geo-localization information system;

→ The applicability of Topic Maps for the semantic-augmented layer;

→ Automatic semantic extraction of metadata from text and images to enrich blog snippets;

→ Semantic metadata enabling richer view, navigation, and query mechanisms;

→ Further use of Topic Maps in deriving relations among different blog entries and developing collaborative spatial- temporal information networks;

→ The importance of topic map merging in collaborative environments where information is dispersed among researchers, experts and students;

→ The use of visualization tools for a Topic Maps-based blog infrastructure that facilitates learning on large number of different subjects.

This layer needs to be extended to better support accessibility, sharing, and rendering of spatial data (maps, images, and vector data) through the implementation of a mapping server that provides mapping services conforming to the recommendation (e.g. GML, G-XML) of the Open Geospatial Consortium. The current implementation will be extended by the use of native XML or native topic maps databases. A case study on Isfahan city in Iran is being conducted as part of the Isfahan Islamic Architectural Database (IIAD) project in cooperation with the Institute of Oriental Studies (The University of Tokyo, Japan).

Acknowledgements

The research presented in this paper would not have been possible without the support and advice of respected professors, and colleagues at the Asian Institute of Technology (Thailand), the National Institute of Informatics (Japan) and the Institute of Oriental Studies (The University of Tokyo, Japan). We would like to thank Professor Darina Dicheva and Professor Christo Dichev (Winston Salem State University) for their valuable comments and cooperation regarding TMblog.

References

1. Andres, F., and Naito, M.: *Dynamic Topic Mapping Using Latent Semantic Indexing*. IEEE International Conference on Information Technology and Applications, Sydney 4th-7th July, 2005. pp 220-225, ISBN 0-7695-2316-1
2. Bar-Ilan, J.: *An outsider's view on "topic-oriented blogging"*. In: Proceedings of the 13th International World Wide Web Conference on Alternate Track Papers Posters New York, NY, USA, (May 19 - 21, 2004). WWW Alt. ACM Press, New York, NY, (2004) 28-34
3. Berners-Lee, T., Hendler, J., Lassila, O.: *The Semantic Web*. Scientific American (2001)
4. Butler, D.: *The web-wide world. Nature*. Publishing Group, Vol. 439, (16 February 2006)
5. Fonseca, F., Egenhofer, M. , Agouris, P., and Câmara, G.: *Using Ontologies for Integrated Geographic Information Systems*. In: Transactions in GIS 6 (3) (2002) 231-257
6. Garshol, L. M.: *Living with Topic Maps and RDF*. In: Proceedings of XML Europe (2003), organized by IDEAlliance, London, UK (2003)
7. Garshol, L. M.: *Metadata? Thesauri? Taxonomies? Topic Maps! Making sense of it all.* Ontopia. (26 October 2004)
8. Grand, L. B., Soto, M.: *Visualisation of the Semantic Web: Topic Maps Visualisation*. Sixth International Conference on Information Visualisation (IV'02) London, England. (2002) 344
9. Gong, Z., Zhang, J.: Layered Semantic Architecture of Multimedia Data. In: *Proceedings of the IASTED International Conference on Internet and Multimedia Systems and Applications*, Honolulu, USA. (August 13-15, 2003) ACTA Press. (2003) 275-280
10. Gruhl, D., Liben-Nowell, D., Guha, R., Tomkins, A.: *Information diffusion through blogspace*. SIGKDD Explor. Newsl. 6, 2 (Dec. 2004) 43-52
11. Güting, R. H. 1989. Gral: an extensible relational database system for geometric applications. In Proceedings of the 15th international Conference on Very Large Data Bases (Amsterdam, The Netherlands). Very Large Data Bases. Morgan Kaufmann Publishers, San Francisco, CA, 33-44.
12. Güting, R. H. 1993. *Second-order signature: a tool for specifying data models*, query processing, and optimization. In *Proceedings of the 1993 ACM SIGMOD international Conference on Management of Data* (Washington, D.C., United States, May 25 - 28, 1993). P. Buneman and S. Jajodia, Eds. SIGMOD '93. ACM Press, New York, NY, 277-286. DOI= http://doi.acm.org/10.1145/170035.170079

13. International Organization for Standardization (ISO): ISO 639:1998 Code for the representation of names of language, (1998)

14. Lema, J. A. C., Guting, R. H.: *Dual Grid: A New Approach for Robust Spatial Algebra Implementation*. GeoInformatica Volume 6, Number 1. Springer, Netherlands (2002) 57-76

15. Naito, M., and Andres, F.: *Application Framework Based on Topic Maps*. Lecture Notes in Computer Science, Volume 3873, Feb 2006, Pages 42 - 52, DOI 10.1007/11676904_4, URL http://dx.doi.org/10.1007/11676904_4 Charting the Topic Maps Research and Applications Landscape: First International Workshop on Topic Map Research and Applications, TMRA 2005, Leipzig, Germany, October 6-7, 2005, Revised Selected Papers Editors: Lutz Maicher, Jack Park ISBN: 3-540-32527-1

16. Pepper, S. and Moore G.: *XML Topic Maps (XTM) 1.0*. TopicMaps.Org Specification. (2001), http://www.topicmaps.org/xtm/

17. Rath, H. H.: *The Topic Maps Handbook*. Empolis GmbH, Gutersloh, Germany (2003) http://www.empolis.com/downloads/empolis_TopicMaps_Whitepaper20030206.pdf

18. Rodríguez, A., Cruz, I., Egenhofer, M., Levashkin, S. (ed.): *GeoSpatial Semantics*. In: the Proceedings of the 1st International Conference on GeoSpatial Semantics Lecture Notes in Computer Science, Vol. 3799, Springer, New York, (2005)

19. Sachit R., and Andres, F.: *Resource Algebra*. NII report (2007).

20. Shneiderman B.: *Treemaps for space-constrained visualization of hierarchies*. HCIL, University of Maryland. (2005)

21. Zhao, R., Grosky, I. W.: *Bridging the Semantic Gap in Image Retrieval*. Distributed Multimedia Databases: Techniques and Applications, Idea Group Publishing, Hershey, Pennsylvania (2002) 13-36

Topic Maps-Based Semblogging with semblog-tm

Alexander Sigel, Lars Bünten, and Marcus Frank

University of Cologne, Department of Information Systems and Information Management,
Pohligstr. 1, 50969 Köln, Germany
sigel@wim.uni-koeln.de

Abstract. Semantic blogging combines blogs with the Semantic Web for improved metadata. Our analysis of six semblogging approaches and systems reveals that all are RDF-based, suffer from not using Published Subjects as proxies for subjects, and do not employ semantic relations motivated by knowledge organization. In contrast, we introduce and discuss semblog-tm, a prototype of a Topic Maps- and PSI-based semblogging system with a well-motivated set of semantic relations. Its basic requirements have been derived from the three main use cases: managing lightweight ontologies, attaching semantics to blog entries, and providing aggregated semblogging data as semantic knowledge services to other semantically-enabled systems. The four main system components (blogging, topic map, PSI, semantic knowledge services), and its capabilities are sketched. The web application semblog-tm is implemented as a plugin for the blojsom blogging engine, using Java and Tomcat with Velocity templates. Topic map operations are realized via TMAPI with TM4J or OKS, and Axis is employed for web services.

Keywords: semantic blogging; semblogging; social software; published subjects; PSIs; emergent lightweight ontologies; distributed knowledge management; knowledge services.

1 Introduction

The emerging field of semblogging (for short SB) combines blogs with the Semantic Web to enrich blog entries with more explicit and machine-understandable metadata, relating both to structure and content. This semantics is conveyed by semantic tags (semtags), connected by semantic associations.

Blogging [1, 2], in particular knowledge blogging in distributed/decentralized knowledge management (DKM) [3] aids personal and collaborative knowledge work [4, 5]. With this instrument, knowledge workers can easily record and publish rather short notes (blog entries) on subjects they want to discourse about. Blogs and wikis are prominent exponents of social software [6, 7], a paradigm in which effects within human groups emerge, and groups are primary objects within the system. Mechanisms like blogrolls, trackbacks or pingbacks, and tagging can lead to highly internetworked and interactive communities focused around subjects.

To improve findability and syndication of blog entries, knowledge workers associate short text strings (tags) with their blog entries. Those tags are either reused or newly created. A blogger can use or create as tag any string (s)he wants to use as a

L. Maicher, A. Sigel, and L.M. Garshol (Eds.): TMRA 2006, LNAI 4438, pp. 227–242, 2007.

retrieval cue. In general, a tag describes an aspect of the aboutness of an entry, but it can be any pragmatic aspect a user likes to attribute. Collaboratively tagging blog entries is an extreme form of user-oriented, social, or democratic indexing [8]. It leads to folksonomies (which can be visualized as tag clouds), and hence to folksonomic tagging [9-13] as a kind of thematic annotation of blog entries.

1.1 Relevance and Motivation: Why We Need Blogging with More Explicit Structure and Semantics

> *"Blogging, as a subset of the web as a whole, can benefit greatly from the addition of semantic metadata. The result — which we will call Semantic Blogging — provides improved capabilities with respect to search, connectivity and browsing compared to current blogging technology." [14]*

In conventional blogging with tags, structure and semantics are not explicit. According to [14], "(...) blogs, and the posts that they contain, lack sufficient semantic information regarding the topics that they are talking about or how the current topic under discussion relates to previous blog discussion threads". This shortcoming makes syndication of blog entries from different blogs about the same subject difficult, since computers have to guess what is only implicit. Improved blogging systems should thus provide support for both structural and content-related metadata.

Structural metadata identifies and describes elements internal to one blog entry, the relations between those elements, or the form of related blog entries [14]. Structured blogging [15, 16] allows bloggers publishing of structured information such as reviews or events by use of machine-interpretable templates. *Content-related (semantic) metadata* refers to the meaning of tags and relations. It expresses the subjects the entries are about. At present, tags are typically only strings used as names, not connected with a concept. It is not explicitly and publicly described or defined which concept a tag shall denote and be a computer proxy for. Except evolutionary competition, there is no vocabulary control of and no central registry for such tags. This may be regarded as an advantage of social software [17], but may also lead to chaos. Another problem is that tags are "flat", i.e. no typed semantic relations are specified between tags, although bloggers might want to express not only tags, but semantically interrelated tags.

A more explicit semantic markup or annotation of content like blog entries with semantic web means is needed such that semantic web applications can automatically process the content [18]. Some knowledge workers want to express and use knowledge structures (make assertions) while blogging, be it for personal or joint knowledge work. They are longing for tools supporting them in expressing more than just text with simple tags.

A major problem is how to aggregate and virtually collocate blog entries about the same subject of thought, and how to systematically present related blog entries. A simple example of this type of problem are book reviews scattered across blogs [19]. Not only are the entries physically distributed all over the blogosphere, but independent bloggers annotate from their personal perspective, not adhering to a central ontology. Social bookmarking, or folksonomic tagging [7] suffers – more than traditional indexing in knowledge organization – from different yet acceptable viewpoints and conceptualizations, from problems with polysemy and homonymy, quality issues, and from rather arbitrary tags.

1.2 The Semblogging Approach

SB [20] crosses blogs with the semantic web, extending blogging by more explicit semantics. "[B]logs [are] enriched with semantic, machine-understandable metadata" [21]. A few system conceptualizations and implementations exist, see e.g. [14, 18, 20]. SB is a special case of semantic annotation [22-24] in line with distributed knowledge management. Blog contents become a data source for semantic web applications and services and can be aggregated and repurposed on a semantic basis in a smarter way.

Some terminology: [25] calls semantic tags *semtags* and the process of semantic tagging *semtagging*. In analogy we will call the process of blogging with such tags semantic blogging (*semblogging*), and such bloggers *sembloggers*. Occasionally, though not consistently used, *to semtag*, used as verb, stands for associating a single semtag with a blog entry, while *to semblog*, used as a verb, stands for semantic blogging in a more general sense (several acts of semtagging). Although not only semtags in isolation, but semantic relations (*"semrels"*) are used to form complex statements, with semtags playing roles, for the sake of simplicity we will subsume this under semtagging/SB.

The challenge of SB is how to best support bloggers in making key structure and semantics explicit while retaining the ease of blogging. Most needed are lightweight means such that bloggers can optionally define the semantics of their folksonomic tags and relate them to each other with typed semantic relations. Such SB systems can be realized with a variety of semantic technologies, in particular with RDF/OWL vs. Topic Maps.

1.3 Research Gap at Project Start in 2004

Cayzer's seminal SB work has inspired several SB systems, but there is no comparative discussion, and no such system is freely available as open source. There is no work on interoperably interlinking several SB systems such that aggregated assertions can be exchanged and queried. Semantic knowledge services between such systems are only emerging. Published Subjects are not used in SB. No reusable tools and no public registry service can be identified for PSIs [26]. Relation types are often ad-hoc based. Often, rather simple links are employed instead of links with role types. No-one has replicated RDF SB work with Topic Maps to better understand the issues in SB systems. Based on our intuition (or bias?) that Topic Maps have presumed strengths, in particular for the expression of knowledge structures by humans, and on our observation that those strengths are not fully explored and exploited for augmenting SB [26], we wonder how a Topic Maps-based SB system would look like.

1.4 Our Contribution

Within the *kpeer* (knowledge peers) project (2004–2006) we investigated Topic Maps-based SB with particular interest in the exchange of assertions in this setting. Three diploma students significantly contributed to this research, investigating the conceptual design and implementation of the initial system [27], its extension by aspects of distribution and semantic knowledge services [28], and interoperable semantic knowledge services with Topic Maps and RDF, with semblog-tm as a data provider [29]. To have better control, we decided to build our own system.

Our analysis of six SB approaches and systems revealed that all are RDF-based, suffer from not using Published Subjects as proxies for subjects, and do not employ semantic relations motivated by knowledge organization. In contrast, we introduce and discuss semblog-tm, a fully implemented prototype of a Topic Maps- and PSI-based SB system with a well-motivated set of semantic relations. It uniquely combines the features: Topic Maps [30-32] as an interesting alternative to RDF(S)/OWL, Published Subjects [33-36], and Semantic Relations explicitly based on work in knowledge organization [37-38].

We have shown that a Topic Maps-based SB system is both feasible and useful. Compared to other SB systems, some added-value is offered, warranting further work. Our main contributions are:

- Identification and short characterization of six RDF-based SB conceptualizations and systems.
- Conceptualization and prototypical implementation of the first public and open-source Topic Maps- and PSI-based SB system, and of the only SB system based on association types motivated by knowledge organization theory.
- The first SB system with open semantic knowledge services, aggregating the data and providing them back to any topic map fragment consumers. Implementation and initial discussion of Topic Maps-based semantic knowledge services, advancing the interoperability and scalability of SB systems.
- Establishing a stronger argument for Topic Maps-based SB, and for integrating appropriate information architecture and semantic interoperability into other SB systems.

2   Review of Related Work on Semblogging

2.1   RDF-Based Semblogging

The Seminal Semblogging Demonstrator (HP)
Within the European research project SWAD-E (Semantic Web Advanced Development for Europe), Steve Cayzer and colleagues at the Hewlett-Packard laboratories in Bristol coined the term semantic blogging and developed the very first prototypical SB demonstrator [20, 39]. The special application scenario was collaborative bibliography management in a scientific community (SB for bibliographies). The demonstrator can be tried out online,[1] and there is a user guide [40]. Requirements [41] and lessons learnt [42] are documented as SWAD deliverables. This prototype supports better semantic view, navigation and query. In principle, arbitrary vocabularies can be used, e.g. such represented with SKOS [43-45]. The system is implemented using the Java blogging platform blojsom[2] and Jena[3] for RDF.

---

[1] http://www.semanticblogging.org/
[2] http://wiki.blojsom.com/wiki/display/blojsom/About+blojsom
[3] http://jena.sourceforge.net/

A Semblogging Client within Haystack (MIT)

Karger and Quan built a SB client into Haystack[4] ("a platform for authoring end user semantic web applications") incorporating publishing, aggregation, and browsing capabilities. The scenario assumes a scientist attending a conference who wants to know more about the talks presented at the conference. The conference program is available in RDF and can be viewed with Haystack as a semantic web browser. For each abstract, corresponding blog entries discussing the paper are suggested. The relations between blog entries (here: the structure of the discussion) can be graphically depicted. After viewing all blog entries (containing both approving and disagreeing contributions), the scientist can create a blog entry annotating the most convincing blog entry or argument. As with the HP system, blojsom is used.

Semblog - Personal Knowledge Publishing Suite

Ohmukai, Takeda, Numa and colleagues proposed a personal knowledge publishing suite, co-incidentally called "semblog", to support the information exchange between individuals [46-48]. This SB system extends RSS aggregators with two capabilities:

1. users can categorize and republish RSS feeds, and
2. standalone aggregators (for each user one), called glucose, form a p2p network.

A user can recommend feeds read to other users. Links between bloggers are modelled with FOAF. Three methods of egocentric search help finding related entries: entries linked from the annotated resource, entries annotating the same resource, and entries classified with the same keyword.

Semantic Blogging Research Project (KMI)

In the SB research project[5] at Open University, Bertrand Sereno, Marc Eisenstadt, and Simon Buckingham Shum investigate how blogs can be used for distributed knowledge management and construction [49]. SB is seen as a special case of distributed sense-making and argumentation. The knowledge mapping tool "Compendium"[6] helps better structuring and interrelating of blog entries, extending the entries with semantics. Discussions spanning several blogs can be marked up with semantic relations and displayed in structured form.

Aggregating Entries with Language Games in the Tagsocratic Project

Avesani, Cova, Hayes, and Massa [19] describe "problems in aligning similar concepts created by a set of distributed, autonomous users". They claim that, employing their tagsocratic approach, entries about the same topic can be aggregated even if bloggers have used tags with different names. For a given tag in one blog, a (for the moment) central mapping service returns tags from different blogs. As a common reference structure, so-called "global tags" form a kind of meta- or switching thesaurus.

semiBlog – Semblogging to Publish Desktop Data

semiBlog applies the concept of SB to publish existing desktop data with semantic markup to better integrate desktop data in the communication process [14, 21, 50]. As

---

[4] http://haystack.lcs.mit.edu/
[5] http://kmi.open.ac.uk/projects/semanticblog/
[6] http://www.compendiuminstitute.org/

a proof-of-concept, semiBlog,[7] a prototypical SB editor and blog reader has been implemented as a desktop application. High emphasis is put on usability and tight integration with desktop applications. An example scenario assumes annotating a scientific paper after discussing it with a colleague. The blogger can annotate the blog by drag-and-drop-referencing information objects available on the semantic desktop, like his colleague (selecting from his address book), the project (selecting the URL of the project page) and the bibliographic reference (selecting the reference in the bibliographic tool of his choice). Other users can import the annotations from the blog to their desktop applications. SB is thus a way to easily exchange semantic web data. In contrast to the HP demonstrator and the SB client within Haystack which use blojsom, semiBlog uses the WordPress blog engine. The SIOC (Semantically-Interlinked Online Communities) ontology developed by the same authors is employed in a SIOC plugin for WordPress. The recent semiBlog is currently the most advanced RDF SB system and unique in its combination of structural and content metadata (see [14], fig. 5: A combined SIOC and semiBlog graph). Compared to Cayzer's HP demonstrator, some semantic relations are used, but they are not yet very rich.

2.2 Topic Maps-Based Semblogging

At least to Topic Mappers, Topic Maps seem an obvious choice for SB. However, despite all our efforts, we could not identify scientific references or published systems on SB realized with Topic Maps (except our own earlier ideas [26, 55-57]. In 2004, Jack Park had presented SB as one example for Augmented Storytelling [58]. Dmitry Bogachev had informally discussed SB with topic maps, but we have no further details. Lars Marius Garshol had realized a simple SB application using Ontopia's OKS, which he kindly provided to us. In his blog entry on "[t]ags/folksonomies and Topic Maps",[8] he also shared some thoughts why "[t]opic Maps are the perfect way to fill the gap between what tagging is and what it should be." Interest in Topic Maps-based SB is slowly rising, see e.g. [59].

2.3 Discussion

There seems no lack of motivation for SB, but a lack of adaption in blogging communities. Until recently, this was partially because there were no tools available in public, but we expected the first usable SB systems to become public in the near future. Except in the semiBlog project, usability issues have been neglected. It should be easier to use SB systems, and they should be tighter integrated into the work environment and knowledge processes of knowledge workers.

To the best of our knowledge, the very few existing SB systems are based on RDF, not on Topic Maps. For example, Karger and Quan, in stating "[w]e characterize the notion of semantic blogging – the publication of RDF-encoded Web logs" [18], do not even seem to be aware of Topic Maps as an alternative for encoding semblog metainformation. No discussion can be found on using Topic Maps vs. RDF(S)/OWL

---

[7] http://semiblog.semanticweb.org/
[8] http://www.garshol.priv.no/blog/33.html

for SB. RDF and Topic Maps can be made semantically interoperable in some way [60-65], and to a certain extent this is also true for RDF(S) and OWL, e.g. using TMCL. Compared to RDF alone, Topic Maps seem better suited for humans to express knowledge, and converting "down" from Topic Maps to RDF is losing information (context and identity) [66]. This suggests that it is worthwhile to explore basing SB directly on Topic Maps, at least as an alternative.

Although PSIs are useful to ground semantics both with RDF and Topic Maps, all the systems suffer from the Web's "identity crisis" [34], because subject indicators [33, 35, 36] are not used, In addition, some systems lack semantic relationships between tags, or the relations are rather simple.

3 semblog-tm, a Topic Maps-Based Semblogging System

We shortly report on semblog-tm as demonstrated at TMRA 06. A demonstrator was available online.[9] Because a demonstration video, together with a transcript [67] and slides [68] is available, screenshots are not included here. The source code with a system installation guide is available via anonymous SVN sourceforge checkout.[10]

3.1 Conceptual Design and Main Capabilities

With the solution elements Topic Maps, Published Subjects and a predefined set of semantic relations already in mind, we developed several scenarios [28, 29], decomposed them into main use cases, and derived basic requirements. Starting from a rather centralized approach, we later explored aspects of distribution, and provided semantic knowledge services both internally and externally. We grouped into three main use cases:

1. Managing lightweight, decentrally governed ontologies: Defining ontologies (semtags connected by semantic associations)
2. SB: Attaching semantics to blog entries by connecting semblog entries with entries from those ontologies, and displaying them
3. Managing aggregated SB data as semantic knowledge services: Provide other semantically-enabled systems with services on topic map fragments.

System capabilities as seen from the user's perspective include:
Semtag: discover, display/follow, copy third-party semtag to own ontology space, attach semtag to blog entry, define own semtag from scratch, mint PSI for semtag, associate two semtags. *Semantic retrieval*: various predefined queries, like: all semtags by all sembloggers, or blog entries for specified semtags, same-server or cross-server retrieval, result display, export to .xtm.

3.2 System Architecture, Tool Selection, and Implementation

We designed semblog-tm to have the following four high-level system components and suggest this as a possible architecture for other systems (cf. fig. 1):

---

[9] http://semblog.wim.uni-koeln.de/blojsom/blog/ (no longer supported).
[10] http://semblog.sf.net/

1. A *blogging component* dealing with all conventional blogging functions.
2. A *topic map component* for manipulating topic maps. It provides capabilities for topic map manipulation, merging and querying, importing, exporting, and format conversion. For each semblogger, a separate topic mapic is held.
3. A *PSI component* allows the creation of new PSIs, thereby aiding in the unambiguous identification of concepts.
4. A *semantic knowledge services component.* Web services manipulating topic map fragments. Internally, these realize a service-oriented architecture, externally, they ease synchronization, aggregation and querying of assertions between SB servers, or a SB server and other semantic applications.

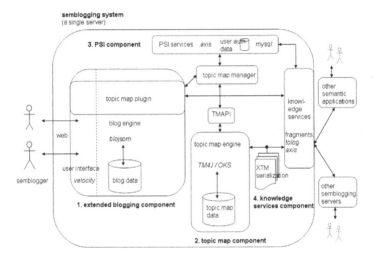

Fig. 1. semblog-tm main components of the system architecture: Simplified view

The core topic map is designed to support both formal (structural) and semantic (content-related) metadata:

Formal metadata: Blog entries are redundantly held in blojsom and in the topic maps. A blog entry is connected via authorship (source – author) with a blogger. The topics *human-aboutness* and *machine-metadata* have been defined to type internal occurrences of Published Subjects, according to the OASIS Published Subjects TC recommendations[11] [33], and the recent proposal by Naito on metadata for Published Subjects [69]. In addition, a topic *primary-topic-subject-identifier* has been defined to discern the designated PSI from additional subject identifiers.

Content-related metadata: This encompasses the semtags themselves, their interrelations, and the relation aboutness between semtag: issue and source: blog entry. Based on a proposal for semantically differentiated thesaurus relations in knowledge

---

[11] Recommendation 1 ("A Published Subject Indicator should provide human-readable metadata about itself"), and recommendation 2 ("A Published Subject Indicator may provide machine-processable metadata about itself").

organization [37, 38],[12] the SB system supports two class-1 relations and all 23 class-2 relations. An example for such a class-2 relation is: "TMRA06" (instrument) is claimed to be instrumental for "Leveraging the semantics" (purpose).

The web application semblog-tm is implemented as a plugin for the blojsom blogging engine, using Java and Tomcat with Velocity[13] templates. Topic map operations are realized via TMAPI[14] with TM4J or OKS. Open source software has been used as far as possible, and portability between Windows and Unix has been achieved. Blojsom was chosen for the *blogging component*, in addition to other advantages, because it is also used for the HP and the Haystack demonstrator. This should make comparison of and interchange between such SB applications easier. The *Topic Map component* is implemented on top of TMAPI, and TM4J (open source) and OKS (commercial) are supported topic map engines. We chose the SOAP web service framework Axis for the *knowledge services component*.

4   Discussion and Suggestions for Further Work

Usability and Users. Maturity: One reviewer found fault with not taking real (empirical) end user requirements into account, which results in additional burden for users, without evaluating and analyzing advantages and disadvantages of the proposed approach. Our primary goal was not provision of a system excelling in usability, albeit desirable. Rather did we pursue design science to better understand how such a system might look like. Thus we first creatively synthesized and imagined potential usage situations. Unfortunately, no user communities could be involved later. Before wider use, several known usability issues would have to be dealt with. We suggest improving the system together with selected users, and evaluating it in a larger, thematically focused community.

Semantic Retrieval vs. Fulltext: It was also recommended to discuss why semantic retrieval with semtags and along their interrelations should outperform searching without additional tags (fulltext). The retrieval results much depend on the context. Although requiring too much metadata can be a heavy, even counterproductive burden, there is sufficient reason to believe fine-grained semantic retrieval has advantages, because precision and recall can be controlled in new ways. We have not evaluated our system with user communities, so future work should look into empirical retrieval tests. Work on SB agents parsing conventional blog entries, heuristically interpreting them, and republishing the adapted contents with semantic markup[15] does not render SB meaningless. This solution cannot fully detect most structures which knowledge workers could explicitly express right from the beginning.

---

[12] In collaboration with Winfried Schmitz-Esser, PSIs for these associations have been defined and published, integrating the PSIs once defined by the company Seruba (now defunct). http://web.archive.org/web/*/http://seruba.com

[13] http://jakarta.apache.org/velocity/

[14] http://www.tmapi.org/

[15] See e.g. ongoing diploma thesis "Entwurf und Realisierung von Semantic Blogging Agents" at Technical University Munich, http://www11.in.tum.de/lehre/da/proj-776.phtml, last accessed 2006-06-12.

Knowledge Organization: One reviewer missed a more detailed justification of why we chose an approach for semantic relations based on knowledge organization, and why this particular one. Any approach based on one or more sound theories of semantic relations (e.g. knowledge organization, rhetorical structure theory, or didactic theory) would be better than ad-hoc relations. The Schmitz-Esser set of relations was chosen because the first author has long-standing experience in knowledge organization and is involved in work on transferring this particular relation set to Topic Maps-based applications. We do not claim that this particular arsenal of relations is the most useful or complete. However, this set turned out as quite powerful, although additional sets such as rhetorical ones (like agreeing/disagreeing) should be integrated in further work. By design, only semtags can be copied to own ontology views, not semrels (associations). Further improvements should support sembloggers in adding new relation types and subtypes, not only instances, and in changing the particular fixed (but configurable) set of predefined association types to a more flexible approach. For ease of use, relation types could be coupled with templates.

RDF(S)/OWL: One reviewer criticized why we value RDF-based approaches without detailed reasons. Another correctly pointed out that the graph model RDF cannot be blamed for the fact that some RDF-based prototypical blogging software does not support semantic relations between blog entries and semtags, as this could be added with RDFS/OWL, both well integrated into RDF. Therefore, we should not base our argument for using Topic Maps on dismissing RDF. In this paper, we were not at all interested in arguing pro or contra RDF(S)/OWL vs. Topic Maps in general, but in drawing from Topic Maps for improved SB. Our main motivation was design science-oriented. We do not claim that Topic Maps are in general superior to other approaches, or that certain Topic Maps-based SB features could not be achieved with other means. In fact, both Published Subjects and well-founded semantic relations can be integrated into other semantic technologies, and should so. However, we do claim that our combination of features:

- was lacking in or not the focus of previous work,
- is useful for SB systems in general, independent of their technical basis, and
- can be well realized with Topic Maps in a more natural way than with RDF alone, or with RDFS/OWL.

We did neither intend nor achieve an in-depth review and feature comparison of all the SB systems. We are aware that some RDF-based systems partially exhibit more sophisticated features, or can be used more easily. In particular, a closer look and intertwining with the recent semiBlog system is desirable. In general, the RDF(S)/OWL and Topic Maps communities should still come closer together, better connecting research, learning from each other, and fostering convergence and interoperability. Future work should better amalgamate advantages of both approaches.

Semwikis, e.g. ArtificialMemory: Related to SB, but not treated here, are semantic wikis (semwikis) [6, 10, 51, 52]. After finishing this paper, we became aware of Artificial Memory[16], a SemWiki developed by Lars Ludwig [53, 54]. Facts treated as subdocuments can be expressed and linked with semantic relations, also in blog style.

---

[16] http://www.artificialmemory.net/

Blogging Component: Future work might adapt our blojsom plugin to other blogging engines.

PSI Component: We only implemented it because a reusable third-party solution did not exist. Future work should integrate more flexible and sophisticated third-party services.

TMAPI and Topic Map Engines: Basing all topic map operations on TMAPI by design has also several major drawbacks: Only the TMAPI layer operations can be used, which are slower and more cumbersome than directly using the more powerful capabilities of engine-specific native framework APIs. This forces some duplication in navigation and querying capabilities. Tolog via TMAPI is not yet supported, so we had to awkwardly access topics with the TMAPI index system, and for complex queries, the engines had to be queried directly. Because the tolog version in TM4J was not sufficient for our purposes, semantic retrieval in semblog-tm currently depends on OKS. Future work should implement higher-level operations on top of TMAPI. Support for more backends using TMAPI, and for different topic map engines not using TMAPI is also desirable. semblog-tm should also be changed from in-memory to database backend, although the topic maps are frequently serialized as .xtm.

Semantic Knowledge Services: We had to decide for one of the different approaches for topic maps services. As shown with TMShare (TopicMapster) [70], topic map fragments can be generated and p2p-like shared. Some alternatives are the TMRAP protocol [71-73], including capabilities for tolog queries, or TMIP [74]. We decided not to use TMRAP, although very useful, because TMAPI does not yet support it. Except Axis, we could not look into other service frameworks, like e.g. WSMO tools[17] Better service interoperability as tackled by a recent harmonization initiative would be nice, and so would be more open semantic knowledge services.

For the **future of Topic Maps-based SB research**, we foresee more research on:

- p2p-like distribution for all components, e.g. TMRAP and semantic overlay in p2p networks with topic map data, or distributed search over PSIs.
- federated interoperability of PSI and topic map aggregation services, as well as more work on interoperability between Topic Maps and RDF(S)/OWL, between topic map query languages and Sparql, and work on semantic knowledge services.
- experiments with PSI registries with additional metadata for Published Subjects
- trust and reputation building for semtags
- empirical research with and actual use in SB communities
- open distributed knowledge management applications with topic maps in general.

References

1. Walker, J.: Weblog. In: Herman, D.H., Jahn, M., Ryan, M.-L. (eds.): The Routledge Encyclopedia of Narrative Theory. Routledge, London and New York (2005) 45
2. Picot, A., Fischer, T. (eds.): Weblogs professionell. Grundlagen, Konzepte und Praxis im unternehmerischen Umfeld. d.punkt (2005)

---

[17] http://www.wsmo.org/

3. Staab, S., Stuckenschmidt, H. (eds.): Semantic Web and Peer-to-Peer. Decentralized Management and Exchange of Knowledge and Information. Springer, Berlin (2006)

4. Röll, M.: Knowledge Blogs: Persönliche Weblogs im Intranet als Werkzeuge im Wissensmanagement. In: Picot, A., Fischer, T. (eds.): Weblogs professionell. Grundlagen, Konzepte und Praxis im unternehmerischen Umfeld. d.punkt (2005) 95-111

5. Kleske, J.: Wissensarbeit mit Social Software. Konzeption & Entwicklung eines Systems für die kollaborative Wissensarbeit in der Forschung basierend auf Social Software. Diplomarbeit Fachhochschule Darmstadt, Darmstadt (2006)

6. Schuster, M., Rappold, D.: Social Semantic Software – was soziale Dynamik im Semantic Web auslöst In: Pellegrini, T., Blumauer, A. (eds.): Semantic Web: Wege zur vernetzten Wissensgesellschaft. Springer (2006) 189-199

7. Hammond, T., Hannay, T., Lund, B., Scott, J.: Social Bookmarking Tools (I) – A General Review. D-Lib Magazine 11(4) (2005) http://www.dlib.org/dlib/april05/hammond/ 04hammond.html

8. Sigel, A.: How can user-oriented depth analysis be constructively guided? In: Beghtol, C., Howarth, L.C., Williamson, N.J. (eds.): Dynamism and Stability in Knowledge Organization. Procs. 6th Int. ISKO Conference. 10-13 July 2000, Toronto, Canada. Ergon, Würzburg (2000) 247-253

9. Golder, S.A., Huberman, B.A.: Usage patterns of collaborative tagging systems. Journal of Information Science 32(2) (2006) 198-208

10. Voß, J.: Collaborative thesaurus tagging the Wikipedia way (2006) http://arxiv.org/ abs/cs/0604036

11. Mathes, A.: Folksonomies – Cooperative Classification and Communication Through Shared Metadata. Computer Mediated Communication – LIS590CMC, Graduate School of Library and Information Science, University of Illinois Urbana-Champaign (2004) http://www. adammathes.com/academic/computer-mediated-communication/folksonomies .pdf

12. Quintarelli, E.: Folksonomies: power to the people. ISKO Italy Conference, 2005-06-24, Mailand, Italy (2005) http://www.iskoi.org/doc/folksonomies.htm

13. Folksonomy (2006-06-08) http://en.wikipedia.org/wiki/Folksonomy

14. Möller, K., Bojärs, U., Breslin, J.G.: Using Semantics to Enhance the Blogging Experience. In: Sure, Y., Domingue, J. (eds.): The Semantic Web: Research and Applications, 3rd European Semantic Web Conference, ESWC 2006, Budva, Montenegro, June 11-14, 2006, Proceedings, LNCS 4011. Springer, Berlin (2006) 679-696

15. Structured blogging (2006-06-08) http://www.structuredblogging.org/

16. Paquet, S.: Towards structured blogging [Blog entry] (2003-03-13) http://radio.weblogs.com/0110772/stories/2003/03/13/towardsStructuredBlogging.html

17. Shirkey, C.: Ontology is Overrated: Categories, Links, and Tags (2005) http://shirky.com/ writings/ontology_overrated.html

18. Karger, D.R., Quan, D.: What would it mean to blog on the semantic web? Journal of Web Semantics 3(2) (2005) 147-157

19. Avesani, P., Cova, M., Hayes, C., Massa, P.: Learning Contextualised Weblog Topics. WWW2005, 2nd Annual Workshop on the Weblogging Ecosystem: Aggregation, Analysis and Dynamics, 2005-05-10, Chiba, Japan (2005) http://sra.itc.it/people/cova/data/papers/ paper-www-workshop-05.pdf

20. Cayzer, S.: Semantic Blogging and Decentralized Knowledge Management. Communications of the ACM 47(12) (2004) 47-52

21. Möller, K., Breslin, J.G.B., Decker, S.: semiBlog - Semantic Publishing of Desktop Data. 14th Conference on Information Systems Development (ISD2005), August 2005 Karlstad, Sweden (2005) http://sw.deri.org/~knud/papers/semiBlogISD2005Word/semiBlogISD 2005print.pdf

22. Handschuh, S., Staab, S.: Annotation for the Semantic Web. IOS Press, Amsterdam (2003)
23. Reif, G.: Semantische Annotation. In: Pellegrini, T., Blumauer, A. (eds.): Semantic Web: Wege zur vernetzten Wissensgesellschaft. Springer (2006) 405-418
24. Uren, V., Cimiano, P., Iria, J., Handschuh, S., Vargas-Vera, M., Motta, E., Ciravegna, F.: Semantic annotation for knowledge management: Requirements and a survey of the state of the art. Journal of Web Semantics 4(1) (2006) 14-28
25. Dill, S., Eiron, N., Gibson, D., Gruhl, D., Guha, R., Jhingran, A., Kanungo, T., Rajagopalan, S., Tomkins, A., Tomlin, J.A., Zien, J.Y.: SemTag and Seeker: Bootstrapping the Semantic Web via Automated Semantic Annotation. WWW 2003 (12th Int. Conf. on World Wide Web). ACM, Budapest, Hungary (2003) 178-186
26. Sigel, A.: Report on the Open Space Sessions. In: Maicher, L., Park, J. (eds.): Charting the Topic Maps Research and Applications Landscape. First International Workshop on Topic Map Research and Applications, TMRA 2005, Leipzig, Germany, October 6-7, 2005, Revised Selected Papers, LNAI 3873. Springer (2006) 271-280 http://www.wim.uni-koeln.de/uploads/media/Report_from_the_open_space_sessions_v24_with_Copyright.pdf
27. Frank, M.: Semantic Blogging mit Topic Maps – Entwurf und Implementierung eines Prototypen. Diplomarbeit. Wirtschaftsinformatik, insbesondere Informationsmanagement. Universität zu Köln, Köln (2005)
28. Bünten, L.: Verteiltheit und semantische Wissensdienste für Topic Maps-basiertes Semblogging: Konzeption und prototypische Implementierung. Diplomarbeit. Wirtschaftsinformatik, insbesondere Informationsmanagement. Universität zu Köln, Köln (2006)
29. Jansen, S.: Interoperable semantische Wissensdienste mit Topic Maps und RDF: Konzeption und prototypische Implementierung. Diplomarbeit. Wirtschaftsinformatik, insbesondere Informationsmanagement. Universität zu Köln, Köln (2006)
30. Biezunski, M., Bryan, M., Newcomb, S.R.: ISO/IEC 13250 Topic Maps (Second Edition). Approved revised text (2002) http://www.jtc1sc34.org/repository/0322.htm
31. Garshol, L.M., Moore, G.: Topic Maps — Data Model. International Standard (for review). (2006-06-18) http://www.isotopicmaps.org/sam/sam-model/
32. Garshol, L.M., Moore, G.: Topic Maps — XML Syntax. Final Draft International Standard Draft (for review). ISO 13250: Topic Maps (2006-06-19) http://www.isotopicmaps.org/sam/sam-xtm/)
33. Pepper, S.: Published Subjects: Introduction and Basic Requirements. OASIS Published Subjects Technical Committee Recommendation (2003-06-24) http://www.oasis-open.org/committees/download.php/3050/pubsubj-pt1-1.02-cs.pdf
34. Pepper, S., Schwab, S.: Curing the Web's Identity Crisis: Subject Indicators for RDF. XML Conference 2003, Philadelphia, Pennsylvania, USA (2003) http://www.idealliance.org/papers/dx_xml03/html/abstract/05-01-05.html
35. Maicher, L.: Subject Identification in Topic Maps in Theory and Practice. In: Tolksdorf, R., Eckstein, R. (eds.): Berliner XML Tage 2004. XML-Clearinghouse, Berlin, Germany (2004) 301-307 http://www.informatik.uni-leipzig.de/~maicher/publications/%5Bmaic04cFINAL%5D.pdf
36. Pepper, S.: The Case for Published Subjects. WWW2006 Workshop: Identity, Reference, and the Web (IRW2006), Edinburgh, Scotland (2006) http://www.ontopia.net/topicmaps/materials/The_Case_for_Published_Subjects.pdf
37. Schmitz-Esser, W.: Thesaurus and Beyond: An Advanced Formula for Linguistics Engineering and Information Retrieval. Knowledge Organization 26(1) (1999) 10-22
38. Introduction to Integrative Cross-Language Ontology (ICLO): Formalizing and interrelating textual knowledge to enable intelligent action and knowledge sharing. In: Schmitz-Esser, W. & Sigel, A. (2006): Introducing Terminology-based Ontologies. http://eprints.rclis.org/archive/00006612/), pp. 54-113. Ninth International ISKO Conference 2006

39. Cayzer, S.: Semantic Blogging: Spreading the Semantic Web Meme. XML Europe 2004, 18-21 April, Amsterdam, NL (2004) http://idealliance.org/papers/dx_xmle04/papers/03-05-03/03-05-03.pdf

40. Cayzer, S.: Semblogging - a guide to the HP Labs semantic blogging demonstrator (2003) http://www.semanticblogging.org/semblog/whatisit.html

41. Cayzer, S., Shabajee, P.: SWAD-Europe deliverable 12.1.2: Semantic Blogging and Bibliographies – Requirements Specification (2003) http://www.w3.org/2001/sw/Europe/reports/pdf/12.1.2.pdf

42. Reynolds, D., Cayzer, S., Shabajee, P., Steer, D.: SWAD-Europe deliverable 12.1.8: SWAD-E Demonstrators – Lessons Learnt (2004) http://www.w3.org/2001/SW/Europe/reports/demo-lessons-report/

43. Miles, A., Brickley, D.: SKOS Core Vocabulary Specification. W3C Working Draft 2 November 2005 (2005) http://www.w3.org/TR/swbp-skos-core-spec

44. Miles, A., Brickley, D.: SKOS Core Guide. W3C Working Draft 2 November 2005 (2005) http://www.w3.org/TR/2005/WD-swbp-skos-core-guide-20051102/

45. Miles, A., Matthews, B., Beckett, D., Brickley, D., Wilson, M., Rogers, N.: SKOS: A language to describe simple knowledge structures for the web. XTech 2005: XML, the Web and beyond. Idealliance, Amsterdam, NL (2005) http://www.idealliance.org/proceedings/xtech05/papers/03-04-01/

46. Ohmukai, I., Numa, K., Takeda, H.: Egocentric Search Method for Authoring Support in Semantic Weblog. Workshop on Knowledge Markup and Semantic Annotation (Semannot2003), collocated with the Second International Conference on Knowledge Capture (K-CAP2003), 2003. (2003)

47. Ohmukai, I., Takeda, H., Numa, K., Hamasaki, M., Adachi, S.: Personal Knowledge Publishing Suite with Weblog. 13th International World Wide Web Conference (WWW2004), Workshop on the Weblogging Ecosystem: Aggregation, Analysis and Dynamics, 2004-05-18. New York, NY, USA (2004)
http://www-kasm.nii.ac.jp/papers/takeda/03/kcap03_ohmukai.pdf

48. Ohmukai, I., Takeda, H.: Semblog: Personal Publishing Platform with RSS and FOAF. In: Brickley, D., Decker, S., Guha, R.V., Miller, L. (eds.): Proceedings of the 1st Workshop on Friend of a Friend, Social Networking and the (Semantic) Web, September 2004, Galway, IE (2005) 217-221 http://www.w3.org/2001/sw/Europe/events/foaf-galway/papers/pp/semblog_personal_publishing_platform/

49. Sereno, B.: Knowledge Mapping as a blogging approach [Blog entry] (2005) http://kmi.open.ac.uk/people/bertrand/index.php/2005/07/15/knowledgemapping-as-a-blogging-approach/

50. Möller, K., Decker, S.: Harvesting Desktop Data for Semantic Blogging. In: Decker, S., Park, J., Quan, D., Sauermann, L. (eds.): Proceedings of 1st Workshop on The Semantic Desktop - Next Generation Information Management & Collaboration Infrastructure. ISWC 2005, November 6, 2005 (CEUR Workshop Proceedings), Galway, Ireland (2005) 79-91
http://sw.deri.org/~knud/papers/semiBlogSemDesk2005/semiBlogSemDesk2005.pdf

51. Völkel, M., Krötzsch, M., Vrandecic, D., Haller, H., Studer, R.: Semantic Wikipedia. 15th International Conference on World Wide Web, WWW 2006, May 23-26, 2006, Edinburgh, Scotland (2006)

52. Völkel, M., Schaffert, S.: Proceedings of the First Workshop on Semantic Wikis - From Wiki to Semantics (SemWiki2006), co-located with the 3rd Annual European Semantic Web Conference (ESWC 2006). Budva, Montenegro, June 12, 2006 (2006) http://www.aifb.uni-karlsruhe.de/WBS/hha/papers/SemanticWikipedia.pdf

53. Ludwig, L., O'Sullivan, D., Zhou, X.: Artificial Memory Prototype for Personal Semantic Subdocument Knowledge Management (PS-KM). Demonstration Proposal. ISWC 2004 (2004) http://iswc2004.semanticweb.org/demos/36/paper.pdf

54. Zhou, X., Li, Q., Ludwig, L., Chen, Y.: Subject-Oriented Knowledge Formalization: Method and Prototype. IEEE/WIC/ACM International Conference on Web Intelligence (WI 2006 Main Conference Proceeding. IEEE Computer Society, 18-22 December 2006, Hong Kong, China (2006) 853-858

55. Sigel, A.: Organisation verteilten Wissens mit semantischen Wissensnetzen und der Aggregation semantischer Wissensdienste am Beispiel Digitale Bibliotheken/Kulturelles Erbe. In: Ohly, H.P., Sieglerschmidt, J., Swertz, C. (eds.): Wissensorganisation und Verantwortung. Gesellschaftliche, ökonomische und technische Aspekte. Ergon, Würzburg (2006) 276-292 http://www.wim.uni-koeln.de/uploads/media/ ISKO2004_SIGEL_Organisation_verteilten_Wissens_v16_01.pdf

56. Sigel, A.: Content Intelligence durch Verknüpfung semantischer Wissensdienste am Beispiel von Semblogging. 2. Kongress Semantic Web und Wissenstechnologien. Semantic Web Services, Darmstadt, Germany (2005) http://www.wim.uni-koeln.de/uploads/media/ Content_Intelligence_ZGDV05_v16.pdf

57. Sigel, A.: kPeer (Knowledge Peers): Informationssuche beim verteilten SemBloggen. Workshop "P2P Information Retrieval in Deutschland", Leipzig (2005) http://www.sempir.informatik.uni-leipzig.de/folien/sigel.pdf

58. Park, J.: Augmented Storytelling on the Web. National Storytelling Conference, July 2004, Bellingham, WA, USA (2004) http://www.nexist.org/nsc2004/index.html

59. Rajbhandari, S., Andres, F., Naito, M., Wuwongse, V.: Semantic-augmented support in Spatial-Temporal Multimedia Blog Management. In: Procs. Of TMRA 2006, this volume (2007).

60. Garshol, L.M.: Living with Topic Maps and RDF: Topic Maps, RDF, DAML, OIL, OWL, TMCL. XML Europe Conference 2003, London, England (2003) http:// www.idealliance.org/papers/dx_xmle03/index/title/ da78f2d953553c194e0c0dbed6.html

61. Garshol, L.M., Naito, M.: RDF and Topic Maps Interoperability in Practice / Realization of seamless knowledge: connecting distributed RDF and Topic Maps. 3rd International Semantic Web Conference (ISWC2004) / SIG-SWO, Hiroshima, Japan (2004) http://iswc2004.semanticweb.org/demos/19/paper.pdf

62. Ontopia: The RTM RDF to Topic Maps Mapping: Definition and Introduction. [Ontopia technical report]. Version 0.2. Ontopia (2003) http://www.ontopia.net/topicmaps/materials/ rdf2tm.html

63. Pepper, S., Presutti, V., Garshol, L.M., Vitali, F.: Guidelines for RDF/Topic Maps Inter-operability. W3C Editor's Draft 30 June 2006 (2006) http://www.w3.org/2001/sw/ BestPractices/RDFTM/guidelines-20060630.html

64. Pepper, S., Vitali, F., Garshol, L.M., Gessa, N., Presutti, V.: A Survey of RDF/Topic Maps Interoperability Proposals. W3C Working Group Note 10 February 2006 (2006) http://www.w3.org/TR/rdftm-survey/

65. Pepper, S., Vitali, F., Garshol, L.M., Gessa, N., Presutti, V.: Approaches to RDF/Topic Maps Interoperability. XTech 2005: XML, the Web and beyond, Amsterdam, NL (2005) http://www.idealliance.org/proceedings/xtech05/papers/03-03-01/

66. Garshol, L.M.: Q: A model for topic maps: Unifying RDF and topic maps. Extreme Markup Languages 2005 (2005) http://www.mulberrytech.com/Extreme/Proceedings/ html/2005/Garshol01/EML2005Garshol01.html

67. Sigel, A., Bünten, L.: Topic Maps-based Semblogging with semblog-tm: System demonstration at TMRA06. Video and edited transcript (2006) http://www.wim.uni-koeln.de/uploads/media/semblog-tm-demo-at-TMRA06.zip

68. Sigel, A., Bünten, L.: Topic Maps-based Semblogging with semblog-tm: System demonstration at TMRA06. Slides (2006) http://www.wim.uni-koeln.de/uploads/media/TMRA_Semblogging_Demo_v15_2006-10-11.pdf

69. Naito, M.: Metadata for Published Subjects. Proposal for a new work item (ISO/IEC JTC 1/SC 34) (2006) Private communication

70. Ahmed, K.: TMShare - Topic Map Fragment Exchange in a Peer-To-Peer Application. XML Europe Conference 2003, London, England (2003) http://www.idealliance.org/papers/dx_xmle03/papers/02-03-03/02-03-03.html

71. Garshol, L.M.: TMRAP - Topic Maps Remote Access Protocol. In: Maicher, L., Park, J. (eds.): Charting the Topic Maps Research and Applications Landscape, First International Workshop on Topic Maps Research and Applications, TMRA 2005, Leipzig, Germany, October 6-7, 2005, Revised Selected Papers, LNAI 3873. Springer (2006) 53-68 http://www.garshol.priv.no/download/text/tmrap.pdf

72. Pepper, S.: Towards Seamless Knowledge. Integrating Public Sector Portals. XML 2004 Conference, Washington, D.C., USA (2004) http://www.ontopia.net/topicmaps/materials/Towards%20Seamless%20Knowledge.ppt

73. Pepper, S., Garshol, L.M.: Seamless Knowledge. Spontaneous Knowledge Federation using TMRAP. Extreme Markup 2004 Conference, Montréal, Canada (2004) http://www.ontopia.net/topicmaps/materials/Seamless%20Knowledge%20with%20TMRAP.ppt

74. Barta, R.: TMIP, a RESTful Topic Maps Interaction Protocol. Extreme Markup Languages Conference 2005. IDEAlliance, Montréal, Canada (2005) http://www.mulberrytech.com/Extreme/Proceedings/xslfo-pdf/2005/Barta01/EML2005Barta01.pdf

Report from the Open Space and Poster Sessions

Lars Marius Garshol[1] and Lutz Maicher[2]

[1] Ontopia AS, Oslo, Norway
larsga@ontopia.net
http://www.ontopia.net
[2] University of Leipzig, Johannisgasse 26, 04103 Leipzig
maicher@informatik.uni-leipzig.de
http://www.informatik.uni-leipzig.de/~maicher/

Abstract. This is a summary of the presentations made in the poster session and the two open space sessions at the TMRA 2006 conference. The poster session consists of peer-reviewed conference submissions accepted as posters, while the open space sessions were free-form sessions where anyone could sign up to do a short presentation. The result is a collection of reports on works in progress and interesting ideas, some of which are likely to appear as papers at next year's conference.

1 The Poster Session

This report summarizes the six contributions to the poster session of TMRA 2006, based on the submitted abstracts, the actual posters, and impressions from the presentations. All posters were submitted to the Program Committee, refereed and accepted as poster presentation for the conference. All posters were exhibited during the whole conference and presented in a series of ten minute presentations during the poster session. The poster session was moderated by Steve Newcomb. All posters are available online at the conference website.

1.1 TMAPI-Implementation for Shared Accessed Topic Maps

Jan Hellich and Martin Krüger introduced a TMAPI implementation in Java[1] that delegates to a remote server (also implemented in Java) using a web service interface. This allows multiple clients to connect to the same remote server, using the same interface as if the accessed topic map had been local. The remote server uses a persistent implementation based on a relational database. The solution uses a 3-tier approach to divide the tasks of handling the user interface, processing the topic maps (inserting, finding and deleting information), and persistent storage.

Using the solution Java applications implemented against the (Java interpretation of) TMAPI[2] can use a shared and remote relational database. Each access or modification of information stored in the Topic Maps backend will be translated into web services communication. The requests correspond roughly to TMAPI method calls, and

---

[1] http://www.informatik.uni-leipzig.de/~tmra/2006/contributions/POSTER_HellichKrueger.pdf
[2] http://www.tmapi.org

L. Maicher, A. Sigel, and L.M. Garshol (Eds.): TMRA 2006, LNAI 4438, pp. 243–255, 2007.

the application server transforms these calls into SQL. The application server used is Glassfish,[3] and the database is MySQL. The architecture of the solution allows the replacement of the application and relational database servers by any conformant product.

The implementation is only a proof of concept, but successfully passes the TMAPI test suite. Performance tests yield encouraging results.

1.2   A Tiny, Simple, and Versatile Topic Map

Motomu Naito presented a Topic Map which could be used as a common test bed[4] within the community when new technologies emerge within the standardization or research process. The Opera Topic Map[5] authored by Steve Pepper is commonly used for these purposes, but Naito-san argued that a new common test bed is needed which is easy to understand for many people, is applicable to various problems, and is open content.

For this purpose, he proposes a "family tree topic map". This is a small and flexible ontology (including a modeling method [Maicher06]) for the creation of topic maps representing family relationships. The vocabulary consists of one topic type "person" and three association types "brother-sister", "married-couple" and "parent-child" (with role types). Using these types, family relationships can be modeled. Within the contribution it is shown how the given vocabulary has to be used to model family relationships as Topic Map.

Topic Maps using the given ontology (and modeling method) can be used to discuss querying, constraints, and numerous other application issues.

1.3   PHPTMAPI

Johannes Schmidt and Andreas Stephan introduced PHPTMAPI,[6] which is an adaptation of TMAPI to PHP5. TMAPI is the common programming interface for accessing and manipulating data held in Topic Maps, defined in Java. PHPTMAPI[7] is Open Source and allows developers to write Topic Maps-based applications in PHP against a common interface. Although PHPTMAPI is intended to be a full implementation of the TMAPI, some small derivations are introduced by the authors (ie. locators are directly represented as strings, not as locator objects).

They also introduced QuaaxTM,[8] a Topic Maps engine implementing PHPTMAPI. QuaaxTM uses MySQL with InnoDB as storage engine and therefore benefits from transaction support and referential integrity. Version 0.2 is available (2007-01-16), but does not implement the merging mechanism of the TMDM.

PHP and MySQL are commonly used to build web applications. Full featured Topic Maps engines for these environments will be very valuable to put Topic Maps into the web.

---

[3] http://glassfish.dev.java.net/

[4] http://www.informatik.uni-leipzig.de/~tmra/2006/contributions/tmra2006-posternaito.ppt

[5] http://www.ontopia.net/omnigator/models/topicmap_complete.jsp?tm=opera.ltm

[6] http://www.informatik.uni-leipzig.de/~tmra/2006/contributions/tmra2006-PHPTMAPI.png

[7] http://phptmapi.sourceforge.net

[8] http://quaaxtm.sourceforge.net/

1.4 Natural Language User Interface to Topic Maps with Prolog

Thomas Flemming presented an approach for a natural language user interface to Topic Maps.[9] Flemming used Prolog as a backend for storing, querying, and updating Topic Maps. Generally, approaches for natural language user interfaces to Topic Maps can be used to increase the search quality and create human-centric interfaces to the database. Another issue will be the ability of the modification of topic maps using (nearly) natural language phrases.

In the first part of the contribution it is shown how Prolog can be used as backend for Topic Maps. Prolog, one of the veterans in logical programming, with a long-standing history starting in 1972, has the benefit of being a mature programming language well suited for Topic Maps. Besides the declarative part, rules can be used to define views on the backend. Even the possibility of the definition of constraints is given. There is a Java implementation of the backend.

In a second step, information given in the topic maps is mapped to some generic natural language elements, like nouns, proper nouns, verb phrases, and transitive verbs. Lexical knowledge is added to the domain models represented in the topic aps. As example the topic with the basename "Johan Sebastian Bach" is given, which is a proper name, a proper noun, and a noun phrase. Further, association types normally consist of Verb Phrases like "has composed". This lexical knowledge can be assigned manually or automatically (using NLP techniques) to the topic map.

So called pattern of interests can be defined or identified (as example the pattern "ProperNoun VerbPhrase NounPhrase" is given) and further translated into Prolog queries (with unfilled slots). Completely filled patterns (facts) are almost natural language, so that search results can be represented in this way.

In the context of this contribution the thematically closely related project AIOBCT[10] [Sigel05] should be mentioned, where a natural language interface to Topic Maps is implemented based on Toma [Pinchuk06].

1.5 SIREN–A Topic Maps-Based Semantic Information Retrieval Environment for Digital Libraries

Hendrik Thomas (Bernd Markscheffel and Torsten Brix) presented SIREN,[11] a scientific framework of a Topic Maps-based "Semantic Information Retrieval Environment for Digital Libraries". The core of the system is a domain model expressed as a topic map which acts as a semantic layer improving the information retrieval. SIREN is developed within the "Digital Mechanism and Gear Library" (DMG-Lib[12]) project.

SIREN integrates existing prototypes to improve information retrieval in the digital library using Topic Maps. The information retrieval process is seen as a four step chain, starting with the creation and population of the domain model and ending with the visualisation of the request results.

---

[9] http://www.informatik.uni-leipzig.de/~tmra/2006/contributions/POSTER_thomasfl.pdf

[10] http://www.informatik.uni-leipzig.de/~tmra05/PRES/RP.pdf

[11] http://www.informatik.uni-leipzig.de/~tmra/2006/contributions/POSTER_SIREN.pdf

[12] http://www.dmg-lib.org/dmglib/main/portal.jsp

The first step is subject analysis. The first part of this step is creating a domain model (in the project context: about mechanisms and gears) as topic map. For this manual task the Topic Maps Wiki Editor TMwiki[13] [Sigel05], is used. The second part of this step is assigning of relevant digital content to the subjects in the domain model. For the creation of these occurrences three indexing levels are foreseen and partly implemented: (1) automatic indexing based on statistical analysis, (2) expensive and reliable content creation by experts, and (3) flexible collaborative tagging approaches.

The second step of the chain is the specification of information needs. To express the information needs the users can exploratively browse through the domain model by using the Topic Map Visualiser (TMV), even developed by the project team. Additionally, the users can express their information needs by (simple and complex) queries or the selection of a set of topics in interest.

The third step of the chain is the search process where the information satisfying the expressed information needs have to be found. This classical information retrieval task uses both the domain model and the indexed digital content.

The last step is the visualisation of the search results. The Topic Maps Viewer presents the search result in the context expressed by the domain model.

The presented work introduced the conceptualisation of a framework for improving information retrieval in digital libraries based on Topic Maps technologies. To get a stable framework in future, the prototypes have to be developed further to stable and scalable solutions which have to be integrated on a reliable platform.

1.6   Visualisation of Intellectual Content for Topic Maps Conceptualisation

Patricia Cheryl Liebetrau presented the challenges faced by a national pilot digitization project in South Africa:[14] making the transition from a project-centric site to an information-centric resource. The cultural heritage project, entitled Southern African Freedom Struggles, 1950 to 1994, has been an attempt to provide a comprehensive archive of literature and online resources to support a changing higher education curriculum in South Africa and to provide an important resource for historians, political scientists and students of African Studies in a global context. The digitalized materials which have to be integrated is everything from underground journals, minutes of political meetings, ANC materials, etc. The aim of the project is to ease the access to this heterogeneous information by implementing a subject-centric knowledge organization.

Within the DISA[15] project a thesaurus was developed which helps to organize apartheid related subjects from a scholar perspective. In future, this thesaurus should be the backbone of a Topic Maps-based solution for organizing the digitalized content and for visualizing the conceptual relationships between them. The poster presented conceptual work in progress.

---

[13] http://www.informatik.uni-leipzig.de/ tmra05/PRES/HTa.pdf

[14] http://www.informatik.uni-leipzig.de/˜tmra/2006/contributions/tmra2006-liebetrau.jpg

[15] http://www.disa.ukzn.ac.za/

2   The Open Space Sessions

The following is a summary of the open space sessions in chronological order based on the slides used by the presenters, a blog summary of the conference,[16] and impressions from the conference itself. The contributions were informal and non-refereed, since workshop attendants had been given the opportunity to sign up to short talks on a flip chart during the conference, and the suggested format for each presentation was: one slide, five minutes presentation, and five minutes discussion. Both sessions were moderated by Lars Marius Garshol. The outcome of this "playground for visionaries" is this report on forward-looking work in progress.

2.1   A Topic Map for Botanical Art

Motomu Naito presented a topic map about various species of flowers that has two points of interest. Firstly, it was produced from a relational database of botanical information merged with a hand-written topic map. Secondly, the topic map was used to produce a PDF document using XSLT and XSL-FO.

The database is actually a CSV file with a standard biological classification of 386 families of flowers into 83 orders, 11 subclasses, 2 classes, and 1 phylum. The hand-written LTM file [Garshol06a] has individual species of flowers and the families to which they belong, people, dates, places, and pictures. Naito-san has created the data flow shown in 1 on the following page, converting this into a PDF document. (DB2TM is a commercial tool for integrating relational data with Topic Maps described in 2.8 on page 253.)

Once the two data sources have been merged into a single topic map that topic map is exported to TM/XML [Garshol06b]. This is an XML syntax for Topic Maps that is much easier to process with XSLT than XTM, and this is what Naito-san has done. The XSLT stylesheet produces XSL-FO output, which is again converted to PDF.

2.2   A Standard Web Service Interface for Topic Maps

Graham Moore spoke on the need for a standard web service interface to Topic Maps servers. His rationale was that although an interchange format (like XTM) allows data to be moved between applications it isn't actually sufficient to enable applications to interoperate. Given that web services are currently the most common method for accessing remote applications independently of platform having a common standard web service interface for Topic Maps servers seems the best way to achieve this.

Graham listed a number of such web services already in use:

– The interface to NetworkedPlanet's commercial TMCore Topic Maps engine.[17]
– Ontopia's TMRAP interface used in their commercial OKS product[Garshol06c].
– Robert Barta's TMIP interface implemented in his open source Perl engine [Barta05a].

---

[16] http://www.garshol.priv.no/blog/73.html
[17] http://www.networkedplanet.com/technology/webservices/intro.html

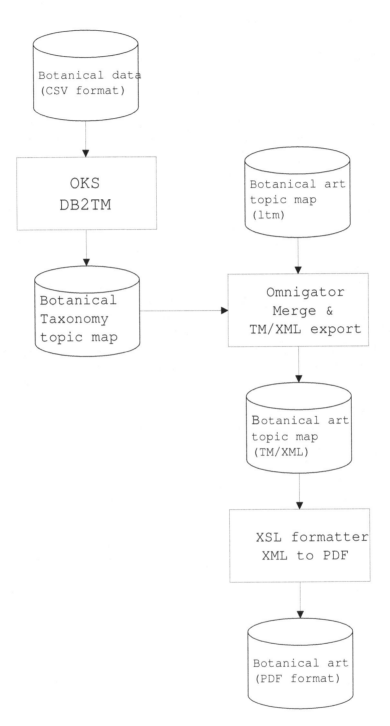

Fig. 1. Data flow

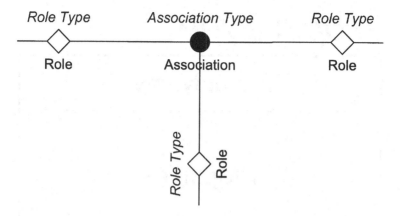

Fig. 2. Associations

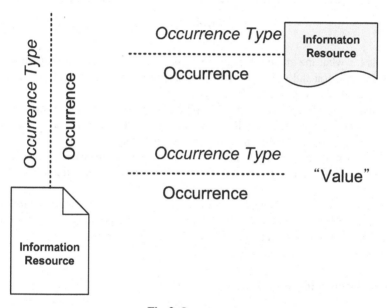

Fig. 3. Occurrences

- The interface used by Robert Cerny to make Topincs[Cerny07].
- The interface used by Jan Hellich and Martin Krger for their remote TMAPI implementation (see 1.1 on page 243).

According to Graham this shows both the need for such a service, and that there is sufficient experience in the field already that a useful common standard can be created.

2.3 Proposals for Graphical Topic Maps Notations

Professor Jaeho Lee presented two proposals for graphical Topic Maps notations. ISO is currently working to create a standard for this, and professor Lee's work was two

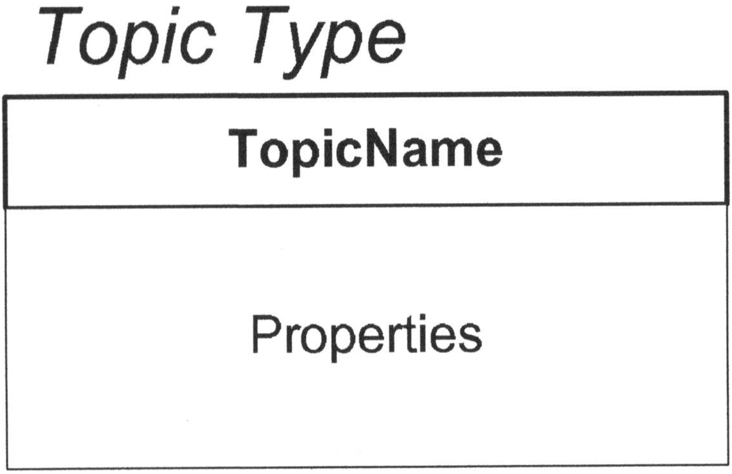

Topic Type

TopicName
Properties

Fig. 4. Topic

proposals for what the standard might look like. The ISO standard will support both schema information and visualization of instance information, but professor Lee's proposals covered only instance information.

The first proposal uses a fixed set of graphical shapes, with boxes for topics and lines for associations and occurrences. Reification is done with identifiers and references to identifiers. The shapes are shown in 4, 2 on the preceding page, and 3 on the previous page. Professor Lee demonstrated an Eclipse plug-in which can be used to create models using this graphical notation, and expressed surprise at how easy creating the plug-in was.

The other proposal was more free-form and allowed any shape to be used for individual topics, together with a "legend", which maps sets of shapes to the topic type they are used to represent. It was not clear how other Topic Maps constructs were represented in this notation.

2.4 The Atmo Topic Maps Editor

Xuan Baldauf presented Atmo, a Topic Maps editor written in Java. Atmo does not use a schema to guide the editing, which means that when creating, for example, a binary association, the user has to choose four topics (the association type, two role types, and the topic at the other end). The difficulty with this is that without a schema any topic could potentially appear in any of these four positions, which makes it awkward for the user to choose the correct topic.

The distinguishing feature of Atmo is that it uses a probabilistic model to compute the most likely topics to be chosen in each position and presents them in order of descending probability. This greatly simplifies selection of the correct topic for the user.

The model is computed from existing data in the topic map, so that the more often a topic is used as an association type (for example), the more likely Atmo considers it as the chosen association type. Similarly, it models which association roles are used together with which association types, and what types of topics play what association role types.

2.5   A Visual Ontology Editor

Graham Moore described what he called "a visual ontology editor", which is part of NetworkedPlanet's commercial offering. It's based on Microsoft Visual Studio, and has predefined shapes which can be used to model Topic Maps ontologies. It supports topic, association, and occurrence types, creating a type hierarchy, as well as cardinality constraints. It's also possible to create PSIs for the ontology topics by defining a base URI to which all identifiers get appended to create PSIs.

A standard feature of Visual Studio is the ability to export such graphical models created from predefined shapes into an XML representation. NetworkedPlanet's tools can then process and load this into a topic map.

2.6   Creating Topic Maps in Pidgin English

Lars Heuer presented AsTMa= 2.0[Barta05b], a compact plain-text syntax for Topic Maps, which allows Topic Maps to be written in a style that is quite close to English. There is also a more formal style, and this allows Topic Maps information to be written in two different styles. One style is close to the original AsTMa= syntax, and can look as shown below.

```
paul-mccartney
http://en.wikipedia.../Paul_McCartney
name: Paul McCartney
homepage: http://mccartney.com
shoesize: 42
date-of-birth: 1942-06-18
sings: Yesterday, all my troubles seemed...
```

This creates a topic with an identifier (first line), a PSI (second), a name, and four occurrences of different types. The datatypes of the occurrence values are automatically recognized from the syntax of the values.

However, what is more unusual is the new style, which allows topics to be written in something approaching English. (Or pidgin English, as Lars called it.)

```
paul-mccartney plays-for The-Beatles,
   which isa music-group and which
   is-located-in London,
plays piano
and has shoesize 42
```

The first line is an association, where the roles are left out, because `plays-for` has been defined as a template (which is explained below). The `,` `which` starts a relative clause (a nested block), where the `which` refers back to the last topic mentioned before the start of the clause. The second comma ends the relative clause, and so on the fourth line we have another association. The general rule is that a new association with no which or who refers to the left-hand topic of the previous association, so on the fourth line it's paul-mccartney who plays the piano, and not The-Beatles. In the final line, the has indicates that what follows is an occurrence type and a value for the occurrence. The ands are ignored.

This means that we could rewrite the previous example to the following (note that a blank line after each association would be necessary to make this correct AsTMa=), where all topic references are given explicitly.

```
paul-mccartney plays-for The-Beatles
The-Beatles isa music-group
The-Beatles is-located-in London
paul-mccartney plays piano
paul-mccartney
shoesize: 42
```

As stated above, this works because plays-for is defined as a template, as follows:

```
plays-for isa astma:template
astma:body:  """
    plays-for(player: $_left, group: $_right)
"""
```

The $_left variable is automatically bound to the value on the left of plays-for, and $_right to the value on the right of it.

It's also possible to do queries in a similar style. The following returns all topics of type person:

```
$who isa person?
```

The next example returns all members of the Beatles who play the drums.

```
select $who
  is-member-of(group: The-Beatles
  member: $who)
  and $who plays drums
```

2.7   A Topic Maps Module in Perl

Robert Barta presented his Perl Topic Maps engine.[18] The current version is a revision of his earlier, more XTM-based engine. The new version is based on the TMRM, and has an implementation of TMDM on top of the TMRM. It supports AsTMa 1.x and LTM[Garshol06a]. There is also support for volatile and persistent indexes. Further, there are the beginnings of support for TMQL.

---

[18] http://search.cpan.org/search?query=tm&mode=dist

2.8 Converting Relational Data to Topic Maps

Lars Marius Garshol presented DB2TM, which is part of Ontopia's commercial OKS product.[19] This module (mentioned in Motomu Naito's presentation above) can convert relational data (via either CSV files or JDBC) to Topic Maps using a simple configuration file that defines the mapping.

A simple example of such a mapping can be seen below:

```
<relation name="organizations.csv" columns="id name url">
  <topic type="ex:organization">
    <item-identifier>#org${id}</item-identifier>
    <topic-name>${name}</topic-name>
    <occurrence type="ex:homepage">${url}</occurrence>
  </topic>
</relation>
```

This maps each row in the CSV file to a topic of type organization, and creates an item identifier for that topic based on the `id` column. A name is assigned from the `name` column, and an occurrence from the `url` column. More advanced mappings are possible, of course.

It's possible to add static data simply by leaving out the column references, and values can be transformed using either a mapping table in the XML file or a call to an external Java function. There is also support for filtering the incoming rows.

The most important functionality, however, is the ability to periodically synchronize the topic map with updates from the data sources.

2.9 Using SQL in AsTMA=

The previous presentation inspired Robert Barta to argue that instead of a dedicated syntax to import relational data into Topic Maps, one could use templates, as proposed for CTM, and one of the "include/import" mechanisms which are necessary anyway.

In AsTMa 2.0[Barta05b] there is already an 'include' directive to load (and merge) external topic maps:

```
%include http://example.org/included.xtm
```

This directive can also be used with a UNIX pipe:

```
%include echo "SELECT ...." | mysql | awk '...' |
```

whereby the pipe creates AsTMa= text on the fly, which is then processed. A small extension would allow this mechanism to generate tabular content from, for example, a SQL database or an Excel spreadsheet, and then use a template to convert each incoming line into an AsTMa fragment:

```
%include 'echo "SELECT id, name, age FROM persons" |
    mysql --batch company_db - |' tperson
```

This requires `tperson` to be defined earlier as a template:

---

[19] http://www.ontopia.net/solutions/products.html

```
tperson isa astma:template
return : """

    {$0}  # use that as topic item identifier
    name : {$1}
    age  : {$2}
    desc : Welcome to corporate hell

    is-employed-at (
       employer : my_big_corporation
       employee : {$0}
    )
"""
```

2.10   A Topic Maps API in Python

Lars Heuer presented Mappa,[20] a Topic Maps engine written in Python which has some slightly unusual features in its API. The API allows occurrence values to be retrieved and set as though the topic object were a dict (or hash), as shown in the example below. (Note that >>> is the prompt of the Python interpreter.)

```
>>> person = myMap.topicBySubjectIdentifier('http://psi.beatles.com/Paul')
>>> person['homepage']
['http://www.paulmccartney.com', 'http://www.paulmccartney.de']
>>> person['homepage @de']
['http://www.paulmccartney.de']
>>> person['shoesize']
[]
>>> person['shoesize'] = 42
>>> person['shoesize]
[42]
```

An extra point to note here is that because the occurrence value is an integer (it's given as a Python integer value) the engine detects this and automatically assignes the correct XSD datatype URI. It's also possible to represent types which are not directly supported by setting the datatype URI explicitly, as shown below.

```
person['something'] = 'this is not a string', 'http://....'
```

References

[Sigel05]   Sigel, A.: *Report on the Open Space Sessions*. In: Maicher, L.; Park, J.: Charting the Topic Maps Research and Applications Landscape, TMRA 2005. LNAI 3873, Springer, (2006).

[Pinchuk06]   Pinchuk, R.; Aked, R.; de Orus, J. et al: *Toma - TMQL, TMCL, TMML*. In: Procs. of TMRA 2006, this volume (2007).

---

[20] http://code.google.com/p/mappa/

[Maicher06]   Maicher, L.; Bttcher, M.: *Closing the Semantic Gap in Topic Maps and OWL Ontologies with Modelling Workflow Patterns*. In: Journal of Universal Computer Science, Special Issue I-Know 2006, pp. 261-269, (2006).

[Garshol06a]   Garshol, L. M.: *The Linear Topic Map Notation–Definition and introduction, version 1.3*. Ontopia Technical Report.
http://www.ontopia.net/download/ltm.html

[Garshol06b]   Garshol, L. M.: *TM/XML – Topic Maps fragments in XML*. In: Maicher, L.; Park, J.: Charting the Topic Maps Research and Applications Landscape, TMRA 2005. Lecture Notes in Artificial Intelligence, Springer Verlag, LNAI 3873, 2006.

[Garshol06c]   Garshol, L. M.: *TMRAP – Topic Maps Remote Access Protocol*. In: Maicher, L.; Park, J.: Charting the Topic Maps Research and Applications Landscape, TMRA 2005. Lecture Notes in Artificial Intelligence, Springer Verlag, LNAI 3873, 2006.

[Barta05a]   Barta, R.: *TMIP, A RESTful Topic Maps Interaction Protocol*; Extreme Markup 2005, Montral, Canada. http://www.mulberrytech.com/ Extreme/Proceedings/html/2005/Barta01/ EML2005Barta01.html

[Barta05b]   Barta, R.; Heuer, L.: *AsTMa= 2.0 Language Definition*; Bond University, 2005. http://astma.it.bond.edu.au/astma=-spec-2.0r1.0.dbk

[Cerny07]   Cerny, R.: *Topincs: Topic Maps, REST and JSON*; In: Procs. of TMRA 2006, this volume (2007).

Author Index

Lecture Notes in Artificial Intelligence (LNAI)

Vol. 4211: P. Vogt, Y. Sugita, E. Tuci, C.L. Nehaniv (Eds.), Symbol Grounding and Beyond. VIII, 237 pages. 2006.

Vol. 4203: F. Esposito, Z.W. Raś, D. Malerba, G. Semeraro (Eds.), Foundations of Intelligent Systems. XVIII, 767 pages. 2006.

Vol. 4201: Y. Sakakibara, S. Kobayashi, K. Sato, T. Nishino, E. Tomita (Eds.), Grammatical Inference: Algorithms and Applications. XII, 359 pages. 2006.

Vol. 4200: I.F.C. Smith (Ed.), Intelligent Computing in Engineering and Architecture. XIII, 692 pages. 2006.

Vol. 4198: O. Nasraoui, O. Zaïane, M. Spiliopoulou, B. Mobasher, B. Masand, P.S. Yu (Eds.), Advances in Web Mining and Web Usage Analysis. IX, 177 pages. 2006.

Vol. 4196: K. Fischer, I.J. Timm, E. André, N. Zhong (Eds.), Multiagent System Technologies. X, 185 pages. 2006.

Vol. 4188: P. Sojka, I. Kopeček, K. Pala (Eds.), Text, Speech and Dialogue. XV, 721 pages. 2006.

Vol. 4183: J. Euzenat, J. Domingue (Eds.), Artificial Intelligence: Methodology, Systems, and Applications. XIII, 291 pages. 2006.

Vol. 4180: M. Kohlhase, OMDoc – An Open Markup Format for Mathematical Documents [version 1.2]. XIX, 428 pages. 2006.

Vol. 4177: R. Marín, E. Onaindía, A. Bugarín, J. Santos (Eds.), Current Topics in Artificial Intelligence. XV, 482 pages. 2006.

Vol. 4160: M. Fisher, W. van der Hoek, B. Konev, A. Lisitsa (Eds.), Logics in Artificial Intelligence. XII, 516 pages. 2006.

Vol. 4155: O. Stock, M. Schaerf (Eds.), Reasoning, Action and Interaction in AI Theories and Systems. XVIII, 343 pages. 2006.

Vol. 4149: M. Klusch, M. Rovatsos, T.R. Payne (Eds.), Cooperative Information Agents X. XII, 477 pages. 2006.

Vol. 4140: J.S. Sichman, H. Coelho, S.O. Rezende (Eds.), Advances in Artificial Intelligence - IBERAMIA-SBIA 2006. XXIII, 635 pages. 2006.

Vol. 4139: T. Salakoski, F. Ginter, S. Pyysalo, T. Pahikkala (Eds.), Advances in Natural Language Processing. XVI, 771 pages. 2006.

Vol. 4133: J. Gratch, M. Young, R. Aylett, D. Ballin, P. Olivier (Eds.), Intelligent Virtual Agents. XIV, 472 pages. 2006.

Vol. 4130: U. Furbach, N. Shankar (Eds.), Automated Reasoning. XV, 680 pages. 2006.

Vol. 4120: J. Calmet, T. Ida, D. Wang (Eds.), Artificial Intelligence and Symbolic Computation. XIII, 269 pages. 2006.

Vol. 4118: Z. Despotovic, S. Joseph, C. Sartori (Eds.), Agents and Peer-to-Peer Computing. XIV, 173 pages. 2006.

Vol. 4114: D.-S. Huang, K. Li, G.W. Irwin (Eds.), Computational Intelligence, Part II. XXVII, 1337 pages. 2006.

Vol. 4108: J.M. Borwein, W.M. Farmer (Eds.), Mathematical Knowledge Management. VIII, 295 pages. 2006.

Vol. 4106: T.R. Roth-Berghofer, M.H. Göker, H.A. Güvenir (Eds.), Advances in Case-Based Reasoning. XIV, 566 pages. 2006.

Vol. 4099: Q. Yang, G. Webb (Eds.), PRICAI 2006: Trends in Artificial Intelligence. XXVIII, 1263 pages. 2006.

Vol. 4095: S. Nolfi, G. Baldassarre, R. Calabretta, J.C.T. Hallam, D. Marocco, J.-A. Meyer, O. Miglino, D. Parisi (Eds.), From Animals to Animats 9. XV, 869 pages. 2006.

Vol. 4093: X. Li, O.R. Zaïane, Z. Li (Eds.), Advanced Data Mining and Applications. XXI, 1110 pages. 2006.

Vol. 4092: J. Lang, F. Lin, J. Wang (Eds.), Knowledge Science, Engineering and Management. XV, 664 pages. 2006.

Vol. 4088: Z.-Z. Shi, R. Sadananda (Eds.), Agent Computing and Multi-Agent Systems. XVII, 827 pages. 2006.

Vol. 4087: F. Schwenker, S. Marinai (Eds.), Artificial Neural Networks in Pattern Recognition. IX, 299 pages. 2006.

Vol. 4068: H. Schärfe, P. Hitzler, P. Øhrstrøm (Eds.), Conceptual Structures: Inspiration and Application. XI, 455 pages. 2006.

Vol. 4065: P. Perner (Ed.), Advances in Data Mining. XI, 592 pages. 2006.

Vol. 4062: G.-Y. Wang, J.F. Peters, A. Skowron, Y. Yao (Eds.), Rough Sets and Knowledge Technology. XX, 810 pages. 2006.

Vol. 4049: S. Parsons, N. Maudet, P. Moraitis, I. Rahwan (Eds.), Argumentation in Multi-Agent Systems. XIV, 313 pages. 2006.

Vol. 4048: L. Goble, J.-J.C.. Meyer (Eds.), Deontic Logic and Artificial Normative Systems. X, 273 pages. 2006.

Vol. 4045: D. Barker-Plummer, R. Cox, N. Swoboda (Eds.), Diagrammatic Representation and Inference. XII, 301 pages. 2006.

Vol. 4031: M. Ali, R. Dapoigny (Eds.), Advances in Applied Artificial Intelligence. XXIII, 1353 pages. 2006.

Vol. 4029: L. Rutkowski, R. Tadeusiewicz, L.A. Zadeh, J.M. Zurada (Eds.), Artificial Intelligence and Soft Computing – ICAISC 2006. XXI, 1235 pages. 2006.

Vol. 4027: H.L. Larsen, G. Pasi, D. Ortiz-Arroyo, T. Andreasen, H. Christiansen (Eds.), Flexible Query Answering Systems. XVIII, 714 pages. 2006.

Vol. 4021: E. André, L. Dybkjær, W. Minker, H. Neumann, M. Weber (Eds.), Perception and Interactive Technologies. XI, 217 pages. 2006.

Vol. 4020: A. Bredenfeld, A. Jacoff, I. Noda, Y. Takahashi (Eds.), RoboCup 2005: Robot Soccer World Cup IX. XVII, 727 pages. 2006.

Vol. 4013: L. Lamontagne, M. Marchand (Eds.), Advances in Artificial Intelligence. XIII, 564 pages. 2006.

Vol. 4012: T. Washio, A. Sakurai, K. Nakajima, H. Takeda, S. Tojo, M. Yokoo (Eds.), New Frontiers in Artificial Intelligence. XIII, 484 pages. 2006.

Vol. 4008: J.C. Augusto, C.D. Nugent (Eds.), Designing Smart Homes. XI, 183 pages. 2006.